Scottish Folk Tales

2017. Miculásra
Soktól

A közeli Kilmahog
Woolen Mill-ben
vettük, amikor
Marianntal ? Balázssal
volt Clunie Highland - minde.

LOMOND BOOKS
www.lomondbooks.com

This edition published 2017 for Lomond Books Ltd
13–14 Freskyn Place, East Mains Industrial Estate,
Broxburn, EH52 5NF, Scotland
www.lomondbooks.com
by Waverley Books,
an imprint of The Gresham Publishing Company Ltd, Academy Park,
Building 4000, Gower Street, Glasgow, G51 1PR, Scotland

ISBN 978 1 84204 247 2

Printed and bound by MBM Print SCS Ltd, Glasgow

Contents

Thomas the Rhymer   5
Gold-Tree and Silver-Tree   16
Whippety-Stourie   28
The Red-Etin   34
The Seal Catcher and the Merman   46
The Page-Boy and the Silver Goblet   53
The Black Bull of Norroway   58
The Wee Bannock   73
The Elfin Knight   79
What to Say to the New Mune   88
Habetrot the Spinstress   89
Nippit Fit and Clippit Fit   100
The Fairies of Merlin's Crag   105
The Wedding of Robin Redbreast and Jenny Wren   110
The Dwarfie Stone   115
Canonbie Dick and Thomas of Ercildoune   128
The Laird O' Co'   135
Poussie Baudrons   140
The Milk-White Doo   141
The Draiglin' Hogney   146
The Brownie O' Ferne-Den   152
The Witch of Fife   157
Assipattle and the Mester Stoorworm   163
The Fox and the Wolf   180
Katherine Crackernuts   186
The Well O' The World's End   197
Farquhar MacNeill   201
Peerifool   206

The Battle of the Birds	217
The Sea-Maiden	232
Rashin-Coatie	241
The Fox Outwitted	245
How the Wolf Lost his Tail	246
The Worme of Linton	247
The Legend of Linton Church	249
Michael Scott	250
The Tale of Sir James Ramsay O' Bamff	256
The Lee Penny	260
The Craig Liath Mhor	262
Fiddler's Well	265
The Fairies of Scotland	267
The Fairy and the Miller's Wife	269
Water Fairies	271
Fairy Transportation	273
The Fairy Boy of Leith	275
The Smith and the Fairies	278
Redemption from Fairy-land	282
Thom and Willie	287
The Scottish Brownie	291
The Brownie of Bodsbeck	293
The Bogle	294
The Doomed Rider	295
Nuckelavee	298
The Witch of Laggan	301
The Blacksmith's Wife of Yarrowfoot	306
The Missing Web of Linen	309
The Witches of Delnabo	311
The Old Lady of Littledean	316
The Island Cave	318
The Spectre Piper	320
Prince Charlie's Cave	322
Adam Bell	324
The Winding Sheet	330
The Tale of the Shifty Lad, the Widow's Son	332
Lothian Tom	346
Cousin Mattie	353
Elphin Irving	365
The Haunted Ships	380

Thomas the Rhymer

Of all the young gallants in Scotland in the thirteenth century, there was none more gracious and debonair than Thomas Learmont, Laird of the Castle of Ercildoune, in Berwickshire.

He loved books, poetry, and music, which were uncommon tastes in those days; and, above all, he loved to study nature, and to watch the habits of the beasts and birds that made their abode in the fields and woods round about his home.

Now it chanced that, one sunny May morning, Thomas left his Tower of Ercildoune, and went wandering into the woods that lay about the Huntly Burn, a little stream that came rushing down from the slopes of the Eildon Hills. It was a lovely morning—fresh, and bright, and warm, and everything was so beautiful that it looked as Paradise might look.

The tender leaves were bursting out of their sheaths, and covering all the trees with a fresh soft mantle of green; and amongst the carpet of moss under the young man's feet, yellow primroses and starry anemones were turning up their faces to the morning sky.

The little birds were singing like to burst their throats, and hundreds of insects were flying backwards and forwards in the sunshine; while down by the burnside the bright-eyed water-rats were poking their noses out of their holes, as if they knew that summer had come, and wanted to have a share in all that was going on.

Thomas felt so happy with the gladness of it all, that he threw himself down at the root of a tree, to watch the living things around him.

As he was lying there, he heard the trampling of a horse's hooves, as it forced its way through the bushes; and, looking up, he saw the most beautiful Lady that he had ever seen coming riding towards him on a grey palfrey.

She wore a hunting dress of glistening silk, the colour of the fresh spring grass; and from her shoulders hung a velvet mantle, which matched the riding-skirt exactly. Her yellow hair, like rippling gold, hung loosely round her shoulders, and on her head sparkled a diadem of precious stones, which flashed like fire in the sunlight.

Her saddle was of pure ivory, and her saddle-cloth of blood-red satin, while her saddle girths were of corded silk and her stirrups of cut crystal. Her horse's reins were of beaten gold, all hung with little silver bells, so that, as she rode along, she made a sound like fairy music.

Apparently she was bent on the chase, for she carried a hunting-horn and a sheaf of arrows; and she led seven greyhounds along in a leash, while as many scenting hounds ran loose at her horse's side.

As she rode down the glen, she lilted a bit of an old Scotch song; and she carried herself with such a queenly air, and her dress was so magnificent, that Thomas was like to kneel by the side of the path and worship her, for he thought that it must be the Blessed Virgin herself.

But when the rider came to where he was, and understood his thoughts, she shook her head sadly.

"I am not that Blessed Lady, as thou thinkest," she said. "Men call me Queen, but it is of a far other country; for I am the Queen of Fairy-land, and not the Queen of Heaven."

And certainly it seemed as if what she said were true; for, from that moment, it was as if a spell were cast over Thomas, making him forget prudence, and caution, and common-sense itself.

For he knew that it was dangerous for mortals to meddle with Fairies, yet he was so entranced with the Lady's beauty that he begged her to give him a kiss. This was just what she wanted, for she knew that if she once kissed him she had him in her power.

And, to the young man's horror, as soon as their lips had met, an awful change came over her. For her beautiful mantle and riding-skirt of silk seemed to fade away, leaving her clad in a long grey garment, which was just the colour of ashes. Her beauty seemed to fade away also, and she grew old and wan; and, worst of all, half of her abundant yellow hair went grey before his very eyes. She saw the poor man's astonishment and terror, and she burst into a mocking laugh.

"I am not so fair to look on now as I was at first," she said, "but that matters little, for thou hast sold thyself, Thomas, to be my servant for seven long years. For whoso kisseth the Fairy Queen must e'en go with her to Fairy-land, and serve her there till that time is past."

When he heard these words poor Thomas fell on his knees and begged for mercy. But mercy he could not obtain. The Elfin Queen only laughed in his face, and brought her dapple-grey palfrey close up to where he was standing.

"No, no," she said, in answer to his entreaties.

"Thou didst ask the kiss, and now thou must pay the price. So dally no longer, but mount behind me, for it is full time that I was gone."

So Thomas, with many a sigh and groan of terror, mounted behind her; and as soon as he had done so, she shook her bridle rein, and the grey steed galloped off.

On and on they went, going swifter than the wind; till they

left the land of the living behind, and came to the edge of a great desert, ,which stretched before them, dry, and bare, and desolate, to the edge of the far horizon.

At least, so it seemed to the weary eyes of Thomas of Ercildoune, and he wondered if he and his strange companion had to cross this desert; and, if so, if there were any chance of reaching the other side of it alive.

But the Fairy Queen suddenly tightened her rein, and the grey palfrey stopped short in its wild career.

"Now must thou descend to earth, Thomas," said the Lady, glancing over her shoulder at her unhappy captive, "and lout down, and lay thy head on my knee, and I will show thee hidden things, which cannot be seen by mortal eyes."

So Thomas dismounted, and louted down, and rested his head on the Fairy Queen's knee; and lo, as he looked once more over the desert, everything seemed changed. For he saw three roads leading across it now, which he had not noticed before, and each of these three roads was different.

One of them was broad, and level, and even, and it ran straight on across the sand, so that no one who was travelling by it could possibly lose his way.

And the second road was as different from the first as it well could be. It was narrow, and winding, and long; and there was a thorn hedge on one side of it, and a briar hedge on the other; and those hedges grew so high, and their branches were so wild and tangled, that those who were travelling along that road would have some difficulty in persevering on their journey at all.

And the third road was unlike any of the others. It was a bonnie, bonnie road, winding up a hillside among brackens, and heather, and golden-yellow whins, and it looked as if it would be pleasant travelling, to pass that way.

"Now," said the Fairy Queen, "an' thou wilt, I shall tell thee where these three roads lead to. The first road, as thou seest, is broad, and even, and easy, and there be many that choose it to travel on. But though it be a good road, it leadeth to a bad end, and the folk that choose it repent their choice for ever.

"And as for the narrow road, all hampered and hindered by the thorns and the briars, there be few that be troubled to ask where that leadeth to. But did they ask, perchance more of them might be stirred up to set out along it. For that is the road of righteousness; and, although it be hard and irksome, yet it endeth in a glorious city, which is called the City of the Great King.

"And the third road—the bonnie road—that runs up the brae among the ferns, and leadeth no mortal kens whither, but I ken where it leadeth, Thomas—for it leadeth unto fair Elf-land; and that road take we.

"And, mark 'ee, Thomas, if ever thou hopest to see thine own Tower of Ercildoune again, take care of thy tongue when we reach our journey's end, and speak no single word to anyone save me—for the mortal who openeth his lips rashly in Fairy-land must bide there for ever."

Then she bade him mount her palfrey again, and they rode on. The ferny road was not so bonnie all the way as it had been at first, however. For they had not ridden along it very far before it led them into a narrow ravine, which seemed to go right down under the earth, where there was no ray of light to guide them, and where the air was dank and heavy. There was a sound of rushing water everywhere, and at last the grey palfrey plunged right into it; and it crept up, cold and chill, first over Thomas's feet, and then over his knees.

His courage had been slowly ebbing ever since he had been parted from the daylight, but now he gave himself up for lost; for it seemed to him certain that his strange companion and he would never come safe to their journey's end.

He fell forward in a kind of swoon; and, if it had not been that he had tight hold of the Fairy's ash-grey gown, I warrant he had fallen from his seat, and had been drowned.

But all things, be they good or bad, pass in time, and at last the darkness began to lighten, and the light grew stronger, until they were back in broad sunshine.

Then Thomas took courage, and looked up; and lo, they were riding through a beautiful orchard, where apples and pears, dates and figs and wineberries grew in great abundance. And his tongue was so parched and dry, and he felt so faint, that he longed for some of the fruit to restore him.

He stretched out his hand to pluck some of it; but his companion turned in her saddle and forbade him.

"There is nothing safe for thee to eat here," she said, "save an apple, which I will give thee presently. If thou touch aught else thou art bound to remain in Fairy-land for ever."

So poor Thomas had to restrain himself as best he could; and they rode slowly on, until they came to a tiny tree all covered with red apples. The Fairy Queen bent down and plucked one, and handed it to her companion.

"This I can give thee," she said, "and I do it gladly, for these apples are the Apples of Truth; and whoso eateth them gaineth this reward, that his lips will never more be able to frame a lie."

Thomas took the apple, and ate it; and for evermore the Grace of Truth rested on his lips; and that is why, in after years, men called him "True Thomas".

They had only a little way to go after this, before they came in sight of a magnificent Castle standing on a hillside.

"Yonder is my abode," said the Queen, pointing to it proudly. "There dwelleth my Lord and all the Nobles of his court; and, as my Lord hath an uncertain temper, and shows no liking for any strange gallant whom he sees in my company, I pray thee, both for thy sake and mine, to utter no word to anyone who speaketh to thee; and, if anyone should ask me who and what thou art, I will tell them that thou art dumb. So wilt thou pass unnoticed in the crowd."

With these words the Lady raised her huntinghorn, and blew a loud and piercing blast; and, as she did so, a marvellous change came over her again; for her ugly ash-covered gown dropped off her, and the grey in her hair vanished, and she appeared once more in her green riding-skirt and mantle, and her face grew young and fair.

And a wonderful change passed over Thomas also; for, as he chanced to glance downwards, he found that his rough country clothes had been transformed into a suit of fine brown cloth, and that on his feet he wore satin shoon.

Immediately the sound of the horn rang out, the doors of the Castle flew open, and the King hurried out to meet the Queen, accompanied by such a number of Knights and Ladies, Minstrels and Pageboys, that Thomas, who had slid from his palfrey, had no difficulty in obeying her wishes and passing into the Castle unobserved.

Everyone seemed very glad to see the Queen back again, and they crowded into the Great Hall in her train, and she spoke to them all graciously, and allowed them to kiss her hand. Then she passed, with her husband, to a dais at the far end of the huge apartment, where two thrones stood, on which the Royal pair seated themselves to watch the revels which now began.

Poor Thomas, meanwhile, stood far away at the other end of the Great Hall, feeling very lonely, yet fascinated by the extraordinary scene on which he was gazing.

For, although all the fine Ladies, and Courtiers, and Knights were dancing in one part of the Great Hall, there were huntsmen coming and going in another part, carrying in great antlered deer, which apparently they had killed in the chase, and throwing them down in heaps on the floor. And there were rows of cooks standing beside the dead animals, cutting them up into joints, and bearing away the joints to be cooked.

Altogether it was such a strange, fantastic scene that Thomas took no heed of how the time flew, but stood and gazed, and gazed, never speaking a word to anybody. This went on for three long days, then the Queen rose from her throne, and, stepping from the dais, crossed the Hall to where he was standing.

"'Tis time to mount and ride, Thomas," she said, "if thou wouldst ever see the fair Castle of Ercildoune again."

Thomas looked at her in amazement. "Thou spokest of seven long years, Lady," he exclaimed, "and I have been here but three days."

The Queen smiled. "Time passeth quickly in Fairy-land, my friend," she replied. "Thou thinkest that thou hast been here but three days. 'Tis seven years since we two met. And now it is time for thee to go. I would fain have had thy presence with me longer, but I dare not, for thine own sake. For every seventh year an evil Spirit cometh from the Regions of Darkness, and carrieth back with him one of our followers, whomsoever he chanceth to choose. And, as thou art a goodly fellow, I fear that he might choose thee.

"So, as I would be loth to let harm befall thee, I will take thee back to thine own country this very night."

Once more the grey palfrey was brought, and Thomas and the Queen mounted it; and, as they had come, so they returned to the Eildon Tree near the Huntly Burn.

Then the Queen bade Thomas farewell; and, as a parting gift, he asked her to give him something that would let people know that he had really been to Fairy-land.

"I have already given thee the Gift of Truth," she replied. "I will now give thee the Gifts of Prophecy and Poesie; so that thou wilt be able to foretell the future, and also to write wondrous verses. And, besides these unseen gifts, here is something that mortals can see with their own eyes—a Harp that was fashioned in Fairy-land. Fare thee well, my friend. Some day, perchance, I will return for thee again.

With these words the Lady vanished, and Thomas was left

alone, feeling a little sorry, if the truth must be told, at parting with such a radiant Being and coming back to the ordinary haunts of men.

After this he lived for many a long year in his Castle of Ercildoune, and the fame of his poetry and of his prophecies spread all over the country, so that people named him True Thomas, and Thomas the Rhymer.

I cannot write down for you all the prophecies which Thomas uttered, and which most surely came to pass, but I will tell you one or two.

He foretold the Battle of Bannockburn in these words:

> "The Burn of Breid
> Shall rin fou reid,"

which came to pass on that terrible day when the waters of the little Bannockburn were reddened by the blood of the defeated English.

He also foretold the Union of the Crowns of England and Scotland, under a Prince who was the son of a French Queen, and who yet bore the blood of Bruce in his veins.

> "A French Quen shall bearre the Sonne;
> Shall rule all Britainne to the sea,
> As neere as is the ninth degree,"

which thing came true in 1603, when King James, son of Mary, Queen of Scots, became Monarch of both countries.

Fourteen long years went by, and people were beginning to forget that Thomas the Rhymer had ever been in Fairy-land; but at last a day came when Scotland was at war with England, and the Scottish army was resting by the banks of the Tweed, not far from the Tower of Ercildoune.

And the Master of the Tower determined to make a feast,

and invite all the Nobles and Barons who were leading the army to sup with him.

That feast was long remembered.

For the Laird of Ercildoune took care that everything was as magnificent as it could possibly be; and when the meal was ended he rose in his place, and, taking his Elfin harp, he sang to his assembled guests song after song of the days of long ago.

The guests listened breathlessly, for they felt that they would never hear such wonderful music again. And so it fell out.

For that very night, after all the Nobles had gone back to their tents, a soldier on guard saw, in the moonlight, a snow-white Hart and Hind moving slowly down the road that ran past the camp.

There was something so unusual about the animals that he called to his officer to come and look at them. And the officer called to his brother officers, and soon there was quite a crowd softly following the dumb creatures, who paced solemnly on, as if they were keeping time to music unheard by mortal ears.

"There is something uncanny about this," said one soldier at last. "Let us send for Thomas of Ercildoune, perchance he may be able to tell us if it be an omen or no."

"Ay, send for Thomas of Ercildoune," cried every one at once. So a little page was sent in haste to the old Tower to rouse the Rhymer from his slumbers.

When he heard the boy's message, the Seer's face grew grave and wrapt.

"'Tis a summons," he said softly, "a summons from the Queen of Fairy-land. I have waited long for it, and it hath come at last."

And when he went out, instead of joining the little company of waiting men, he walked straight up to the snow-white Hart and Hind. As soon as he reached them they paused for a moment as if to greet him. Then all three moved slowly down a steep bank that sloped to the little River Leader, and disappeared in its foaming waters, for the stream was in full flood.

And, although a careful search was made, no trace of Thomas of Ercildoune was found; and to this day the country folk believe that the Hart and the Hind were messengers from the Elfin Queen, and that he went back to Fairy-land with them.

Gold-Tree and Silver-Tree

In bygone days there lived a little Princess named Gold-Tree, and she was one of the prettiest children in the whole world. Although her mother was dead, she had a very happy life, for her father loved her dearly, and thought that nothing was too much trouble so long as it gave his little daughter pleasure. But by and by he married again, and then the little Princess's sorrows began.

For his new wife, whose name, curious to say, was Silver-Tree, was very beautiful, but she was also very jealous, and she made herself quite miserable for fear that, some day, she should meet someone who was better looking than she was herself.

When she found that her step-daughter was so very pretty, she took a dislike to her at once, and was always looking at her and wondering if people would think her prettier than she was. And because, in her heart of hearts, she was afraid that they would do so, she was very unkind indeed to the poor girl.

At last, one day, when Princess Gold-Tree was quite grown up, the two ladies went for a walk to a little well which lay, all surrounded by trees, in the middle of a deep glen.

Now the water in this well was so clear that everyone who looked into it saw his face reflected on the surface; and the proud Queen loved to come and peep into its depths, so that she could see her own picture mirrored in the water.

But to-day, as she was looking in, what should she see but

a little trout, which was swimming quietly backwards and forwards not very far from the surface.

"Troutie, troutie, answer me this one question," said the Queen. "Am not I the most beautiful woman in the world?"

"No, indeed, you are not," replied the trout promptly, jumping out of the water, as he spoke, in order to swallow a fly.

"Who is the most beautiful woman, then?" asked the disappointed Queen, for she had expected a far different answer.

"Thy step-daughter, the Princess Gold-Tree, without a doubt," said the little fish; then, frightened by the black look that came upon the jealous Queen's face, he dived to the bottom of the well.

It was no wonder that he did so, for the Queen's expression was not pleasant to look at, as she darted an angry glance at her fair young step-daughter, who was busy picking flowers some little distance away.

Indeed, she was so annoyed at the thought that anyone should say that the girl was prettier than she was, that she quite lost her self-control; and when she reached home she went up, in a violent passion, to her room, and threw herself on the bed, declaring that she felt very ill indeed.

It was in vain that Princess Gold-Tree asked her what the matter was, and if she could do anything for her. She would not let the poor girl touch her, but pushed her away as if she had been some evil thing. So at last the Princess had to leave her alone, and go out of the apartment, feeling very sad indeed.

By and by the King came home from his hunting, and he at once asked for the Queen. He was told that she had been seized with sudden illness, and that she was lying on her bed in her own room, and that no one, not even the Court Physician, who had been hastily summoned, could make out what was wrong with her.

In great anxiety—for he really loved her—the King went up to her bedside, and asked the Queen how she felt, and if there was anything that he could do to relieve her.

"Yes, there is one thing that thou couldst do," she answered harshly, "but I know full well that, even although it is the only thing that will cure me, thou wilt not do it."

"Nay," said the King, "I deserve better words at thy mouth than these; for thou knowest that I would give thee aught thou carest to ask, even if it be the half of my Kingdom."

"Then give me thy daughter's heart to eat," cried the Queen, "for unless I can obtain that, I will die, and that speedily."

She spoke so wildly, and looked at him in such a strange fashion, that the poor King really thought that her brain was turned, and he was at his wits' end what to do. He left the room, and paced up and down the corridor in great distress, until at last he remembered that that very morning the son of a Great King had arrived from a country far over the sea, asking for his daughter's hand in marriage.

"Here is a way out of the difficulty," he said to himself. "This marriage pleaseth me well, and I will have it celebrated at once. Then, when my daughter is safe out of the country, I will send a lad up the hillside, and he shall kill a he-goat, and I will have its heart prepared and dressed, and send it up to my wife. Perhaps the sight of it will cure her of this madness."

So he had the strange Prince summoned before him, and told him how the Queen had taken a sudden illness that had wrought on her brain, and had caused her to take a dislike to the Princess, and how it seemed as if it would be a good thing if, with the maiden's consent, the marriage could take place at once, so that the Queen might be left alone to recover from her strange malady.

Now the Prince was delighted to gain his bride so easily, and the Princess was glad to escape from her step-mother's hatred, so the marriage took place at once, and the newly wedded pair set off across the sea for the Prince's country.

Then the King sent a lad up the hillside to kill a he-goat; and when it was killed he gave orders that its heart should be dressed and cooked, and sent to the Queen's apartment on a silver dish. And the wicked woman tasted it, believing it to be the heart of her step-daughter; and when she had done so, she rose from her bed and went about the Castle looking as well and hearty as ever.

I am glad to be able to tell you that the marriage of Princess Gold-Tree, which had come about in such a hurry, turned out to be a great success; for the Prince whom she had wedded was rich, and great, and powerful, and he loved her dearly, and she was as happy as the day was long.

So things went peacefully on for a year. Queen Silver-Tree was satisfied and contented, because she thought that her step-daughter was dead; while all the time the Princess was happy and prosperous in her new home.

But at the end of the year it chanced that the Queen went once more to the well in the little glen, in order to see her face reflected in the water.

And it chanced also that the same little trout was swimming backwards and forwards, just as he had done the year before. And the foolish Queen determined to have a better answer to her question this time than she had last.

"Troutie, troutie," she whispered, leaning over the edge of the well, "am not I the most beautiful woman in the world?"

"By my troth, thou art not," answered the trout, in his very straightforward way.

"Who is the most beautiful woman, then?" asked the Queen, her face growing pale at the thought that she had yet another rival.

"Why, your Majesty's step-daughter, the Princess Gold-Tree, to be sure," answered the trout.

The Queen threw back her head with a sigh of relief. "Well, at any rate, people cannot admire her now," she said, "for it is a year since she died. I ate her heart for my supper."

"Art thou sure of that, your Majesty?" asked the trout, with a twinkle in his eye. "Methinks it is but a year since she married the gallant young Prince who came from abroad to seek her hand, and returned with him to his own country."

When the Queen heard these words she turned quite cold with rage, for she knew that her husband had deceived her; and she rose from her knees and went straight home to the Palace, and, hiding her anger as best she could, she asked him if he would give orders to have the Long Ship made ready, as she wished to go and visit her dear step-daughter, for it was such a very long time since she had seen her.

The King was somewhat surprised at her request, but he was only too glad to think that she had got over her hatred towards his daughter, and he gave orders that the Long Ship should be made ready at once.

Soon it was speeding over the water, its prow turned in the direction of the land where the Princess lived, steered by the Queen herself; for she knew the course that the boat ought to take, and she was in such haste to be at her journey's end that she would allow no one else to take the helm.

Now it chanced that Princess Gold-Tree was alone that day, for her husband had gone a-hunting. And as she looked out of one of the Castle windows she saw a boat coming sailing over the sea towards the landing place. She recognised it as her father's Long Ship, and she guessed only too well whom it carried on board.

She was almost beside herself with terror at the thought, for she knew that it was for no good purpose that Queen Silver-Tree had taken the trouble to set out to visit her, and she felt that she would have given almost anything she possessed if her husband had but been at home. In her distress she hurried into the servants' hall.

"Oh, what shall I do, what shall I do?" she cried, "for I see my father's Long Ship coming over the sea, and I know that my step-mother is on board. And if she hath a chance she will kill me, for she hateth me more than anything else upon earth."

Now the servants worshipped the ground that their young Mistress trod on, for she was always kind and considerate to them, and when they saw how frightened she was, and heard her piteous words, they crowded round her, as if to shield her from any harm that threatened her.

"Do not be afraid, your Highness," they cried, "we will defend thee with our very lives if need be. But in case thy Lady Step-Mother should have the power to throw any evil spell over thee, we will lock thee in the great Mullioned Chamber, then she cannot get nigh thee at all."

Now the Mullioned Chamber was a strong-room, which was in a part of the castle all by itself, and its door was so thick that no one could possibly break through it; and the Princess knew that if she were once inside the room, with its stout oaken door between her and her step-mother, she would be perfectly safe from any mischief that that wicked woman could devise.

So she consented to her faithful servants' suggestion, and allowed them to lock her in the Mullioned Chamber.

So it came to pass that when Queen Silver-Tree arrived at the great door of the Castle, and commanded the lackey who opened it to take her to his Royal Mistress, he told her, with a low bow, that that was impossible, because the Princess was locked in the strong-room of the castle, and could not get out, because no one knew where the key was.

(Which was quite true, for the old butler had tied it round the neck of the Prince's favourite sheepdog, and had sent him away to the hills to seek his master.)

"Take me to the door of the apartment," commanded the Queen. "At least I can speak to my dear daughter through it." And the lackey, who did not see what harm could possibly come from this, did as he was bid.

"If the key is really lost, and thou canst not come out to

welcome me, dear Gold-Tree," said the deceitful Queen, "at least put thy little finger through the keyhole that I may kiss it."

The Princess did so, never dreaming that evil could come to her through such a simple action. But it did. For instead of kissing the tiny finger, her stepmother stabbed it with a poisoned needle, and, so deadly was the poison, that, before she could utter a single cry, the poor Princess fell, as one dead, on the floor.

When she heard the fall, a smile of satisfaction crept over Queen Silver-Tree's face. "Now I can say that I am the handsomest woman in the world," she whispered; and she went back to the lackey who stood waiting at the end of the passage, and told him that she had said all that she had to say to her daughter, and that now she must return home.

So the man attended her to the boat with all due ceremony, and she set sail for her own country; and no one in the Castle knew that any harm had befallen their dear Mistress until the Prince came home from his hunting with the key of the Mullioned Chamber, which he had taken from his sheepdog's neck, in his hand.

He laughed when he heard the story of Queen Silver-Tree's visit, and told the servants that they had done well; then he ran upstairs to open the door and release his wife.

But what was his horror and dismay, when he did so, to find her lying dead at his feet on the floor.

He was nearly beside himself with rage and grief; and, because he knew that a deadly poison such as Queen Silver-Tree had used would preserve the Princess's body so that it had no need of burial, he had it laid on a silken couch and left in the Mullioned Chamber, so that he could go and look at it whenever he pleased.

He was so terribly lonely, however, that in a little time he married again, and his second wife was just as sweet and as good as the first one had been. This new wife was very happy, there was only one little thing that caused her any trouble at all, and she was too sensible to let it make her miserable.

That one thing was that there was one room in the Castle—a room which stood at the end of a passage by itself—which she could never enter, as her husband always carried the key. And as, when she asked him the reason of this, he always made an excuse of some kind, she made up her mind that she would not seem as if she did not trust him, so she asked no more questions about the matter.

But one day the Prince chanced to leave the door unlocked, and as he had never told her not to do so, she went in, and there she saw Princess Gold-Tree lying on the silken couch, looking as if she were asleep.

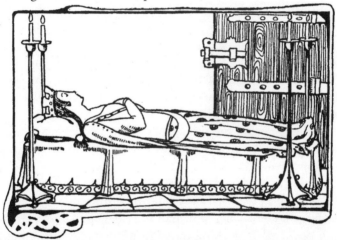

"Is she dead, or is she only sleeping?" she said to herself, and she went up to the couch and looked closely at the Princess. And there, sticking in her little finger, she discovered a curiously shaped needle.

"There hath been evil work here," she thought to herself. "If that needle be not poisoned, then I know naught of medicine." And, being skilled in leechcraft, she drew it carefully out.

In a moment Princess Gold-Tree opened her eye and sat up, and presently she had recovered sufficiently to tell the Other Princess the whole story.

Now, if her step-mother had been jealous, the Other Princess was not jealous at all; for, when she heard all that had happened, she clapped her little hands, crying, "Oh, how glad the Prince will be; for although he hath married again, I know that he loves thee best."

That night the Prince came home from hunting looking very tired and sad, for what his second wife had said was quite true. Although he loved her very much, he was always mourning in his heart for his first dear love, Princess Gold-Tree.

"How sad thou art!" exclaimed his wife, going out to meet him. "Is there nothing that I can do to bring a smile to thy face?"

"Nothing," answered the Prince wearily, laying down his bow, for he was too heart-sore even to pretend to be gay.

"Except to give thee back Gold-Tree," said his wife mischievously. "And that can I do. Thou wilt find her alive and well in the Mullioned Chamber."

Without a word the Prince ran upstairs, and, sure enough, there was his dear Gold-Tree, sitting on the couch ready to welcome him.

He was so overjoyed to see her that he threw his arms round her neck and kissed her over and over again, quite forgetting his poor second wife, who had followed him upstairs, and who now stood watching the meeting that she had brought about.

She did not seem to be sorry for herself, however. "I always knew that thy heart yearned after Princess Gold-Tree," she said. "And it is but right that it should be so. For she was thy first love, and, since she hath come to life again, I will go back to mine own people."

"No, indeed thou wilt not," answered the Prince, "for it is

thou who hast brought me this joy. Thou wilt stay with us, and we shall all three live happily together. And Gold-Tree and thee will become great friends."

And so it came to pass. For Princess Gold-Tree and the Other Princess soon became like sisters, and loved each other as if they had been brought up together all their lives.

In this manner another year passed away, and one evening, in the old country, Queen Silver-Tree went, as she had done before, to look at her face in the water of the little well in the glen.

And, as had happened twice before, the trout was there. "Troutie, troutie," she whispered, "am not I the most beautiful woman in the world?"

"By my troth, thou art not," answered the trout, as he had answered on the two previous occasions.

"And who dost thou say is the most beautiful woman now?" asked the Queen, her voice trembling with rage and vexation.

"I have given her name to thee these two years back," answered the trout. "The Princess Gold-Tree, of course."

"But she is dead," laughed the Queen. "I am sure of it this time, for it is just a year since I stabbed her little finger with a poisoned needle, and I heard her fall down dead on the floor."

"I would not be so sure of that," answered the trout, and without saying another word he dived straight down to the bottom of the well.

After hearing his mysterious words the Queen could not rest, and at last she asked her husband to have the Long Ship prepared once more, so that she could go and see her step-daughter.

The King gave the order gladly; and it all happened as it had happened before.

She steered the Ship over the sea with her own hands, and when it was approaching the land it was seen and recognised by Princess Gold-Tree.

The Prince was out hunting, and the Princess ran, in great terror, to her friend, the Other Princess, who was upstairs in her chamber.

"Oh, what shall I do, what shall I do?" she cried, "for I see my father's Long Ship coming, and I know that my cruel step-mother is on board, and she will try to kill me, as she tried to kill me before. Oh! Come, let us escape to the hills."

"Not at all," replied the Other Princess, throwing her arms round the trembling Gold-Tree. "I am not afraid of thy Lady Step-Mother. Come with me, and we will go down to the sea-shore to greet her."

So they both went down to the edge of the water, and when Queen Silver-Tree saw her step-daughter coming she pretended to be very glad, and sprang out of the boat and ran to meet her, and held out a silver goblet full of wine for her to drink.

"'Tis rare wine from the East," she said, "and therefore very precious. I brought a flagon with me, so that we might pledge each other in a loving cup."

Princess Gold-Tree, who was ever gentle and courteous, would have stretched out her hand for the cup, had not the Other Princess stepped between her and her step-mother.

"Nay, Madam," she said gravely, looking the Queen straight in the face, "it is the custom in this land for the one who offers a loving cup to drink from it first herself."

"I will follow the custom gladly," answered the Queen, and she raised the goblet to her mouth. But the Other Princess, who was watching her closely, noticed that she did not allow the wine that it contained to touch her lips. So she stepped forward and, as if by accident, struck the bottom of the goblet with her shoulder. Part of its contents flew into the Queen's face, and part, before she could shut her mouth, went down her throat.

So, because of her wickedness, she was, as the Good Book says, caught in her own net. For she had made the wine so poisonous that, almost before she had swallowed it, she fell dead at the two Princesses' feet.

No one was sorry for her, for she really deserved her fate; and they buried her hastily in a lonely piece of ground, and very soon everybody had forgotten all about her.

As for Princess Gold-Tree, she lived happily and peacefully with her husband and her friend for the remainder of her life.

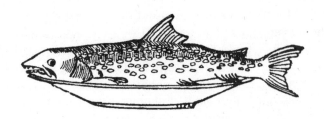

Whippety-Stourie

I am going to tell you a story about a poor young widow woman, who lived in a house called Kittlerumpit, though whereabouts in Scotland the house of Kittlerumpit stood nobody knows.

Some folk think that it stood in the neighbourhood of the Debateable Land, which, as all the world knows, was on the Borders, where the old Border Reivers were constantly coming and going; the Scotch stealing from the English, and the English from the Scotch. Be that as it may, the widowed Mistress of Kittlerumpit was sorely to be pitied.

For she had lost her husband, and no one quite knew what had become of him. He had gone to a fair one day, and had never come back again, and although everybody believed that he was dead, no one knew how he died.

Some people said that he had been persuaded to enlist, and had been killed in the wars; others, that he had been taken away to serve as a sailor by the press-gang, and had been drowned at sea.

At any rate, his poor young wife was sorely to be pitied, for she was left with a little baby boy to bring up, and, as times were bad, she had not much to live on.

But she loved her baby dearly, and worked all day amongst her cows, and pigs, and hens, in order to earn enough money to buy food and clothes for both herself and him.

Now, on the morning of which I am speaking, she rose very early and went out to feed her pigs, for rent-day was coming on, and she intended to take one of them, a great, big, fat creature, to the market that very day, as she thought that the price that it would fetch would go a long way towards paying her rent.

And because she thought so, her heart was light, and she hummed a little song to herself as she crossed the yard with her bucket on one arm and her baby boy on the other.

But the song was quickly changed into a cry of despair when she reached the pig-stye, for there lay her cherished pig on its back, with its legs in the air and its eyes shut, just as if it were going to breathe its last breath.

"What shall I do? What shall I do?" cried the poor woman, sitting down on a big stone and clasping her boy to her breast, heedless of the fact that she had dropped her bucket, and that the pig's meat was running out, and that the hens were eating it.

"First I lost my husband, and now I am going to lose my finest pig. The pig that I hoped would fetch a deal of money."

Now I must explain to you that the house of Kittlerumpit stood on a hillside, with a great fir wood behind it, and the ground sloping down steeply in front.

And as the poor young thing, after having a good cry to herself, was drying her eyes, she chanced to look down the hill, and who should she see coming up it but an old woman, who looked like a Lady born.

She was dressed all in green, with a white apron, and she wore a black velvet hood on her head, and a steeple-crowned beaver hat over that, something like those, as I have heard tell, that the women wear in Wales. She walked very slowly, leaning on a long staff, and she gave a bit hirple now and then, as if she were lame.

As she drew near, the young widow felt it was becoming

to rise and curtsey to the gentlewoman, for such she saw her to be.

"Madam," she said, with a sob in her voice, "I bid you welcome to the house of Kittlerumpit, although you find its Mistress one of the most unfortunate women in the world."

"Hout-tout," answered the old woman, in such a harsh voice that the young woman started, and grasped her baby tighter in her arms. "Ye have little need to say that. Ye have lost your husband, I grant ye, but there were waur losses at Shirra-Muir. And now your pig is like to die—I could, maybe, remedy that. But I must first hear how much ye wad gie me if I cured him."

"Anything that your Ladyship's Madam likes to ask," replied the widow, too much delighted at having the animal's life saved to think that she was making rather a rash promise.

"Very good," said the old woman, and without wasting any more words she walked straight into the pig-stye.

She stood and looked at the dying creature for some minutes, rocking to and fro and muttering to herself in words which the widow could not understand; at least, she could only understand four of them, and they sounded something like this:

"Pitter-patter,
Haly water."

Then she put her hand into her pocket and drew out a tin bottle with a liquid that looked like oil in it. She took the cork out, and dropped one of her long lady-like fingers into it; then she touched the pig on the snout and on his ears, and on the tip of his curly tail.

No sooner had she done so than up the beast jumped, and, with a grunt of contentment, ran off to its trough to look for its breakfast.

A joyful woman was the Mistress of Kittlerumpit when she saw it do this, for she felt that her rent was safe; and in her relief and gratitude she would have kissed the hem of the strange Lady's green gown, if she would have allowed it, but she would not.

"No, no," said she, and her voice sounded harsher than ever. "Let us have no fine meanderings, but let us stick to our bargain. I have done my part, and mended the pig; now ye must do yours, and give me what I like to ask—your son."

Then the poor widow gave a piteous cry, for she knew now what she had not guessed before—that the green-clad Lady was a Fairy, and a Wicked Fairy too, else had she not asked such a terrible thing.

It was too late now, however, to pray, and beseech, and beg for mercy; the Fairy stood her ground, hard and cruel.

"Ye promised me what I liked to ask, and I have asked your son; and your son I will have," she replied, "so it is useless making such a din about it. But one thing I may tell you, for I know well that the knowledge will not help you. By the laws of Fairy-land, I cannot take the bairn till the third day after this, and if by that time you have found out my name I cannot take him even then. But ye will not be able to find it out, of that I am certain. So I will call back for the boy in three days."

And with that she disappeared round the back of the pig-stye, and the poor mother fell down in a dead faint beside the stone.

All that day, and all the next, she did nothing but sit in her kitchen and cry, and hug her baby tighter in her arms; but on the day before that on which the Fairy said that she was coming back, she felt as if she must get a little breath of fresh air, so she went for a walk in the fir wood behind the house.

Now in this fir wood there was an old quarry hole, in the bottom of which was a bonnie spring well, the water of which was always sweet and pure. The young widow was walking near this quarry hole, when, to her astonishment, she heard the whirr of a spinning-wheel and the sound of a voice lilting a song. At first she could not think where the sound came from; then, remembering the quarry, she laid down her child at a tree root, and crept noiselessly through the bushes on her hands and knees to the edge of the hole and peeped over.

She could hardly believe her eyes! For there, far below her, at the bottom of the quarry, beside the spring well, sat the cruel Fairy, dressed in her green frock and tall felt hat, spinning away as fast as she could at a tiny spinning-wheel. And what should she be singing but:

"Little kens our guid dane at hame,
Whippety-Stourie is my name."

The widow woman almost cried aloud for joy, for now she had learned the Fairy's secret, and her child was safe. But she dare not, in case the wicked old Dame heard her and threw some other spell over her.

So she crept softly back to the place where she had left her child; then, catching him up in her arms, she ran through the wood to her house, laughing, and singing, and tossing him in the air in such a state of delight that, if anyone had met her, they would have been in danger of thinking that she was mad.

Now this young woman had been a merry-hearted maiden, and would have been merry-hearted still, if, since her marriage, she had not had so much trouble that it had made her grow old and sober-minded before her time; and she began to think what fun it would be to tease the Fairy for a few minutes before she let her know that she had found out her name.

So next day, at the appointed time, she went out with her boy in her arms, and seated herself on the big stone where she had sat before; and when she saw the old woman coming up the hill, she crumpled up her nice clean cap, and screwed up her face, and pretended to be in great distress and to be crying bitterly.

The Fairy took no notice of this, however, but came close up to her, and said, in her harsh, merciless voice, "Goodwife of Kittlerumpit, ye ken the reason of my coming; give me the bairn."

Then the young mother pretended to be in sorer distress than ever, and fell on her knees before the wicked old woman and begged for mercy.

"Oh, sweet Madam Mistress," she cried, "spare me my bairn, and take, an' thou wilt, the pig instead."

"We have no need of bacon where I come from," answered the Fairy coldly, "so give me the laddie and let me begone—I have no time to waste in this wise."

"Oh, dear Lady mine," pleaded the Goodwife, "if thou wilt not have the pig, wilt thou not spare my poor bairn and take me myself?"

The Fairy stepped back a little, as if in astonishment. "Art thou mad, woman," she cried contemptuously, "that thou proposest such a thing? Who in all the world would care to take a plain-looking, red-eyed, dowdy wife like thee with them?"

Now the young Mistress of Kittlerumpit knew that she was no beauty, and the knowledge had never vexed her; but something in the Fairy's tone made her feel so angry that she could contain herself no longer.

"In troth, fair Madam, I might have had the wit to know that the like of me is not fit to tie the shoestring of the High and Mighty Princess, WHIPPETY-STOURIE!"

If there had been a charge of gunpowder buried in the ground, and if it had suddenly exploded beneath her feet, the Wicked Fairy could not have jumped higher into the air.

And when she came down again she simply turned round and ran down the brae, shrieking with rage and disappointment, for all the world, as an old book says, "like an owl chased by Witches".

The Red-Etin

There were once two widows who lived in two cottages which stood not very far from one another. And each of those widows possessed a piece of land on which she grazed a cow and a few sheep, and in this way she made her living.

One of these poor widows had two sons, the other had one; and as these three boys were always together, it was natural that they should become great friends.

At last the time arrived when the eldest son of the widow who had two sons, must leave home and go out into the world to seek his fortune. And the night before he went away his mother told him to take a can and go to the well and bring back some water, and she would bake a cake for him to carry with him.

"But remember," she added, "the size of the cake will depend on the quantity of water that thou bringest back. If thou bringest much, then will it be large; and, if thou bringest little, then will it be small. But, big or little, it is all that I have to give thee."

The lad took the can and went off to the well, and filled it with water, and came home again. But he never noticed that the can had a hole in it, and the water was running out; so that, by the time that he arrived at home, there was very little water left. So his mother could only bake him a very little cake.

But, small as it was, she asked him, as she gave it to him, to choose one of two things. Either to take the half of it with her blessing, or the whole of it with her curse. "For," said she, "thou canst not have both the whole cake and a blessing along with it."

The lad looked at the cake and hesitated. It would have been pleasant to have left home with his mother's blessing upon him; but he had far to go, and the cake was little; the half of it would be a mere mouthful, and he did not know when he would get any more food. So at last he made up his mind to take the whole of it, even if he had to bear his mother's curse.

Then he took his younger brother aside, and gave him his hunting-knife, saying, "Keep this by thee, and look at it every morning. For as long as the blade remains clear and bright, thou wilt know that it is well with me; but should it grow dim and rusty, then know thou that some evil hath befallen me."

After this he embraced them both and set out on his travels. He journeyed all that day, and all the next, and on the afternoon of the third day he came to where an old shepherd was sitting beside a flock of sheep.

"I will ask the old man whose sheep they are," he said to himself, "for mayhap his master might engage me also as a shepherd." So he went up to the old man, and asked him to whom the sheep belonged. And this was all the answer he got:

> "The Red-Etin of Ireland
> Ance lived in Ballygan,
> And stole King Malcolm's daughter,
> The King of fair Scotland.
> He beats her, he binds her,
> He lays her on a band,
> And every day he dings her
> With a bright silver wand.
> Like Julian the Roman,
> He's one that fears no man.

It's said there's ane predestinate
To be his mortal foe,
But that man is yet unborn,
And lang may it be so."

"That does not tell me much; but somehow I do not fancy this Red-Etin for a master," thought the youth, and he went on his way.

He had not gone very far, however, when he saw another old man, with snow-white hair, herding a flock of swine; and as he wondered to whom the swine belonged, and if there was any chance of him getting a situation as a swineherd, he went up to the countryman, and asked who was the owner of the animals.

He got the same answer from the swineherd that he had got from the shepherd:

"The Red-Etin of Ireland
Ance lived in Ballygan,
And stole King Malcolm's daughter,
The King of fair Scotland.
He beats her, he binds her,
He lays her on a band,
And every day he dings her
With a bright silver wand.
Like Julian the Roman,
He's one that fears no man.
It's said there's ane predestinate
To be his mortal foe,
But that man is yet unborn,
And lang may it be so."

"Plague on this old Red-Etin; I wonder when I will get out of his domains," he muttered to himself; and he journeyed still further.

Presently he came to a very, very old man—so old, indeed, that he was quite bent with age—and he was herding a flock of goats.

Once more the traveller asked to whom the animals belonged, and once more he got the same answer:

> "The Red-Etin of Ireland
> Ance lived in Ballygan,
> And stole King Malcolm's daughter,
> The King of fair Scotland.
> He beats her, he binds her,
> He lays her on a band,
> And every day he dings her
> With a bright silver wand.
> Like Julian the Roman,
> He's one that fears no man.
> It's said there's ane predestinate
> To be his mortal foe,
> But that man is yet unborn,
> And lang may it be so."

But this ancient goatherd added a piece of advice at the end of his rhyme. "Beware, stranger," he said, "of the next herd of beasts that ye shall meet. Sheep, and swine, and goats will harm nobody; but the creatures ye shall now encounter are of a sort that ye have never met before, and they are not harmless."

The young man thanked him for his counsel, and went on his way, and he had not gone very far before he met a herd of very dreadful creatures, unlike anything that he had ever dreamed of in all his life.

For each of them had three heads, and on each of its three heads it had four horns; and when he saw them he was so frightened that he turned and ran away from them as fast as he could.

Up hill and down dale he ran, until he was wellnigh exhausted; and, just when he was beginning to feel that his legs would not carry him any further, he saw a great Castle in front of him, the door of which was standing wide open.

He was so tired that he went straight in, and after wandering through some magnificent Halls, which appeared to be quite deserted, he reached the kitchen, where an old woman was sitting by the fire.

He asked her if he might have a night's lodging, as he had come a long and weary journey, and would be glad of somewhere to rest.

"You can rest here, and welcome, for me," said the old Dame, "but for your own sake I warn you that this is an ill house to bide in; for it is the Castle of the Red-Etin, who is a fierce and terrible Monster with three heads, and he spareth neither man nor woman, if he can get hold of them."

Tired as he was, the young man would have made an effort to escape from such a dangerous abode had he not remembered the strange and awful beasts from which he had just been fleeing, and he was afraid that, as it was growing dark, if he set out again he might chance to walk right into their midst. So he begged the old woman to hide him in some dark corner, and not to tell the Red-Etin that he was in the Castle.

"For," thought he, "if I can only get shelter until the morning, I will then be able to avoid these terrible creatures and go on my way in peace."

So the old Dame hid him in a press under the back stairs, and, as there was plenty of room in it, he settled down quite comfortably for the night.

But just as he was going off to sleep he heard an awful roaring and trampling overhead. The Red-Etin had come home, and it was plain that he was searching for something.

And the terrified youth soon found out what the "something"

was, for very soon the horrible Monster came into the kitchen, crying out in a voice like thunder:

"Seek but, and seek ben,
I smell the smell of an earthly man!
Be he living, or be he dead,
His heart this night I shall eat with my bread."

And it was not very long before he discovered the poor young man's hiding-place and pulled him roughly out of it.

Of course, the lad begged that his life might be spared, but the Monster only laughed at him.

"It will be spared if thou canst answer three questions," he said; "if not, it is forfeited."

The first of these three questions was, "Whether Ireland or Scotland was first inhabited?"

The second, "How old was the world when Adam was made?"

And the third, "Whether men or beasts were created first?"

The lad was not skilled in such matters, having had but little book-learning, and he could not answer the questions. So the Monster struck him on the head with a queer little hammer which he carried, and turned him into a piece of stone.

Now every morning since he had left home his younger brother had done as he had promised, and had carefully examined his hunting-knife.

On the first two mornings it was bright and clear, but on the third morning he was very much distressed to find that it was dull and rusty. He looked at it for a few moments in great dismay; then he ran straight to his mother, and held it out to her.

"By this token I know that some mischief hath befallen my brother," he said, "so I must set out at once to see what evil hath come upon him."

"First must thou go to the well and fetch me some water," said his mother, "that I may bake thee a cake to carry with thee, as I baked a cake for him who is gone. And I will say to thee what I said to him. That the cake will be large or small according as thou bringest much or little water back with thee."

So the lad took the can, as his brother had done, and went off to the well, and it seemed as if some evil spirit directed him to follow his example in all things, for he brought home little water, and he chose the whole cake and his mother's curse, instead of the half and her blessing, and he set out and met the shepherd, and the swineherd, and the goatherd, and they all gave the same answers to him which they had given to his brother.

And he also encountered the same fierce beasts, and ran from them in terror, and took shelter from them in the Castle; and the old Dame hid him, and the Red-Etin found him, and, because he could not answer the three questions, he, too, was turned into a pillar of stone.

And no more would ever have been heard of these two youths had not a kind Fairy, who had seen all that had happened, appeared to the other widow and her son, as they were sitting at supper one night in the gloaming, and told them the whole story, and how their two poor young neighbours had been turned into pillars of stone by a cruel enchanter called Red-Etin.

Now the third young man was both brave and strong, and he determined to set out to see if he could in anywise help his two friends. And, from the very first moment that he had made up his mind to do so, things went differently with him than they had with them. I think, perhaps, that this was because he was much more loving and thoughtful than they were.

For, when his mother sent him to fetch water from the well so that she might bake a cake for him, just as the other mother had done for her sons, a raven, flying above his head, croaked out that his can was leaking, and he, wishing to please his mother by bringing her a good supply of water, patched up the hole with clay, and so came home with the can quite full.

Then, when his mother had baked a big bannock for him, and giving him his choice between the whole cake and her curse, or half of it and her blessing, he chose the latter. "For," said he, throwing his arms round her neck, "I may light on other cakes to eat, but I will never light on another blessing such as thine."

And the curious thing was, that, after he had said this, the half cake which he had chosen seemed to spread itself out, and widen, and broaden, till it was bigger by far than it had been at first.

Then he started on his journey, and, after he had gone a good way he began to feel hungry. So he pulled the cake out of his pocket and began to eat it.

Just then he met an old woman, who seemed to be very poor, for her clothing was thin, and worn, and old, and she stopped and spoke to him.

"Of thy charity, kind Master," she said, stretching out one of her withered hands, "spare me a bit of the cake that thou art eating."

Now the youth was very hungry, and he could have eaten it all himself, but his kind heart was touched by the woman's pinched face, so he broke it in two, and gave her half of it.

Instantly she was changed into the Fairy who had appeared to his mother and himself as they had sat at supper the night before, and she smiled graciously at the generous lad, and held out a little wand to him.

"Though thou knowest it not, thy mother's blessing and thy kindness to an old and poor woman hath gained thee many blessings, brave boy," she said. "Keep that as thy reward; thou wilt need it ere thy errand be done." Then, bidding him sit down on the grass beside her, she told him all the dangers that he would meet on his travels, and the way in which he could overcome them, and then, in a moment, before he could thank her, she vanished out of his sight.

But with the little wand, and all the instructions that she had given him, he felt that he could face fearlessly any danger that he might be called on to meet, so he rose from the grass and went his way, full of a cheerful courage.

After he had walked for many miles further, he came, as each of his friends had done, to the old shepherd herding his sheep. And, like them, he asked to whom the sheep belonged. And this time the old man answered:

> "The Red-Etin of Ireland
> Ance lived in Ballygan,
> And stole King Malcolm's daughter,
> The King of fair Scotland.
> He beats her, he binds her,
> He lays her on a band,
> And every day he dings her
> With a bright silver wand.
> Like Julian the Roman,
> He's one that fears no man.
> But now I fear his end is near,
> And destiny at hand;
> And you're to be, I plainly see,
> The heir of all his land."

Then the young man went on, and he came to the swineherd, and to the goatherd; and each of them in turn repeated the same words to him.

And, when he came to where the droves of monstrous beasts were, he was not afraid of them, and when one came running up to him with its mouth wide open to devour him, he just struck it with his wand, and it dropped down dead at his feet.

At last he arrived at the Red-Etin's Castle, and he knocked boldly at the door. The old Dame answered his knock, and, when he had told her his errand, warned him gravely not to enter.

"Thy two friends came here before thee," she said, "and they are now turned into two pillars of stone; what advantage is it to thee to lose thy life also?"

But the young man only laughed. "I have knowledge of an art of which they knew nothing," he said. "And methinks I can fight the Red-Etin with his own weapons."

So, much against her will, the old Dame let him in, and hid him where she had hid his friends.

It was not long before the Monster arrived, and, as on former occasions, he came into the kitchen in a furious rage, crying:

"Seek but, and seek ben,
I smell the smell of an earthly man!
Be he living, or be he dead,
His heart this night I shall eat with my bread."

Then he peered into the young man's hiding-place, and called to him to come out. And after he had come out, he put to him the three questions, never dreaming that he could answer them; but the Fairy had told the youth what to say, and he gave the answers as pat as any book.

Then the Red-Etin's heart sank within him for fear, for he knew that someone had betrayed him, and that his power was gone.

And gone in very truth it was. For when the youth took an axe and began to fight with him, he had no strength to resist, and, before he knew where he was, his heads were cut off. And that was the end of the Red-Etin.

As soon as he saw that his enemy was really dead, the young man asked the old Dame if what the shepherd, and the swineherd, and the goatherd had told him were true, and if King Malcolm's daughter were really a prisoner in the Castle.

The old Dame nodded. "Even with the Monster lying dead at my feet, I am almost afraid to speak of it," she said. "But come with me, my gallant gentleman, and thou wilt see what grief and misery the Red-Etin hath caused to many a home."

She took a huge bunch of keys, and led him up a long flight of stairs, which ended in a passage with a great many doors on each side of it. She unlocked these doors with her keys, and, as she opened them, she put her head into every room and said, "Ye have naught to fear now, Madam, the Predestinated Deliverer hath come, and the Red-Etin is dead."

And behold, with a cry of joy, out of every room came a beautiful Lady who had been stolen from her home, and shut up there, by the Red-Etin.

Among them was one who was more beautiful and stately than the rest, and all the others bowed down to her and treated her with such great reverence that it was clear to see that she was the Royal Princess, King Malcolm's daughter.

And when the youth stepped forward and did reverence to her also, she spoke so sweetly to him, and greeted him so gladly, and called him her Deliverer, in such a low, clear voice, that his heart was taken captive at once.

But, for all that, he did not forget his friends. He asked the old woman where they were, and she took him into a room at the end of the passage, which was so dark that one could scarcely see in it, and so low that one could scarcely stand upright.

In this dismal chamber stood two blocks of stone.

"One can unlock doors, young Master," said the old Dame, shaking her head forebodingly, "but 'tis hard work to try to turn cauld stane back to flesh and blood."

"Nevertheless, I will do it," said the youth, and, lifting his little wand, he touched each of the stone pillars lightly on the top.

Instantly the hard stone seemed to soften and melt away, and the two brothers started into life and form again. Their gratitude to their friend, who had risked so much to save them, knew no bounds, while he, on his part, was delighted to think that his efforts had been successful.

The next thing to do was to convey the Princess and the other Ladies (who were all Noblemen's daughters) back to the King's Court, and this they did next day.

King Malcolm was so overjoyed to see his dearly loved daughter, whom he had given up for dead, safe and sound, and so grateful to her deliverer, that he said that he should become his son-in-law and marry the Princess, and come and live with them at Court. Which all came to pass in due time; while as for the two other young men, they married Noblemen's daughters, and the two old mothers came to live near their sons, and everyone was as happy as they could possibly be.

The Seal Catcher
and the Merman

Once upon a time there was a man who lived not very far from John o' Groat's house, which, as everyone knows, is in the very north of Scotland. He lived in a little cottage by the sea-shore, and made his living by catching seals and selling their fur, which is very valuable.

He earned a good deal of money in this way, for these creatures used to come out of the sea in large numbers, and lie on the rocks near his house basking in the sunshine, so that it was not difficult to creep up behind them and kill them.

Some of those seals were larger than others, and the country people used to call them "Roane", and whisper that they were not seals at all, but Mermen and Merwomen, who came from a country of their own, down under the ocean, who assumed this strange disguise in order that they might pass through the water, and come up to breathe the air of this earth of ours.

But the seal catcher only laughed at them, and said that those seals were most worth killing, for their skins were so big that he got an extra price for them.

Now it chanced one day, when he was pursuing his calling, that he stabbed a seal with his hunting-knife, and whether the stroke had not been sure enough or not, I cannot say, but with a loud cry of pain the creature slipped off the rock into the sea, and disappeared under the water, carrying the knife along with it.

The seal catcher, much annoyed at his clumsiness, and also at the loss of his knife, went home to dinner in a very downcast frame of mind. On his way he met a horseman, who was so tall and so strange-looking and who rode on such a gigantic horse, that he stopped and looked at him in astonishment, wondering who he was, and from what country he came.

The stranger stopped also, and asked him his trade and on hearing that he was a seal catcher, he immediately ordered a great number of seal skins. The seal catcher was delighted, for such an order meant a large sum of money to him. But his face fell when the horseman added that it was absolutely necessary that the skins should be delivered that evening.

"I cannot do it," he said in a disappointed voice, "for the seals will not come back to the rocks again until tomorrow morning."

"I can take you to a place where there are any number of seals," answered the stranger, "if you will mount behind me on my horse and come with me."

The seal catcher agreed to this, and climbed up behind the rider, who shook his bridle rein, and off the great horse galloped at such a pace that he had much ado to keep his seat.

On and on they went, flying like the wind, until at last they came to the edge of a huge precipice, the face of which went sheer down to the sea. Here the mysterious horseman pulled up his steed with a jerk.

"Get off now," he said shortly.

The seal catcher did as he was bid, and when he found himself safe on the ground, he peeped cautiously over the edge of the cliff, to see if there were any seals lying on the rocks below.

To his astonishment he saw no rocks, only the blue sea, which came right up to the foot of the cliff.

"Where are the seals that you spoke of?" he asked anxiously, wishing that he had never set out on such a rash adventure.

"You will see presently," answered the stranger, who was attending to his horse's bridle.

The seal catcher was now thoroughly frightened, for he felt sure that some evil was about to befall him, and in such a lonely place he knew that it would be useless to cry out for help.

And it seemed as if his fears would prove only too true, for the next moment the stranger's hand was laid upon his shoulder, and he felt himself being hurled bodily over the cliff, and then he fell with a splash into the sea.

He thought that his last hour had come, and he wondered how anyone could work such a deed of wrong upon an innocent man.

But, to his astonishment, he found that some change must have passed over him, for instead of being choked by the water, he could breathe quite easily, and he and his companion, who was still close at his side, seemed to be sinking as quickly down through the sea as they had flown through the air.

Down and down they went, nobody knows how far, till at last they came to a huge arched door, which appeared to be made of pink coral, studded over with cockle-shells. It opened, of its own accord, and when they entered they found themselves in a huge Hall, the walls of which were formed of mother-of-pearl, and the floor of which was of sea-sand, smooth, and firm, and yellow.

The Hall was crowded with occupants, but they were seals, not men, and when the seal catcher turned to his companion to ask him what it all meant, he was aghast to find that he, too, had assumed the form of a seal. He was still more aghast when he caught sight of himself in a large mirror that hung on the wall, and saw that he also no longer bore the likeness of a man, but was transformed into a nice, hairy, brown seal.

"Ah, woe to me," he said to himself, "for no fault of mine own this artful stranger hath laid some baneful charm upon me, and in this awful guise will I remain for the rest of my natural life."

At first none of the huge creatures spoke to him. For some reason or other they seemed to be very sad, and moved gently about the Hall, talking quietly and mournfully to one another, or lay sadly upon the sandy floor, wiping big tears from their eyes with their soft furry fins.

But presently they began to notice him, and to whisper to one another, and presently his guide moved away from him, and disappeared through a door at the end of the Hall. When he returned he held a huge knife in his hand.

"Didst thou ever see this before?" he asked, holding it out to the unfortunate seal catcher, who, to his horror, recognised his own hunting-knife with which he had struck the seal in the morning, and which had been carried off by the wounded animal.

At the sight of it he fell upon his face and begged for mercy, for he at once came to the conclusion that the inhabitants of the cavern, enraged at the harm which had been wrought upon their comrade, had, in some magic way, contrived to capture him, and to bring him down to their subterranean abode, in order to wreak their vengeance upon him by killing him.

But, instead of doing so, they crowded round him, rubbing their soft noses against his fur to show their sympathy, and implored him not to put himself about, for no harm would befall him, and they would love him all their lives long if he would only do what they asked him.

"Tell me what it is," said the seal catcher, "and I will do it, if it lies within my power."

"Follow me," answered his guide, and he led the way to the door through which he had disappeared when he went to seek the knife.

The seal catcher followed him. And there, in a smaller room, he found a great brown seal lying on a bed of pale pink seaweed, with a gaping wound in his side.

"That is my father," said his guide, "whom thou wounded this morning, thinking that he was one of the common seals who live in the sea, instead of a Merman who hath speech, and understanding, as you mortals have. I brought thee hither to bind up his wounds, for no other hand than thine can heal him."

"I have no skill in the art of healing," said the seal catcher, astonished at the forbearance of these strange creatures, whom he had so unwittingly wronged, "but I will bind up the wound to the best of my power, and I am only sorry that it was my hands that caused it."

He went over to the bed, and, stooping over the wounded Merman, washed and dressed the hurt as well as he could; and the touch of his hands appeared to work like magic, for no sooner had he finished than the wound seemed to deaden and die, leaving only the scar, and the old seal sprang up, as well as ever.

Then there was great rejoicing throughout the whole Palace of the Seals. They laughed, and they talked, and they embraced each other in their own strange way, crowding round their comrade, and rubbing their noses against his, as if to show him how delighted they were at his recovery.

But all this while the seal catcher stood alone in a corner, with his mind filled with dark thoughts, for although he saw now that they had no intention of killing him, he did not relish the prospect of spending the rest of his life in the guise of a seal, fathoms deep under the ocean.

But presently, to his great joy, his guide approached him, and said, "Now you are at liberty to return home to your wife and children. I will take you to them, but only on one condition."

"And what is that?" asked the seal catcher eagerly, overjoyed at the prospect of being restored safely to the upper world, and to his family.

"That you will take a solemn oath never to wound a seal again."

"That will I do right gladly," he replied, for although the promise meant giving up his means of livelihood, he felt that if only he regained his proper shape he could always turn his hand to something else.

So he took the required oath with all due solemnity, holding up his fin as he swore, and all the other seals crowded round him as witnesses. And a sigh of relief went through the Halls when the words were spoken, for he was the most noted seal catcher in the North.

Then he bade the strange company farewell, and, accompanied by his guide, passed once more through the outer doors of coral, and up, and up, and up, through the shadowy green water, until it began to grow lighter and lighter and at last they emerged into the sunshine of earth.

Then, with one spring, they reached the top of the cliff, where the great black horse was waiting for them, quietly nibbling the green turf.

When they left the water their strange disguise dropped from them, and they were now as they had been before, a plain seal catcher and a tall, well-dressed gentleman in riding clothes.

"Get up behind me," said the latter, as he swung himself into his saddle. The seal catcher did as he was bid, taking tight hold of his companion's coat, for he remembered how nearly he had fallen off on his previous journey.

Then it all happened as it happened before. The bridle was shaken, and the horse galloped off, and it was not long before the seal catcher found himself standing in safety before his own garden gate.

He held out his hand to say goodbye, but as he did so the stranger pulled out a huge bag of gold and placed it in his hand. "Thou hast done thy part of the bargain—we must do ours," he said. "Men shall never say that we took away an honest man's work without making reparation for it, and here is what will keep thee in comfort to thy life's end."

Then he vanished, and when the astonished seal catcher carried the bag into his cottage, and turned the gold out on the table, he found that what the stranger had said was true, and that he would be a rich man for the remainder of his days.

The Page-Boy
and the Silver Goblet

There was once a little page-boy, who was in service in a stately Castle. He was a very good-natured little fellow, and did his duties so willingly and well that everybody liked him, from the great Earl whom he served every day on bended knee, to the fat old butler whose errands he ran.

Now the Castle stood on the edge of a cliff overlooking the sea, and although the walls at that side were very thick, in them there was a little postern door, which opened on to a narrow flight of steps that led down the face of the cliff to the sea-shore, so that anyone who liked could go down there in the pleasant summer mornings and bathe in the shimmering sea.

On the other side of the Castle were gardens and pleasure grounds, opening on to a long stretch of heather-covered moorland, which, at last, met a distant range of hills.

The little page-boy was very fond of going out on this moor when his work was done, for then he could run about as much as he liked, chasing bumble-bees, and catching butterflies, and looking for birds' nests when it was nesting time.

And the old butler was very pleased that he should do so, for he knew that it was good for a healthy little lad to have plenty of fun in the open air. But before the boy went out the old man always gave him one warning.

"Now, mind my words, laddie, and keep far away from the Fairy Knowe, for the Little Folk are not to be trusted."

This Knowe of which he spoke was a little green hillock, which stood on the moor not twenty yards from the garden gate, and folk said that it was the abode of Fairies, who would punish any rash mortal who came too near them. And because of this the country people would walk a good half-mile out of their way, even in broad daylight, rather than run the risk of going too near the Fairy Knowe and bringing down the Little Folks' displeasure upon them. And at night they would hardly cross the moor at all, for everyone knows that Fairies come abroad in the darkness, and the door of their dwelling stands open, so that any luckless mortal who does not take care may find himself inside.

Now, the little page-boy was an adventurous fellow, and instead of being frightened of the Fairies, he was very anxious to see them, and to visit their abode, just to find out what it was like.

So one night, when everyone else was asleep, he crept out of the Castle by the little postern door, and stole down the stone steps, and along the sea-shore, and up on to the moor, and went straight to the Fairy Knowe.

To his delight he found that what everyone said was true. The top of the Knowe was tipped up, and from the opening that was thus made, rays of light came streaming out.

His heart was beating fast with excitement, but, gathering his courage, he stooped down and slipped inside the Knowe.

He found himself in a large room lit by numberless tiny candles, and there, seated round a polished table, were scores of the Tiny Folk, Fairies, and Elves, and Gnomes, dressed in green, and yellow, and pink; blue, and lilac, and scarlet; in all the colours, in fact, that you can think of.

He stood in a dark corner watching the busy scene in wonder, thinking how strange it was that there should be such a number of these tiny beings living their own lives all unknown to men, at such a little distance from them, when suddenly someone— he could not tell who it was—gave an order

"Fetch the Cup," cried the owner of the unknown voice, and instantly two little Fairy pages, dressed all in scarlet livery, darted from the table to a tiny cupboard in the rock, and returned staggering under the weight of a most beautiful silver cup, richly embossed and lined inside with gold.

They placed it in the middle of the table, and, amid clapping of hands and shouts of joy, all the Fairies began to drink out of it in turn. And the page could see, from where he stood, that no one poured wine into it, and yet it was always full, and that the wine that was in it was not always the same kind, but that each Fairy, when he grasped its stem, wished for the wine that he loved best, and lo! in a moment the cup was full of it.

"'Twould be a fine thing if I could take that cup home with me," thought the page. "No one will believe that I have been here except I have something to show for it." So he bided his time, and watched.

Presently the Fairies noticed him, and, instead of being angry at his boldness in entering their abode, as he expected that they would be, they seemed very pleased to see him, and invited him to a seat at the table. But by and by they grew rude and insolent, and jeered at him for being content to serve mere mortals, telling him that they saw everything that went on at the Castle, and making fun of the old butler, whom the page loved with all his heart. And they laughed at the food he ate, saying that it was only fit for animals; and when any fresh dainty was set on the table by the scarlet-clad pages, they would push the dish across to him, saying, "Taste it, for you will not have the chance of tasting such things at the Castle."

At last he could stand their teasing remarks no longer, besides, he knew that if he wanted to secure the cup he must lose no time in doing so.

So he suddenly stood up, and grasped the stem of it tightly in his hand. "I'll drink to you all in water," he cried, and instantly the ruby wine was turned to clear cold water.

He raised the cup to his lips, but he did not drink from it. With a sudden jerk he threw the water over the candles, and instantly the room was in darkness. Then, clasping the precious cup tightly in his arms, he sprang to the opening of the Knowe, through which he could see the stars glimmering clearly.

He was just in time, for it fell to with a crash behind him; and soon he was speeding along the wet, dew-spangled moor, with the whole troop of Fairies at his heels. They were wild with rage, and from the shrill shouts of fury which they uttered, the page knew well that, if they overtook him, he need expect no mercy at their hands.

And his heart began to sink, for, fleet of foot though he was, he was no match for the Fairy Folk, who gained on him steadily.

All seemed lost, when a mysterious voice sounded out of the darkness:

> "If thou wouldst gain the Castle door,
> Keep to the black stones on the shore."

It was the voice of some poor mortal, who, for some reason or other, had been taken prisoner by the Fairies—who were really very malicious Little Folk—and who did not want a like fate to befall the adventurous page-boy; but the little fellow did not know this.

He had once heard that if anyone walked on the wet sands, where the waves had come over them, the Fairies could not touch him, and this mysterious sentence brought the saying into his mind.

So he turned, and dashed panting down to the shore. His feet sank in the dry sand, his breath came in little gasps, and he felt as if he must give up the struggle; but he persevered, and at last, just as the foremost Fairies were about to lay hands on him, he jumped across the water-mark onto the firm, wet sand, from which the waves had just receded, and then he knew that he was safe.

For the Little Folk could go no step further, but stood on the dry sand uttering cries of rage and disappointment, while the triumphant page-boy ran safely along the shore, his precious cup in his arms, and climbed lightly up the steps in the rock and disappeared through the postern. And for many years after, long after the little page-boy had grown up and become a stately butler, who trained other little page-boys to follow in his footsteps, the beautiful cup remained in the Castle as a witness of his adventure.

The Black Bull of Norroway

In bygone days, long centuries ago, there lived a widowed Queen who had three daughters. And this widowed Queen was so poor, and had fallen upon such evil days, that she and her daughters had often much ado to get enough to eat.

So the eldest Princess determined that she would set out into the world to seek her fortune. And her mother was quite willing that she should do so. "For," said she, " 'tis better to work abroad than to starve at home."

But as there was an old Hen-wife living near the Castle who was said to be a Witch, and to be able to foretell the future, the Queen sent the Princess to her cottage, before she set out on her travels, to ask her in which direction she ought to go, in order to find the best fortune.

"Thou needst gang nae farther than my back door, hinnie," answered the old Dame, who had always felt very sorry for the Queen and her pretty daughters, and was glad to do them a good turn.

So the Princess ran through the passage to the Hen-wife's back door and peeped out, and what should she see but a magnificent coach, drawn by six beautiful cream-coloured horses, coming along the road.

Greatly excited at this unusual sight, she hurried back to the kitchen, and told the Hen-wife what she had seen.

"Aweel, aweel, ye've seen your fortune," said the old Dame,

in a tone of satisfaction, "for that coach-and-six is coming for thee."

Sure enough, the coach-and-six stopped at the gate of the Castle, and the second Princess came running down to the cottage to tell her sister to make haste, because it was waiting for her. Delighted beyond measure at the wonderful luck that had come to her, she hurried home, and, saying farewell to her mother and sisters, took her seat within, and the horses galloped off immediately.

And I've heard tell that they drew her to the Palace of a great and wealthy Prince, who married her; but that is outside my story.

A few weeks afterwards, the second Princess thought that she would do as her sister had done, and go down to the Hen-wife's cottage, and tell her that she, too, was going out into the world to seek her fortune. And, of course, in her heart of hearts she hoped that what had happened to her sister would happen to her also.

And, curious to say, it did. For the old Hen-wife sent her to look out at her back door, and she went, and, lo and behold, another coach-and-six was coming along the road! And when she went and told the old Hen-wife, she smiled upon her kindly, and told her to hurry home, for the coach-and-six was her fortune also, and that it had come for her.

So she, too, ran home, and got into her grand carriage, and was driven away. And, of course, after all these lucky happenings, the youngest Princess was anxious to try what her fortune might be; so that very night, in high good humour, she tripped away down to the old Hen-wife's cottage.

She, too, was told to look out at the back door, and she was only too glad to do so; for she fully expected to see a third coach-and-six coming rolling along the high road, straight for the Castle door.

But, alas and alack, no such sight greeted her eager eyes, for the high road was quite deserted, and in great disappointment she ran back to the Hen-wife to tell her so.

"Then it is clear that thy fortune is not coming to meet thee this day," said the old Dame, "so thou must e'en come back to-morrow."

So the little Princess went home again, and next day she turned up once more at the old Hen-wife's cottage.

But once more she was disappointed, for although she looked out long and eagerly, no glad sight of a coach-and-six, or of any other coach, greeted her eyes. On the third day, however, what should she see but a great Black Bull coming rushing along the road, bellowing as it came, and tossing its head fiercely in the air.

In great alarm, the little Princess shut the door, and ran to the Hen-wife to tell her about the furious animal that was approaching.

"Hech, hinnie," cried the old woman, holding up her hands in dismay, "and who would have thocht that the Black Bull of Norroway wad be your fate!"

At the words, the poor little maiden grew pale. She had come out to seek her fortune, but it had never dawned upon her that her fortune could be anything so terrible as this.

"But the Bull cannot be my fortune," she cried in terror. "I cannot go away with a bull."

"But ye'll need tae," replied the Hen-wife calmly. "For you lookit out of my door with the intent of meeting your fortune; and when your fortune has come tae ye, you must just bear it."

And when the poor Princess ran weeping to her mother, to beg to be allowed to stay at home, she found her mother of the same mind as the old Wise Woman; and so she had to allow herself to be lifted up onto the back of the enormous Black Bull that had come up to the door of the Castle, and was now standing there quietly enough. And when she was settled, he set off again on his wild career, while she sobbed and trembled with terror, and clung to his horns with all her might.

On and on they went, until at last the poor maiden was so faint with fear and hunger that she could scarce keep her seat.

Just as she was losing her hold of the great beast's horns, however, and feeling that she must fall to the ground, he turned his massive head round a little, and, speaking in a wonderfully soft and gentle voice, said, "Eat out of my right ear, and drink out of my left ear, so wilt thou be refreshed for thy journey."

So the Princess put a trembling hand into the Bull's right ear, and drew out some bread and meat, which, in spite of her terror, she was glad to swallow; then she put her hand into his left ear, and found there a tiny flagon of wine, and when she had drunk that, her strength returned to her in a wonderful way.

Long they went, and sore they rode, till, just as it seemed to the Princess that they must be getting near the World's End, they came in sight of a magnificent Castle.

"That's where we maun bide this night," said the Black Bull of Norroway, "for that is the house of one of my brothers."

The Princess was greatly surprised at these words; but by this time she was too tired to wonder very much at anything, so she did not answer, but sat still where she was, until the Bull ran into the courtyard of the Castle and knocked his great head against the door.

The door was opened at once by a very splendid footman, who treated the Black Bull with great respect, and helped the Princess to alight from his back. Then he ushered her into a magnificent Hall, where the Lord of the Castle, and his Lady, and a great and noble company were assembled; while the Black Bull trotted off quite contentedly to the grassy park which stretched all round the building, to spend the night there.

The Lord and his Lady were very kind to the Princess, and gave her her supper, and led her to a richly furnished bedroom, all hung round with golden mirrors, and left her to rest there.

They came in sight of a magnificent castle

And in the morning, just as the Black Bull came trotting up to the front door, they handed her a beautiful apple, telling her not to break it, but to put it in her pocket, and keep it till she was in the greatest strait that mortal could be in. Then she was to break it, and it would bring her out of it.

So she put the apple in her pocket, and they lifted her once more onto the Black Bull's back, and she and her strange companion continued on their journey.

All that day they travelled, far further than I can tell you, and at night they came in sight of another Castle, which was even bigger and grander than the first.

"That's where we maun bide this night," said the Black Bull, "for that is the home of another of my brothers."

And here the Princess rested for the night in a very fine bedroom indeed, all hung with silken curtains; and the Lord and Lady of the Castle did everything to please her and make her comfortable.

And in the morning, before she left, they presented her with the largest pear that she had ever seen, and warned her that she must not break it until she was in the direst strait that she had ever been in, and then, if she broke it, it would bring her out of it.

The third day was the same as the other two had been. The Princess and the Black Bull of Norroway rode many a weary mile, and at sundown they came to another Castle, more splendid by far than the other two.

This Castle belonged to the Black Bull's youngest brother, and here the Princess abode all night; while the Bull, as usual, lay outside in the park. And this time, when they departed, the Princess received a most lovely plum, with the warning not to break it till she was in the greatest strait that mortal could be in. Then she was to break it, and it would set her free.

On the fourth day, however, things were changed. For there was no fine Castle waiting for them at the end of their journey;

on the contrary, as the shadows began to lengthen, they came to a dark, deep glen, which was so gloomy and so awesome-looking that the poor Princess felt her courage sinking as they approached it.

At the entrance the Black Bull stopped. "Light down here, Lady," he said, "for in this glen a deadly conflict awaits me, which I must face unaided and alone. For the dark and gloomy region that lies before us is the abode of a great Spirit of Darkness, who worketh much ill in the world. I would fain fight with him and overcome him; and, by my troth, I have good hope that I shall do so. As for thee, thou must seat thyself on this stone, and stir neither hand, nor foot, nor tongue till I return. For, if thou but so much as move, then the Evil Spirit of the Glen will have thee in his power."

"But how shall I know what is happening to thee," asked the Princess anxiously, for she was beginning to grow quite fond of the huge black creature that had carried her so gallantly these last four days, "if I have neither to move hand nor foot, nor yet to speak?"

"Thou wilt know by the signs around thee," answered the Bull. "For if everything about thee turn blue, then thou wilt know that I have vanquished the Evil Spirit; but if everything about thee turn red, then the Evil Spirit hath vanquished me."

With these words he departed, and was soon lost to sight in the dark recesses of the glen, leaving the little Princess sitting motionless on her stone, afraid to move so much as her little finger, in case some unknown evil fell upon her.

At last, when she had sat there for well-nigh an hour, a curious change began to pass over the landscape. First it turned grey, and then it turned a deep azure blue, as if the sky had descended on the earth.

"The Bull hath conquered," thought the Princess. "Oh! What a noble animal he is!" And in her relief and delight she moved her position and crossed one leg over the other.

Oh, woe-a-day! In a moment a mystic spell fell upon her, which caused her to become invisible to the eyes of the Prince of Norroway, who, having vanquished the Evil Spirit, was loosed from the spell which had lain over him, and had transformed him into the likeness of a great Black Bull, and who returned in haste down the glen to present himself, in his rightful form, to the maiden whom he loved, and whom he hoped to win for his bride.

Long, long he sought, but he could not find her, while all the time she was sitting patiently waiting on the stone; but the spell was on her eyes also, and hindered her seeing him, as it hindered him seeing her.

So she sat on and on, till at last she became so wearied, and lonely, and frightened, that she burst out crying, and cried herself to sleep; and when she woke in the morning she felt that it was no use sitting there any longer, so she rose and took her way, hardly knowing whither she was going.

And she went, and she went, till at last she came to a great Mountain made all of glass, which blocked her way and prevented her going any further. She tried time after time to climb it, but it was all of no avail, for the surface of the Mountain was so slippery that she only managed to climb up a few feet, to slide down again the next moment.

So she began to walk round the bottom of the Glass Mountain, in the hope of finding some path that would lead her over it, but the Mountain was so big, and she was so tired, that it seemed almost a hopeless quest, and her spirit died completely within her. And as she went slowly along, sobbing with despair, she felt that if help did not come soon she must lie down and die.

About midday, however, she came to a little cottage, and beside the cottage there was a smithy, where an old smith was working at his anvil.

She entered, and asked him if he could tell her of any path

that would lead her over the Glass Mountain. The old man laid down his hammer and looked at her, slowly shaking his head as he did so.

"Na, na, lassie," he said, "there is no easy road over the Mountain of Glass. Folk maun either walk round it, which is not an easy thing to do, for the foot of it stretches out for hundreds of miles, and the folk who try to do so are almost sure to lose their way; or they maun walk over the top of it, and that can only be done by those who are shod with iron shoon."

"And how am I to get these iron shoon?" cried the Princess eagerly. "Couldst thou fashion me a pair, good man? I would gladly pay thee for them." Then she stopped suddenly, for she remembered that she had no money.

"These shoon cannot be made for siller," said the old man solemnly. "They can only be earned by service. I alone can make them, and I make them for those who are willing to serve me."

"And how long must I serve thee ere thou makest them for me?" asked the Princess faintly.

"Seven years," replied the old man, "for they be magic shoon, and that is the magic number."

So, as there seemed nothing else for it, the Princess hired herself to the smith for seven long years: to clean his house, and cook his food, and make and mend his clothes.

At the end of that time he fashioned her a pair of iron shoon, with which she climbed the Mountain of Glass with as much ease as if it had been covered with fresh green turf.

When she had reached the summit, and descended to the other side, the first house that she came to was the house of an old washerwoman, who lived there with her only daughter. And as the Princess was now very tired, she went up to the door, and knocked, and asked if she might be allowed to rest there for the night.

The washerwoman, who was old and ugly, with a sly and evil face, said that she might—on one condition, and that was that she should try to wash a white mantle that the Black Knight of Norroway had brought to her to wash, as he had got it stained in a deadly fight.

"Yesterday I spent the lee-long day washing it," went on the old washerwoman, "and I might as well have let it lie on the table. For at night, when I took it out of the washtub, the stains were there as dark as ever. Peradventure, maiden, if thou wouldst try thy hand upon it thou mightest be more successful. For I am loth to disappoint the Black Knight of Norroway, who is an exceeding great and powerful Prince."

"Is he in any way connected with the Black Bull of Norroway?" asked the Princess; for at the name her heart had leaped for joy, for it seemed that mayhap she was going to find once more him whom she had lost.

The old woman looked at her suspiciously. "The two are one," she answered, "for the Black Knight chanced to have a spell thrown over him, which turned him into a Black Bull, and which could not be lifted until he had fought with, and overcome, a mighty Spirit of Evil that lived in a dark glen. He fought with the Spirit, and overcame it and once more regained his true form; but 'tis said that his mind is somewhat clouded at times, for he speaketh ever of a maiden whom he would fain have wedded, and whom he hath lost. Though who, or what she was, no living person kens. But this story can have no interest to a stranger like thee," she added slowly, as if she were sorry for having said so much. "I have no more time to waste in talking. But if thou wilt try and wash the mantle, thou art welcome to a night's lodging; and if not, I must ask thee to go on thy way."

Needless to say, the Princess said that she would try to wash the mantle; and it seemed as if her fingers had some magic power in them, for as soon as she put it into water the stains vanished, and it became as white and clean as when it was new.

Of course, the old woman was delighted, but she was very suspicious also, for it appeared to her that there must be some mysterious link between the maiden and the Knight, if his mantle became clean so easily when she washed it, when it had remained soiled and stained in spite of all the labour which she and her daughter had bestowed upon it.

So, as she knew that the young Gallant intended returning for it that very night, and as she wanted her daughter to get the credit of washing it, she advised the Princess to go to bed early, in order to get a good night's rest after all her labours. And the Princess followed her advice, and thus it came about that she was sound asleep, safely hidden in the big box-bed in the corner, when the Black Knight of Norroway came to the cottage to claim his white mantle.

Now you must know that the young man had carried about this mantle with him for the last seven years—ever since his encounter with the Evil Spirit of the Glen—always trying to find someone who could wash it for him, and never succeeding.

For it had been revealed to him by a Wise Woman that she who could make it white and clean was destined to be his wife—be she bonnie or ugly, old or young. And that, moreover, she would prove a loving, a faithful, and a true helpmeet.

So when he came to the washerwoman's cottage, and received back his mantle white as the driven snow, and heard that it was the washerwoman's daughter who had wrought this wondrous change, he said at once that he would marry her, and that the very next day.

When the Princess awoke in the morning and heard all that had befallen, and how the Black Knight had come to the cottage while she was asleep, and had received his mantle, and had promised to marry the washerwoman's daughter that very day, her heart was like to break. For now she felt that she never would have the chance of speaking to him and telling him who she really was.

And in her sore distress she suddenly remembered the beautiful fruit which she had received on her journey seven long years before, and which she had carried with her ever since.

"Surely I will never be in a sorer strait than I am now," she said to herself, and she drew out the apple and broke it. And, lo and behold! It was filled with the most beautiful precious stones that she had ever seen; and at the sight of them a plan came suddenly into her head.

She took the precious stones out of the apple, and, putting them into a corner of her kerchief, carried them to the washerwoman.

"See," said she, "I am richer than mayhap thou thoughtest I was. And if thou wilt, all these riches may be thine."

"And how could that come about?" asked the old woman eagerly, for she had never seen so many precious stones in her life before, and she had a great desire to become the possessor of them.

"Only put off thy daughter's wedding for one day," replied the Princess. "And let me watch beside the Black Knight as he sleeps this night, for I have long had a great desire to see him."

To her astonishment the washerwoman agreed to this request; for the wily old woman was very anxious to get the jewels, which would make her rich for life, and it did not seem to her that there was any harm in the Princess's request; for she had made up her mind that she would give the Black Knight a sleeping-draught, which would prevent him as much as speaking to this strange maiden.

So she took the jewels and locked them up in her kist, and the wedding was put off, and that night the little Princess slipped into the Black Knight's apartment when he was asleep, and watched all through the long hours by his bedside, singing this song to him in the hope that he would awake and hear it:

> "Seven lang years I served for thee,
> The glassy hill I clamb for thee,
> The mantle white I washed for thee,
> And wilt thou no waken, and turn to me?"

But although she sang it over and over again, as if her heart would burst, he neither listened nor stirred, for the old washerwoman's potion had made sure of that.

Next morning, in her great trouble, the little Princess broke open the pear, hoping that its contents would help her better than the contents of the apple had done. But in it she found just what she had found before—a heap of precious stones. Only these stones were richer and more valuable than the others had been.

So, as it seemed the only thing to do, she carried them to the old woman, and bribed her to put the wedding off for yet another day, and allow her to watch that night also by the Black Prince's bedside.

And the washerwoman did so. "For," said she, as she locked away the stones, "I shall soon grow quite rich at this rate."

But, alas! It was all in vain that the Princess spent the long hours singing with all her might:

> "Seven lang years I served for thee,
> The glassy hill I clamb for thee,
> The mantle white I washed for thee,
> And wilt thou no waken, and turn to me?"

For the young Prince whom she watched so tenderly, remained deaf and motionless as a stone.

By the morning she had almost lost hope, for there was only the plum remaining now, and if that failed her last chance had gone. With trembling fingers she broke it open, and found inside another collection of precious stones, richer and rarer than all the others.

She ran with these to the washerwoman, and, throwing them into her lap, told her she could keep them all and welcome if she would put off the wedding once again, and let her watch by the Prince for one more night. And, greatly wondering, the old woman consented.

Now it chanced that the Black Knight, tired with waiting for his wedding, went out hunting that day with all his attendants behind him. And as the servants rode they talked together about something that had puzzled them sorely these two nights gone by. At last an old huntsman rode up to the Knight, with a question upon his lips.

"Master," he said, "we would fain ken who the sweet singer is who singeth through the night in thy chamber?"

"Singer!" he repeated. "There is no singer. My chamber hath been as quiet as the grave, and I have slept a dreamless sleep ever since I came to live at the cottage."

The old huntsman shook his head. "Taste not the old wife's draught this night, Master," he said earnestly, "then wilt thou hear what other ears have heard."

At other times the Black Knight would have laughed at his words, but today the man spoke with such earnestness that he could not but listen to them. So that evening, when the washerwoman, as was her wont, brought his sleeping-draught of spiced ale to his bedside, he told her that it was not sweet enough for his liking. And when she turned and went to the kitchen to fetch some honey to sweeten it, he jumped out of bed and poured it all out of the window; and when she came back he pretended that he had drunk it.

So it came to pass that he lay awake that night and heard

the Princess enter his room, and listened to her plaintive little song, sung in a voice that was full of sobs:

> "Seven lang years I served for thee,
> The glassy hill I clamb for thee,
> The mantle white I washed for thee,
> And wilt thou no waken, and turn to me?"

And when he heard it, he understood it all; and he sprang up and took her in his arms and kissed her, and asked her to tell him the whole story.

And when he heard it, he was so angry with the old washerwoman and her deceitful daughter that he ordered them to leave the country at once; and he married the little Princess, and they lived happily all their days.

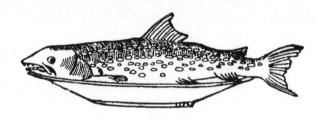

The Wee Bannock

"Some tell about their sweethearts
How they tirled them to the winnock,
But I'll tell you a bonnie tale
About a guid oatmeal bannock."

There was once an old man and his wife, who lived in a dear little cottage by the side of a burn. They were a very cheerful and contented couple, for they had enough to live on, and enough to do. Indeed, they considered themselves quite rich, for, besides their cottage and their garden, they possessed two sleek cows, five hens and a cock, an old cat, and two kittens.

The old man spent his time looking after the cows, and the hens, and the garden; while the old woman kept herself busy spinning.

One day, just after breakfast, the old woman thought that she would like an oatmeal bannock for her supper that evening, so she took down her bakeboard, and put on her girdle, and baked a couple of fine cakes, and when they were ready she put them down before the fire to harden.

While they were toasting, her husband came in from the byre, and sat down to take a rest in his great armchair. Presently his eyes fell on the bannocks, and, as they looked very good, he broke one through the middle and began to eat it.

When the other bannock saw this it determined that it should not have the same fate, so it ran across the kitchen and out of the door as fast as it could. And when the old woman saw it disappearing, she ran after it as fast as her legs would carry her, holding her spindle in one hand and her distaff in the other.

But she was old, and the bannock was young, and it ran faster than she did, and escaped over the hill behind the house. It ran, and it ran, and it ran, until it came to a large newly thatched cottage, and, as the door was open, it took refuge inside, and ran right across the floor to a blazing fire, which was burning in the first room that it came to.

Now, it chanced that this house belonged to a tailor, and he and his two apprentices were sitting cross-legged on the top of a big table by the window, sewing away with all their might, while the tailor's wife was sitting beside the fire carding lint.

When the wee bannock came trundling across the floor, all three tailors got such a fright that they jumped down from the table and hid behind the Master Tailor's wife.

"Hoot," she said, "what a set of cowards ye be! 'Tis but a nice wee bannock. Get hold of it and divide it between you, and I'll fetch you all a drink of milk."

So she jumped up with her lint and her lint cards, and the tailor jumped up with his great shears, and one apprentice grasped the line measure, while another took up the saucer full of pins; and they all tried to catch the wee bannock. But it dodged them round and round the fire, and at last it got safely out of the door and ran down the road, with one of the apprentices after it, who tried to snip it in two with his shears.

It ran too quickly for him, however, and at last he stopped and went back to the house, while the wee bannock ran on until it came to a tiny cottage by the roadside. It trundled in at the door, and there was a weaver sitting at his loom, with his wife beside him, winding a clue of yarn.

"What's that, Tibby?" said the weaver, with a start, as the little cake flew past him.

"Oh!" cried she in delight, jumping to her feet, " 'tis a wee bannock. I wonder where it came from?"

"Dinna bother your head about that, Tibby," said her man, "but grip it, my woman, grip it."

But it was not so easy to get hold of the wee bannock. It was in vain that the Goodwife threw her clue at it, and that the Goodman tried to chase it into a corner and knock it down with his shuttle. It dodged, and turned, and twisted, like a thing bewitched, till at last it flew out at the door again, and vanished down the hill. "For all the world," as the old woman said, "like a new tarred sheep, or a daft cow."

In the next house that it came to it found the Goodwife in the kitchen, churning. She had just filled her churn, and there was still some cream standing in the bottom of her cream jar.

"Come away, little bannock," she cried when she saw it. "Thou art come in just the nick of time, for I am beginning to feel hungry, and I'll have cakes and cream for my dinner."

But the wee bannock hopped round to the other side of the churn, and the Goodwife after it. And she was in such a hurry that she nearly upset the churn; and by the time that she had put it right again, the wee bannock was out at the door and half-way down the brae to the mill.

The miller was sifting meal in the trough, but he straightened himself up when he saw the little cake.

"It's a sign of plenty when bannocks are running about with no one to look after them," he said, " but I like bannocks and cheese, so just come in, and I will give thee a night's lodging."

But the little bannock had no wish to be eaten up by the miller, so it turned and ran out of the mill, and the miller was so busy that he did not trouble himself to run after it.

After this it ran on, and on, and on, till it came to the smithy, and it popped in there to see what it could see.

The smith was busy at the anvil making horseshoe nails, but he looked up as the wee bannock entered.

"If there be one thing I am fond of, it is a glass of ale and a well-toasted cake," he cried. "So come inbye here, and welcome to ye."

But as soon as the little bannock heard of the ale, it turned and ran out of the smithy as fast as it could, and the disappointed smith picked up his hammer and ran after it. And when he saw that he could not catch it, he flung his heavy hammer at it, in the hope of knocking it down, but, luckily for the little cake, he missed his aim.

After this the bannock came to a farmhouse, with a great stack of peats standing at the back of it. In it went, and ran to the fireside. In this house the master had all the flax spread out on the floor, and was cloving it with an iron rod, while the mistress was heckling what he had already cloven.

"Oh, Janet," cried the Goodman in surprise, "here comes in a little bannock. It looks rare and good to eat. I'll have one half of it."

"And I'll have the other half," cried the Goodwife. "Hit it over the back with your cloving-stick, Sandy, and knock it down. Quick, or it will be out at the door again."

But the bannock played "jook-about", and dodged behind a chair. "Hoot!" cried Janet contemptuously, for she thought that her husband might easily have hit it, and she threw her heckle at it.

But the heckle missed it, just as her husband's cloving-rod had done, for it played "jook-about" again, and flew out of the house.

This time it ran up a burn-side till it came to a little cottage standing among the heather.

Here the Goodwife was making porridge for the supper in a pot over the fire, and her husband was sitting in a corner plaiting ropes of straw with which to tie up the cow.

"Oh, Jock! Come here, come here," cried the Goodwife. "Thou art aye crying for a little bannock for thy supper; come here, histie, quick, and help me to catch it."

"Ay, ay," assented Jock, jumping to his feet and hurrying across the little room. "But where is it? I cannot see it."

"There, man, there," cried his wife, "under that chair. Run thou to that side; I will keep to this."

So Jock ran into the dark corner behind the chair; but, in his hurry, he tripped and fell, and the wee bannock jumped over him and flew laughing out at the door.

Through the whins and up the hillside it ran, and over the top of the hill, to a shepherd's cottage on the other side.

The inmates were just sitting down to their porridge, and the Goodwife was scraping the pan.

"Save us and help us," she exclaimed, stopping with the spoon halfway to her mouth. "There's a wee bannock come in to warm itself at our fireside."

"Sneck the door," cried the husband, "and we'll try to catch it. It would come in handy after the porridge."

But the bannock did not wait until the door was sneckit. It turned and ran as fast as it could, and the shepherd and his wife and all the bairns ran after it, with their spoons in their hands, in hopes of catching it.

And when the shepherd saw that it could run faster than they could, he threw his bonnet at it, and almost struck it; but it escaped all these dangers, and soon it came to another house, where the folk were just going to bed.

The Goodman was half-undressed, and the Goodwife was raking the cinders carefully out of the fire.

"What's that?" said he. "For the bowl of brose that I had at suppertime wasna' very big."

"Catch it, then," answered his wife, "and I'll have a bit, too. Quick! Quick! Throw your coat over it or it will be away."

So the Goodman threw his coat right on the top of the little bannock, and almost managed to smother it; but it struggled bravely, and got out, breathless and hot, from under it. Then it ran out into the grey light again, for night was beginning to fall, and the Goodman ran out after it, without his coat. He chased it and chased it through the stackyard and across a field, and in amongst a fine patch of whins. Then he lost it; and, as he was feeling cold without his coat, he went home.

As for the poor little bannock, it thought that it would creep under a whin bush and lie there till morning, but it was so dark that it never saw that there was a fox's hole there. So it fell down the fox's hole, and the fox was very glad to see it, for he had had no food for two days.

"Oh, welcome, welcome," he cried; and he snapped it through the middle with his teeth, and that was the end of the poor wee bannock.

And if a moral be wanted for this tale, here it is: That people should never be too uplifted or too cast down over anything, for all the good folk in the story thought that they were going to get the bannock, and, lo and behold, the fox got it after all!

The Elfin Knight

There is a lone moor in Scotland, which, in times past, was said to be haunted by an Elfin Knight. This Knight was only seen at rare intervals, once in every seven years or so, but the fear of him lay on all the country round, for every now and then someone would set out to cross the moor and would never be heard of again.

And although men might search every inch of the ground, no trace of him would be found, and with a thrill of horror the searching party would go home again, shaking their heads and whispering to one another that he had fallen into the hands of the dreaded Knight.

So, as a rule, the moor was deserted, for nobody dare pass that way, much less live there; and by and by it became the haunt of all sorts of wild animals, which made their lairs there, as they found that they never were disturbed by mortal huntsmen.

Now in that same region lived two young earls, Earl St. Clair and Earl Gregory, who were such friends that they rode, and hunted, and fought together, if need be.

And as they were both very fond of the chase, Earl Gregory suggested one day that they should go a-hunting on the haunted moor, in spite of the Elfin King.

"Certes, I hardly believe in him at all," cried the young man, with a laugh. "Methinks 'tis but an old wife's tale to frighten the bairns withal, lest they go straying amongst the heather and lose themselves. And 'tis pity that such fine sport should be lost because we—two bearded men—pay heed to such gossip."

But Earl St. Clair looked grave. "'Tis ill meddling with unchancy things," he answered, "and 'tis no bairn's tale that travellers have set out to cross that moor who have vanished bodily, and never mair been heard of; but it is, as thou sayest, a pity that so much good sport be lost, all because an Elfin Knight choosest to claim the land as his, and make us mortals pay toll for the privilege of planting a foot upon it. I have heard tell, however, that one is safe from any power that the Knight may have if one wearest the Sign of the Blessed Trinity. So let us bind that on our arm and ride forth without fear."

Sir Gregory burst into a loud laugh at these words. "Dost thou think that I am one of the bairns," he said, "first to be frightened by an idle tale, and then to think that a leaf of clover will protect me? No, no, carry that Sign if thou wilt; I will trust to my good bow and arrow."

But Earl St. Clair did not heed his companion's words, for he remembered how his mother had told him, when he was a little lad at her knee that whoso carried the Sign of the Blessed Trinity need never fear any spell that might be thrown over him by Warlock or Witch, Elf or Demon.

So he went out to the meadow and plucked a leaf of clover, which he bound on his arm with a silken scarf; then he mounted his horse and rode with Earl Gregory to the desolate and lonely moorland.

For some hours all went well; and in the heat of the chase the young men forgot their fears. Then suddenly both of them reined in their steeds and sat gazing in front of them with affrighted faces.

For a horseman had crossed their track, and they both would fain have known who he was and whence he came.

"By my troth, but he rideth in haste, whoever he may be,"

said Earl Gregory at last, "and tho' I always thought that no steed on earth could match mine for swiftness, I reckon that for every league that mine goeth, his would go seven. Let us follow him, and see from what part of the world he cometh."

"The Lord forbid that thou shouldst stir thy horse's feet to follow him," said Earl St. Clair devoutly. "Why, man, 'tis the Elfin Knight! Canst thou not see that he doth not ride on the solid ground, but flieth through the air, and that, although he rideth on what seemeth a mortal steed, he is really carried by mighty pinions, which cleave the air like those of a bird? Follow him forsooth! It will be an evil day for thee when thou seekest to do that."

But Earl St. Clair forgot that he carried a Talisman which his companion lacked, that enabled him to see things as they really were, while the other's eyes were holden, and he was startled and amazed when Earl Gregory said sharply, "Thy mind hath gone mad over this Elfin King. I tell thee he who passed was a goodly Knight, clad in a green vesture, and riding on a great black jennet. And because I love a gallant horseman, and would fain learn his name and degree, I will follow him till I find him, even if it be at the world's end."

And without another word he put spurs to his horse and galloped off in the direction which the mysterious stranger had taken, leaving Earl St. Clair alone upon the moorland, his fingers touching the sacred Sign and his trembling lips muttering prayers for protection.

For he knew that his friend had been bewitched, and he made up his mind, brave gentleman that he was, that he would follow him to the world's end, if need be, and try to deliver him from the spell that had been cast over him.

Meanwhile Earl Gregory rode on and on, ever following in the wake of the Knight in green, over moor, and burn, and moss, till he came to the most desolate region that he had ever been in in his life; where the wind blew cold, as if from snowfields, and where the hoar-frost lay thick and white on the withered grass at his feet.

And there, in front of him, was a sight from which mortal man might well shrink back in awe and dread. For he saw an enormous Ring marked out on the ground, inside of which the grass, instead of being withered and frozen, was lush, and rank, and green, where hundreds of shadowy Elfin figures were dancing, clad in loose transparent robes of dull blue, which seemed to curl and twist round their wearers like snaky wreaths of smoke.

These weird Goblins were shouting and singing as they danced, and waving their arms above their heads, and throwing themselves about on the ground, for all the world as if they had gone mad; and when they saw Earl Gregory halt on his horse just outside the Ring they beckoned to him with their skinny fingers.

"Come hither, come hither," they shouted, "come tread a measure with us, and afterwards we will drink to thee out of our Monarch's loving cup."

And, strange as it may seem, the spell that had been cast over the young Earl was so powerful that, in spite of his fear, he felt that he must obey the eldrich summons, and he threw his bridle on his horse's neck and prepared to join them.

But just then an old and grizzled Goblin stepped out from among his companions and approached him.

Apparently he dare not leave the charmed Circle, for he stopped at the edge of it; then, stooping down and pretending to pick up something, he whispered in a hoarse whisper:

"I know not whom thou art, nor from whence thou comest, Sir Knight, but if thou lovest thy life, see to it that thou comest not within this Ring, nor joinest with us in our feast. Else wilt thou be for ever undone."

But Earl Gregory only laughed. "I vowed that I would follow the Green Knight," he replied, "and I will carry out my vow, even if the venture leadeth me close to the nethermost world."

And with these words he stepped over the edge of the Circle, right in amongst the ghostly dancers.

At his coming they shouted louder than ever, and danced more madly, and sang more lustily; then, all at once, a silence fell upon them, and they parted into two companies, leaving a way through their midst, up which they signed to the Earl to pass.

He walked through their ranks till he came to the middle of the Circle; and there, seated at a table of red marble, was the Knight whom he had come so far to seek, clad in his grass-green robes. And before him, on the table, stood a wondrous goblet, fashioned from an emerald, and set round the rim with blood-red rubies.

And this cup was filled with heather ale, which foamed up over the brim; and when the Knight saw Earl Gregory, he lifted it from the table, and handed it to him with a stately bow, and Earl Gregory, being very thirsty, drank.

And as he drank he noticed that the ale in the goblet never grew less, but ever foamed up to the edge; and for the first time his heart misgave him, and he wished that he had never set out on this strange adventure.

But, alas! The time for regrets had passed, for already a strange numbness was stealing over his limbs, and a chill pallor was creeping over his face, and before he could utter a single cry for help the goblet dropped from his nerveless fingers, and he fell down before the Elfin King like a dead man.

Then a great shout of triumph went up from all the company; for if there was one thing which filled their hearts with joy, it was to entice some unwary mortal into their Ring and throw their uncanny spell over him, so that he must needs spend long years in their company.

But soon their shouts of triumph began to die away, and they muttered and whispered to each other with looks of something like fear on their faces.

For their keen ears heard a sound which filled their hearts with dread. It was the sound of human footsteps, which were so free and untrammelled that they knew at once that the stranger, whoever he was, was as yet untouched by any charm. And if this were so he might work them ill, and rescue their captive from them.

And what they dreaded was true; for it was the brave Earl St. Clair who approached, fearless and strong because of the Holy Sign he bore.

And as soon as he saw the charmed Ring and the eldrich dancers, he was about to step over its magic border, when the little grizzled Goblin who had whispered to Earl Gregory, came and whispered to him also.

"Alas! Alas!" he exclaimed, with a look of sorrow on his wrinkled face. "Hast thou come, as thy companion came, to pay thy toll of years to the Elfin King? Oh! If thou hast wife or child behind thee, I beseech thee, by all that thou holdest sacred, to turn back ere it be too late."

"Who art thou, and from whence hast thou come?" asked the Earl, looking kindly down at the little creature in front of him.

"I came from the country that thou hast come from," wailed the Goblin. "For I was once a mortal man, even as thou. But I set out over the enchanted moor, and the Elfin King appeared in the guise of a beauteous Knight, and he looked so brave, and noble, and generous that I followed him hither, and drank of his heather ale, and now I am doomed to bide here till seven long years be spent.

"As for thy friend, Sir Earl, he, too, hath drunk of the accursed draught, and he now lieth as dead at our lawful Monarch's feet. He will wake up, 'tis true, but it will be in such a guise as I wear, and to the bondage with which I am bound."

"Is there naught that I can do to rescue him," cried Earl St. Clair eagerly, "ere he taketh on him the Elfin shape? I have no fear of the spell of his cruel captor, for I bear the Sign of One Who is stronger than he. Speak speedily, little man, for time presseth."

"There is something that thou couldst do, Sir Earl," whispered the Goblin, "but to essay it were a desperate attempt. For if thou failest, then could not even the Power of the Blessed Sign save thee."

"And what is that?" asked the Earl impatiently.

"Thou must remain motionless," answered the old man, "in the cold and frost till dawn break and the hour cometh when they sing Matins in the Holy Church. Then must thou walk slowly nine times round the edge of the enchanted Circle, and after that thou must walk boldly across it to the red marble table where sits the Elfin King. On it thou wilt see an emerald goblet studded with rubies and filled with heather ale. That must thou secure and carry away; but whilst thou art doing so let no word cross thy lips. For this enchanted ground whereon we dance may look solid to mortal eyes, but in reality it is not so. 'Tis but a quaking bog, and under it is a great lake, wherein dwelleth a fearsome Monster, and if thou so much as utter a word while thy foot resteth upon it, thou wilt fall through the bog and perish in the waters beneath."

So saying the grisly Goblin stepped back among his companions, leaving Earl St. Clair standing alone on the outskirts of the charmed Ring.

There he waited, shivering with cold, through the long, dark hours, till the grey dawn began to break over the hill tops, and, with its coming, the Elfin forms before him seemed to dwindle and fade away.

And at the hour when the sound of the Matin Bell came softly pealing from across the moor, he began his solemn walk. Round and round the Ring he paced, keeping steadily on his way, although loud murmurs of anger, like distant thunder, rose from the Elfin Shades, and even the very ground seemed to heave and quiver, as if it would shake this bold intruder from its surface.

But through the power of the Blessed Sign on his arm Earl St. Clair went on unhurt.

When he had finished pacing round the Ring he stepped boldly onto the enchanted ground, and walked across it; and what was his astonishment to find that all the ghostly Elves and Goblins whom he had seen, were lying frozen into tiny blocks of ice, so that he was sore put to it to walk amongst them without treading upon them.

And as he approached the marble table the very hairs rose on his head at the sight of the Elfin King sitting behind it, stiff and stark like his followers; while in front of him lay the form of Earl Gregory, who had shared the same fate.

Nothing stirred, save two coal-black ravens, who sat, one on each side of the table, as if to guard the emerald goblet, flapping their wings, and croaking hoarsely.

When Earl St. Clair lifted the precious cup, they rose in the air and circled round his head, screaming with rage, and threatening to dash it from his hands with their claws; while the frozen Elves, and even their mighty King himself, stirred in their sleep, and half sat up, as if to lay hands on this presumptuous intruder. But the Power of the Holy Sign restrained them, else had Earl St. Clair been foiled in his quest.

As he retraced his steps, awesome and terrible were the sounds that he heard around him. The ravens shrieked, and the frozen Goblins screamed; and up from the hidden lake below came the sound of the deep breathing of the awful Monster who was lurking there, eager for prey.

But the brave Earl heeded none of these things, but kept steadily onwards, trusting in the Might of the Sign he bore. And it carried him safely through all the dangers; and just as

the sound of the Matin Bell was dying away in the morning air he stepped onto solid ground once more, and flung the enchanted goblet from him.

And lo! Every one of the frozen Elves vanished, along with their King and his marble table, and nothing was left on the rank green grass save Earl Gregory, who slowly woke from his enchanted slumber, and stretched himself, and stood up, shaking in every limb. He gazed vaguely round him, as if he scarce remembered where he was.

And when, after Earl St. Clair had run to him and had held him in his arms till his senses returned and the warm blood coursed through his veins, the two friends returned to the spot where Earl St. Clair had thrown down the wondrous goblet, they found nothing but a piece of rough grey whinstone, with a drop of dew hidden in a little crevice which was hollowed in its side.

What to Say
to the New Mune

New Mune, true Mune,
Tell unto me,
If my ane true love
He will marry me.

If he marry me in haste,
Let me see his bonny face;

If he marry me betide,
Let me see his bonnie side;

Gin he marry na me ava',
Turn his back and gae awa'.

Habetrot the Spinstress

In byegone days, in an old farmhouse which stood by a river, there lived a beautiful girl called Maisie. She was tall and straight, with auburn hair and blue eyes, and she was the prettiest girl in all the valley. And one would have thought that she would have been the pride of her mother's heart.

But, instead of this, her mother used to sigh and shake her head whenever she looked at her. And why?

Because, in those days, all men were sensible; and instead of looking out for pretty girls to be their wives, they looked out for girls who could cook and spin, and who gave promise of becoming notable housewives.

Maisie's mother had been an industrious spinster; but, alas! to her sore grief and disappointment, her daughter did not take after her.

The girl loved to be out of doors, chasing butterflies and plucking wild flowers, far better than sitting at her spinning-wheel. So when her mother saw one after another of Maisie's companions, who were not nearly so pretty as she was, getting rich husbands, she sighed and said:

"Woe's me, child, for methinks no brave wooer will ever pause at our door while they see thee so idle and thoughtless." But Maisie only laughed.

At last her mother grew really angry, and one bright Spring morning she laid down three heads of flax on the table, saying sharply, "I will have no more of this dallying. People will say that it is my blame that no wooer comes to seek thee. I cannot have thee left on my hands to be laughed at, as the idle maid who would not marry. So now thou must work; and if thou hast not these heads of flax spun into seven hanks of thread in three days, I will e'en speak to the Mother at St. Mary's Convent, and thou wilt go there and learn to be a nun."

Now, though Maisie was an idle girl, she had no wish to be shut up in a nunnery; so she tried not to think of the sunshine outside, but sat down soberly with her distaff.

But, alas! She was so little accustomed to work that she made but slow progress; and although she sat at the spinning-wheel all day, and never once went out of doors, she found at night that she had only spun half a hank of yarn.

The next day it was even worse, for her arms ached so much she could only work very slowly. That night she cried herself to sleep; and next morning, seeing that it was quite hopeless to expect to get her task finished, she threw down her distaff in despair, and ran out of doors.

Near the house was a deep dell, through which ran a tiny stream. Maisie loved this dell, the flowers grew so abundantly there.

This morning she ran down to the edge of the stream, and seated herself on a large stone. It was a glorious morning, the hazel trees were newly covered with leaves, and the branches nodded over her head, and showed like delicate tracery against the blue sky. The primroses and sweet-scented violets peeped out from among the grass, and a little water wagtail came and perched on a stone in the middle of the stream, and bobbed up and down, till it seemed as if he were nodding to Maisie, and as if he were trying to say to her, "Never mind, cheer up."

But the poor girl was in no mood that morning to enjoy the flowers and the birds. Instead of watching them, as she generally did, she hid her face in her hands, and wondered what would become of her. She rocked herself to and fro, as she thought how terrible it would be if her mother fulfilled her threat and shut her up in the Convent of St. Mary, with the grave, solemn-faced sisters, who seemed as if they had completely forgotten what it was like to be young, and run about in the sunshine, and laugh, and pick the fresh Spring flowers.

"Oh, I could not do it, I could not do it," she cried at last. "It would kill me to be a nun."

"And who wants to make a pretty wench like thee into a nun?" asked a queer, cracked voice quite close to her.

Maisie jumped up, and stood staring in front of her as if she had been moonstruck. For, just across the stream from where she had been sitting, there was a curious boulder, with a round hole in the middle of it—for all the world like a big apple with the core taken out.

Maisie knew it well; she had often sat upon it, and wondered how the funny hole came to be there.

It was no wonder that she stared, for, seated on this stone, was the queerest little old woman that she had ever seen in her life. Indeed, had it not been for her silver hair, and the white mutch with the big frill that she wore on her head, Maisie would have taken her for a little girl, she wore such a very short skirt, only reaching down to her knees.

Her face, inside the frill of her cap, was round, and her cheeks were rosy, and she had little black eyes, which twinkled merrily as she looked at the startled maiden. On her shoulders was a black and white checked shawl, and on her legs, which she dangled over the edge of the boulder, she wore black silk stockings and the neatest little shoes, with great silver buckles.

In fact, she would have been quite a pretty old lady had it not been for her lips, which were very long and very thick, and made her look quite ugly in spite of her rosy cheeks and black eyes. Maisie stood and looked at her for such a long time in silence that she repeated her question.

"And who wants to make a pretty wench like thee into a

SEATED ON THIS STONE WAS THE QUEEREST LITTLE OLD WOMAN—

nun? More likely that some gallant gentleman should want to make a bride of thee."

"Oh, no," answered Maisie, "my mother says no gentleman would look at me because I cannot spin."

"Nonsense," said the tiny old woman. "Spinning is all very well for old folks like me—my lips, as thou seest, are long and ugly because I have spun so much, for I always wet my fingers with them, the easier to draw the thread from the distaff. No, no, take care of thy beauty, child; do not waste it over the spinning-wheel, nor yet in a nunnery."

"If my mother only thought as thou dost," replied the girl sadly; and, encouraged by the old woman's kindly face, she told her the whole story.

"Well," said the old woman, "I do not like to see pretty girls weep; what if I were able to help thee, and spin the flax for thee?"

Maisie thought that this offer was too good to be true; but her new friend bade her run home and fetch the flax; and I need not tell you that she required no second bidding.

When she returned she handed the bundle to the little old lady, and was about to ask her where she should meet her in order to get the thread from her when it was spun, when a sudden noise behind her made her look round.

She saw nothing; but what was her horror and surprise, when she turned back again, to find that the old woman had vanished entirely, flax and all.

She rubbed her eyes, and looked all round, but she was nowhere to be seen. The girl was utterly bewildered. She wondered if she could have been dreaming, but no that could not be, there were her footprints leading up the bank and down again, where she had gone for the flax, and brought it back, and there was the mark of her foot, wet with dew, on a stone in the middle of the stream, where she had stood when she had handed the flax up to the mysterious little stranger.

What was she to do now? What would her mother say when, in addition to not having finished the task that had been given her, she had to confess to having lost the greater part of the flax also? She ran up and down the little dell, hunting amongst the bushes, and peeping into every nook and cranny of the bank where the little old woman might have hidden herself. It was all in vain; and at last, tired out with the search, she sat down on the stone once more, and presently fell fast asleep.

When she awoke it was evening. The sun had set, and the yellow glow on the western horizon was fast giving place to the silvery light of the moon. She was sitting thinking of the curious events of the day, and gazing at the great boulder opposite, when it seemed to her as if a distant murmur of voices came from it.

With one bound she crossed the stream, and clambered on to the stone. She was right.

Someone was talking underneath it, far down in the ground. She put her ear close to the stone, and listened.

The voice of the queer little old woman came up through the hole. "Ho, ho, my pretty little wench little knows that my name is Habetrot."

Full of curiosity, Maisie put her eye to the opening, and the strangest sight that she had ever seen met her gaze. She seemed to be looking through a telescope into a wonderful little valley. The trees there were brighter and greener than any that she had ever seen before; and there were beautiful flowers, quite different from the flowers that grew in her country. The little valley was carpeted with the most exquisite moss, and up and down it walked her tiny friend, busily engaged in spinning.

She was not alone, for round her were a circle of other little old women, who were seated on large white stones, and they were all spinning away as fast as they could.

Occasionally one would look up, and then Maisie saw that they all seemed to have the same long, thick lips that her friend had. She really felt very sorry, as they all looked exceedingly kind, and might have been pretty had it not been for this defect.

One of the Spinstresses sat by herself, and was engaged in winding the thread, which the others had spun, into hanks. Maisie did not think that this little lady looked so nice as the others. She was dressed entirely in grey, and had a big hooked nose, and great horn spectacles. She seemed to be called Slantlie Mab, for Maisie heard Habetrot address her by that name, telling her to make haste and tie up all the thread, for it was getting late, and it was time that the young girl had it to carry home to her mother.

Maisie did not quite know what to do, or how she was to get the thread, for she did not like to shout down the hole in case the queer little old woman should be angry at being watched.

However, Habetrot, as she had called herself, suddenly appeared on the path beside her, with the hanks of thread in her hand.

"Oh, thank you, thank you," cried Maisie. "What can I do to show you how thankful I am?"

"Nothing," answered the Fairy. "For I do not work for reward. Only do not tell your mother who span the thread for thee."

It was now late, and Maisie lost no time in running home with the precious thread upon her shoulder. When she walked into the kitchen she found that her mother had gone to bed. She seemed to have had a busy day, for there, hanging up in the wide chimney, in order to dry, were seven large black puddings.

The fire was low, but bright and clear; and the sight of it and the sight of the puddings suggested to Maisie that she was very hungry, and that fried black puddings were very good.

Flinging the thread down on the table, she hastily pulled off her shoes, so as not to make a noise and awake her mother; and, getting down the frying-pan from the wall, she took one of the black puddings from the chimney, and fried it, and ate it.

Still she felt hungry, so she took another, and then another, till they were all gone. Then she crept upstairs to her little bed and fell fast asleep.

Next morning her mother came downstairs before Maisie was awake. In fact, she had not been able to sleep much for thinking of her daughter's careless ways, and had been sorrowfully making up her mind that she must lose no time in speaking to the Abbess of St. Mary's about this idle girl of hers.

What was her surprise to see on the table the seven beautiful hanks of thread, while, on going to the chimney to take down a black pudding to fry for breakfast, she found that every one of them had been eaten. She did not know whether to laugh for joy that her daughter had been so industrious, or to cry for vexation because all her lovely black puddings—which she had expected would last for a week at least—were gone. In her bewilderment she sang out:

> "My daughter's spun se'en, se'en, se'en,
> My daughter's eaten se'en, se'en, se'en,
> And all before daylight."

Now I forgot to tell you that, about half a mile from where the old farmhouse stood, there was a beautiful Castle, where a very rich young Nobleman lived. He was both good and brave, as well as rich; and all the mothers who had pretty daughters used to wish that he would come their way, some day, and fall in love with one of them. But he had never done so, and everyone said, "He is too grand to marry any country girl. One day he will go away to London Town and marry a Duke's daughter."

Well, this fine spring morning it chanced that this young Nobleman's favourite horse had lost a shoe, and he was so afraid that any of the grooms might ride it along the hard road, and not on the soft grass at the side, that he said that he would take it to the smithy himself.

So it happened that he was riding along by Maisie's garden gate as her mother came into the garden singing these strange lines.

He stopped his horse, and said good-naturedly, "Good day, Madam; and may I ask why you sing such a strange song?"

Maisie's mother made no answer, but turned and walked into the house; and the young nobleman, being very anxious to know what it all meant, hung his bridle over the garden gate, and followed her.

She pointed to the seven hanks of thread lying on the table, and said, "This hath my daughter done before breakfast."

Then the young man asked to see the Maiden who was so industrious, and her mother went and pulled Maisie from behind the door, where she had hidden herself when the stranger came in; for she had come downstairs while her mother was in the garden.

She looked so lovely in her fresh morning gown of blue gingham, with her auburn hair curling softly round her brow, and her face all over blushes at the sight of such a gallant young man, that he quite lost his heart, and fell in love with her on the spot.

"Ah," said he, "my dear mother always told me to try and find a wife who was both pretty and useful, and I have succeeded beyond my expectations. Do not let our marriage, I pray thee, good Dame, be too long deferred."

Maisie's mother was overjoyed, as you may imagine, at this piece of unexpected good fortune, and busied herself in getting everything ready for the wedding; but Maisie herself was a little perplexed.

She was afraid that she would be expected to spin a great deal when she was married and lived at the Castle, and if that were so, her husband was sure to find out that she was not really such a good spinstress as he thought she was.

In her trouble she went down, the night before her wedding, to the great boulder by the stream in the glen, and, climbing up on it, she laid her head against the stone, and called softly down the hole, "Habetrot, dear Habetrot."

The little old woman soon appeared, and, with twinkling eyes, asked her what was troubling her so much just when she should have been so happy. And Maisie told her.

"Trouble not thy pretty head about that," answered the Fairy, "but come here with thy bridegroom next week, when the moon is full, and I warrant that he will never ask thee to sit at a spinning-wheel again."

Accordingly, after all the wedding festivities were over and the couple had settled down at the Castle, on the appointed evening Maisie suggested to her husband that they should take a walk together in the moonlight.

She was very anxious to see what the little Fairy would do to help her; for that very day he had been showing her all over her new home, and he had pointed out to her the beautiful new spinning-wheel made of ebony, which had belonged to his mother, saying proudly, "Tomorrow, little one, I shall bring some flax from the town, and then the maids will see what clever little fingers my wife has."

Maisie had blushed as red as a rose as she bent over the lovely wheel, and then felt quite sick, as she wondered whatever she would do if Habetrot did not help her.

So on this particular evening, after they had walked in the garden, she said that she should like to go down to the little dell and see how the stream looked by moonlight. So to the dell they went.

As soon as they came to the boulder Maisie put her head against it and whispered, "Habetrot, dear Habetrot." And in an instant the little old woman appeared.

She bowed in a stately way, as if they were both strangers to her, and said, " Welcome, Sir and Madam, to the Spinsters' Dell." And then she tapped on the root of a great oak tree with a tiny wand which she held in her hand, and a green door, which Maisie never remembered having noticed before, flew open, and they followed the Fairy through it into the other valley which Maisie had seen through the hole in the great stone.

All the little old women were sitting on their white chucky

stones busy at work, only they seemed far uglier than they had seemed at first; and Maisie noticed that the reason for this was, that, instead of wearing red skirts and white mutches as they had done before, they now wore caps and dresses of dull grey, and instead of looking happy, they all seemed to be trying who could look most miserable, and who could push out their long lips furthest, as they wet their fingers to draw the thread from their distaffs.

"Save us and help us! What a lot of hideous old Witches," exclaimed her husband. "Whatever could this funny old woman mean by bringing a pretty child like thee to look at them? Thou wilt dream of them for a week and a day. Just look at their lips." And, pushing Maisie behind him, he went up to one of them and asked her what had made her mouth grow so ugly.

She tried to tell him, but all the sound that he could hear was something that sounded like SPIN-N-N.

He asked another one, and her answer sounded like this: SPAN-N-N. He tried a third, and hers sounded like SPUN-N-N.

He seized Maisie by the hand and hurried her through the green door. "By my troth," he said, "my mother's spinning-wheel may turn to gold ere I let thee touch it, if this is what spinning leads to. Rather than that thy pretty face should be spoilt, the linen chests at the Castle may get empty, and remain so for ever!"

So it came to pass that Maisie could be out of doors all day wandering about with her husband, and laughing and singing to her heart's content. And whenever there was flax at the Castle to be spun, it was carried down to the big boulder in the dell and left there, and Habetrot and her companions spun it, and there was no more trouble about the matter.

Nippit Fit and Clippit Fit

In a country, far across the sea, there once dwelt a great and mighty Prince. He lived in a grand Castle, which was full of beautiful furniture, and curious and rare ornaments. And among them was a lovely little glass shoe, which would only fit the tiniest foot imaginable.

And as the Prince was looking at it one day, it struck him what a dainty little lady she would need to be who wore such a very small shoe. And, as he liked dainty people, he made up his mind that he would never marry until he found a maiden who could wear the shoe, and that, when he found her, he would ask her to be his wife.

And he called all his Lords and Courtiers to him, and told them of the determination that he had come to, and asked them to help him in his quest.

And after they had taken counsel together they summoned a trusty Knight, and appointed him the Prince's Ambassador; and told him to take the slipper, and mount a fleet-footed horse, and ride up and down the whole of the Kingdom until he found a lady whom it would fit.

So the Ambassador put the little shoe carefully in his pocket and set out on his errand.

He rode, and he rode, and he rode, going to every town and castle that came in his way, and summoning all the ladies to appear before him to try on the shoe. And, as he caused a

Proclamation to be made that whoever could wear it should be the Prince's Bride, I need not tell you that all the ladies in the countryside flocked to wherever the Ambassador chanced to be staying, and begged leave to try on the slipper.

But they were all disappointed, for not one of them, try as she would, could make her foot small enough to go into the Fairy Shoe; and there were many bitter tears shed in secret, when they returned home, by countless fair ladies who prided themselves on the smallness of their feet, and who had set out full of lively expectation that they would be the successful competitors.

At last the Ambassador arrived at a house where a well-to-do Laird had lived. But the Laird was dead now, and there was nobody left but his wife and two daughters, who had grown poor of late, and who had to work hard for their living.

One of the daughters was haughty and insolent; the other was little, and young, and modest, and sweet.

When the Ambassador rode into the courtyard of this house, and, holding out the shoe, asked if there were any fair ladies there who would like to try it on, the elder sister, who always thought a great deal of herself, ran forward, and said that she would do so, while the younger girl just shook her head and went on with her work. "For," said she to herself, "though my feet are so little that they might go into the slipper, what would I do as the wife of a great Prince? Folk would just laugh at me, and say that I was not fit for the position. No, no, I am far better to bide as I am."

So the Ambassador gave the glass shoe to the elder sister, who carried it away to her own room; and presently, to every one's astonishment, came back wearing it on her foot.

It is true that her face was very white, and that she walked with a little limp; but no one noticed these things except her younger sister, and she only shook her wise little head, and said nothing.

The Prince's Ambassador was delighted that he had at last found a wife for his master, and he mounted his horse and rode off at full speed to tell him the good news.

When the Prince heard of the success of his errand, he ordered all his Courtiers to be ready to accompany him next day when he went to bring home his Bride.

You can fancy what excitement there was at the Laird's house when the gallant company arrived, with their Prince at their head, to greet the lady who was to be their Princess.

The old mother and the plain-looking maid-of-all-work ran hither and thither, fetching such meat and drink as the house could boast to set before their high-born visitors, while the bonnie little sister went and hid herself behind a great pot which stood in the corner of the courtyard, and which was used for boiling hen's meat.

She knew that her foot was the smallest in the house; and something told her that if the Prince once got a glimpse of her he would not be content till she had tried on the slipper.

Meanwhile, the selfish elder sister did not help at all, but ran up to her chamber, and decked herself out in all the fine clothes that she possessed before she came downstairs to meet the Prince.

And when all the Knights and Courtiers had drunk a stirrup-cup, and wished Good Luck to their Lord and his Bride, she was lifted up behind the Prince on his horse, and rode off so full of her own importance, that she even forgot to say goodbye to her mother and sister.

Alas! Alas! Pride must have a fall. For the cavalcade had not proceeded very far when a little bird which was perched on a branch of a bush by the roadside sang out:

"Nippit fit, and clippit fit, behind the King rides,
But pretty fit, and little fit, ahint the caldron hides."

"What is this that the birdie says?" cried the Prince, who, if the truth be told, did not feel altogether satisfied with the Bride whom fortune had bestowed upon him. "Hast thou another sister, Madam?"

"Only a little one," murmured the lady, who liked ill the way in which things seemed to be falling out.

"We will go back and find her," said the Prince firmly, "for when I sent out the slipper I had no mind that its wearer should nip her foot, and clip her foot, in order to get it on."

So the whole party turned back; and when they reached the Laird's house the Prince ordered a search to be made in the courtyard. And the bonnie little sister was soon discovered and brought out, all blushes and confusion, from her hiding-place behind the caldron.

"Give her the slipper, and let her try it on," said the Prince, and the eldest sister was forced to obey. And what was the horror of the bystanders, as she drew it off, to see that she had cut off the tops of her toes in order to get it on.

But it fitted her little sister's foot exactly, without either paring or clipping; and when the Prince saw that it was so, he lifted the elder sister down from his horse and lifted the little one up in her place, and carried her home to his Palace, where the wedding was celebrated with great rejoicing; and for the rest of their lives they were the happiest couple in the whole kingdom.

The Fairies of Merlin's Crag

About two hundred years ago there was a poor man working as a labourer on a farm in Lanarkshire. He was what is known as an "Orra Man"—that is, he had no special work mapped out for him to do, but he was expected to undertake odd jobs of any kind that happened to turn up.

One day his master sent him out to cast peats on a piece of moorland that lay on a certain part of the farm. Now this strip of moorland ran up at one end to a curiously shaped crag, known as Merlin's Crag, because, so the country folk said, that famous Enchanter had once taken up his abode there.

The man obeyed, and, being a willing fellow, when he arrived at the moor he set to work with all his might and main. He had lifted quite a quantity of peat from near the Crag, when he was startled by the appearance of the very smallest woman that he had ever seen in his life. She was only about two feet high, and she was dressed in a green gown and red stockings, and her long yellow hair was not bound by any ribbon, but hung loosely round her shoulders.

She was such a dainty little creature that the astonished countryman stopped working, stuck his spade into the ground, and gazed at her in wonder.

His wonder increased when she held up one of her tiny fingers and addressed him in these words, "What wouldst thou think if I were to send my husband to uncover thy house? You mortals think that you can do aught that pleaseth you."

Then, stamping her tiny foot, she added in a voice of command, "Put back that turf instantly, or thou shalt rue this day."

Now the poor man had often heard of the Fairy Folk, and of the harm that they could work to unthinking mortals who offended them, so in fear and trembling he set to work to undo all his labour, and to place every divot in the exact spot from which he had taken it.

When he was finished he looked round for his strange visitor, but she had vanished completely; he could not tell how, nor where. Putting up his spade, he wended his way homewards, and going straight to his master, he told him the whole story, and suggested that in future the peats should be taken from the other end of the moor.

But the master only laughed. He was a strong, hearty man, and had no belief in Ghosts, or Elves, or Fairies, or any other creature that he could not see; but although he laughed, he was vexed that his servant should believe in such things, so to cure him, as he thought, of his superstition, he ordered him to take a horse and cart and go back at once, and lift all the peats and bring them to dry in the farm steading.

The poor man obeyed with much reluctance; and was greatly relieved, as weeks went on, to find that, in spite of his having done so, no harm befell him.

In fact, he began to think that his master was right, and that the whole thing must have been a dream.

So matters went smoothly on. Winter passed, and spring, and summer, until autumn came round once more, and the very day arrived on which the peats had been lifted the year before.

That day, as the sun went down, the Orra Man left the farm to go home to his cottage, and as his master was pleased with him because he had been working very hard lately, he had given him a little can of milk as a present to carry home to his wife.

So he was feeling very happy, and as he walked along he was humming a tune to himself. His road took him by the foot of Merlin's Crag, and as he approached it he was astonished to find himself growing strangely tired. His eyelids dropped over his eyes as if he were going to sleep, and his feet grew as heavy as lead.

"I will sit down and take a rest for a few minutes," he said to himself. "The road home never seemed so long as it does today."

So he sat down on a tuft of grass right under the shadow of the Crag, and before he knew where he was he had fallen into a deep and heavy slumber.

When he awoke it was near midnight, and the moon had risen on the Crag. And he rubbed his eyes, when by its soft light he became aware of a large band of Fairies who were dancing round and round him, singing and laughing, pointing their tiny fingers at him, and shaking their wee fists in his face.

A large band of Fairies Dancing Round and Round

The bewildered man rose and tried to walk away from them, but turn in whichever direction he would the Fairies accompanied him, encircling him in a magic ring, out of which he could in no wise go.

At last they stopped, and, with shrieks of Elfin laughter, led the prettiest and daintiest of their companions up to him, and cried, "Tread a measure, tread a measure, oh, Man! Then wilt thou not be so eager to escape from our company."

Now the poor labourer was but a clumsy dancer, and he held back with a shamefaced air; but the Fairy who had been chosen to be his partner reached up and seized his hands, and lo, some strange magic seemed to enter into his veins, for in a moment he found himself waltzing and whirling, sliding and bowing, as if he had done nothing else but dance all his life.

And, strangest thing of all, he forgot about his home and his children; and he felt so happy that he had no longer the slightest desire to leave the Fairies' company.

All night long the merriment went on. The Little Folk danced and danced as if they were mad, and the farm man danced with them, until at last a shrill sound came over the moor. It was the cock from the farmyard crowing its loudest to welcome the dawn.

In an instant the revelry ceased, and the Fairies, with cries of alarm, crowded together and rushed towards the Crag, dragging the countryman along in their midst. As they reached the rock, a mysterious door, which he never remembered having seen before, opened in it of its own accord, and shut again with a crash as soon as the Fairy Host had all trooped through.

The door led into a large, dimly lighted Hall full of tiny couches, and here the Little Folk sank to rest, tired out with their exertions, while the good man sat down on a piece of rock in the corner, wondering what would happen next.

But there seemed to be some kind of spell thrown over his senses, for even when the Fairies awoke and began to go about their household occupations, and to carry out certain curious practices which he had never seen before, and which, as you will hear, he was forbidden to speak of afterwards, he was content to sit and watch them, without in any way attempting to escape.

As it drew toward evening someone touched his elbow, and he turned round with a start to see the little woman with the green dress and scarlet stockings, who had remonstrated with him for lifting the turf the year before, standing by his side.

"The divots which thou took'st from the roof of my house have grown once more," she said, "and once more it is covered with grass; so thou canst go home again, for justice is satisfied— thy punishment hath lasted long enough. But first must thou take thy solemn oath never to tell to mortal ears what thou hast seen whilst thou hast dwelt among us."

The countryman promised gladly, and took the oath with all due solemnity. Then the door was opened, and he was at liberty to depart.

His can of milk was standing on the green, just where he had laid it down when he went to sleep; and it seemed to him as if it were only yesternight that the farmer had given it to him.

But when he reached his home he was speedily undeceived. For his wife looked at him as if he were a ghost, and the children whom he had left wee, toddling things were now well-grown boys and girls, who stared at him as if he had been an utter stranger.

"Where hast thou been these long, long years?" cried his wife when she had gathered her wits and seen that it was really he, and not a spirit. "And how couldst thou find it in thy heart to leave the bairns and me alone?"

And then he knew that the one day he had passed in Fairyland had lasted seven whole years, and he realised how heavy the punishment had been which the Wee Folk had laid upon him.

The Wedding of Robin Redbreast and Jenny Wren

There was once an old grey Poussie Baudrons, and she went out for a stroll one Christmas morning to see what she could see. And as she was walking down the burn-side she saw a little Robin Redbreast hopping up and down on the branches of a briar bush.

"What a tasty breakfast he would make," thought she to herself. "I must try to catch him."

So, "Good morning, Robin Redbreast," quoth she, sitting down on her tail at the foot of the briar bush and looking up at him. "And where mayest thou be going so early on this cold winter's day?"

"I'm on my road to the King's Palace," answered Robin cheerily, "to sing him a song this merry Yule morning."

"That's a pious errand to be travelling on, and I wish you good success," replied Poussie slyly. "But just hop down a minute before thou goest, and I will show thee what a bonnie white ring I have round my neck. 'Tis few cats that are marked like me."

Then Robin cocked his head on one side, and looked down on Poussie Baudrons with a twinkle in his eye. "Ha, ha, grey Poussie Baudrons!" he said. "Ha, ha! For I saw thee worry the little grey mouse, and I have no wish that thou shouldst worry me."

And with that he spread his wings and flew away. And he flew, and he flew, till he lighted on an old sod dyke; and there he saw a greedy old Buzzard sitting, with all his feathers ruffled up as if he felt cold.

"Good morning, Robin Redbreast," cried the greedy old Buzzard, who had had no food since yesterday, and was therefore very hungry. "And where mayest thou be going to, this cold winter's day?"

"I'm on my road to the King's Palace," answered Robin, "to sing to him a song this merry Yule morning." And he hopped away a yard or two from the Buzzard, for there was a look in his eye that he did not quite like.

"Thou art a friendly little fellow," remarked the Buzzard sweetly, "and I wish thee good luck on thine errand; but ere thou go on, come nearer me, I prith'ee, and I will show thee what a curious feather I have in my wing. 'Tis said that no other Buzzard in the countryside hath one like it."

"Like enough," rejoined Robin, hopping still further away, "but I will take thy word for it, without seeing it. For I saw thee pluck the feathers from the wee lintie, and I have no wish that thou shouldst pluck the feathers from me. So I will bid thee good day, and go on my journey."

The next place on which he rested was a piece of rock that overhung a dark, deep glen, and here he saw a sly old Fox looking out of his hole not two yards below him.

"Good morning, Robin Redbreast," said the sly old Fox, who had tried to steal a fat duck from a farmyard the night before, and had barely escaped with his life. "And where mayest thou be going so early on this cold winter's day?"

"I'm on my road to the King's Palace, to sing him a song this merry Yule morning," answered Robin, giving the same answer that he had given to the grey Poussie Baudrons and the greedy Buzzard.

"Thou wilt get a right good welcome, for His Majesty is

fond of music," said the wily Fox. "But ere thou go, just come down and have a look at a black spot which I have on the end of my tail. 'Tis said that there is not a fox 'twixt here and the Border that hath a spot on his tail like mine."

"Very like, very like," replied Robin, "but I chanced to see thee worrying the wee lambie up on the braeside yonder, and I have no wish that thou shouldst try thy teeth on me. So I will e'en go on my way to the King's Palace, and thou canst show the spot on thy tail to the next passer-by."

So the little Robin Redbreast flew away once more, and never rested till he came to a bonnie valley with a little burn running through it, and there he saw a rosy-cheeked Boy sitting on a log eating a piece of bread and butter. And he perched on a branch and watched him.

"Good morning, Robin Redbreast, and where mayest thou be going so early on this cold winter's day?" asked the Boy eagerly; for he was making a collection of stuffed birds, and he had still to get a Robin Redbreast.

"I'm on my way to the King's Palace to sing him a song this merry Yule morning," answered Robin, hopping down to the ground, and keeping one eye fixed on the bread and butter.

"Come a bit nearer, Robin," said the Boy, "and I will give thee some crumbs."

"Na, na, my wee man," chirped the cautious little bird, "for I saw thee catch the goldfinch, and I have no wish to give thee the chance to catch me."

At last he came to the King's Palace and lighted on the window-sill, and there he sat and sang the very sweetest song that he could sing; for he felt so happy because it was the Blessed Yuletide, that he wanted everyone else to be happy too. And the King and the Queen were so delighted with his song, as he peeped in at them at their open window, that they asked each other what they could give him as a reward for his kind thought in coming so far to greet them.

"We can give him a wife," replied the Queen, "who will go home with him and help him to build his nest."

"And who wilt thou give him for a bride?" asked the King. "Methinks 'twould need to be a very tiny lady to match his size."

"Why, Jenny Wren, of course," answered the Queen. "She hath looked somewhat dowie of late, this will be the very thing to brighten her up."

Then the King clapped his hands, and praised his wife for her happy thought, and wondered that the idea had not struck him before.

So Robin Redbreast and Jenny Wren were married, amid great rejoicings, at the King's Palace; and the King and Queen and all the fine Nobles and Court Ladies danced at their wedding. Then they flew away home to Robin's own countryside, and built their nest in the roots of the briar bush, where he had spoken to Poussie Baudrons. And you will be glad to hear that Jenny Wren proved the best little housewife in the world.

The Dwarfie Stone

Far up in a green valley in the Island of Hoy stands an immense boulder. It is hollow inside, and the natives of these northern islands call it "the Dwarfie Stone", because long centuries ago, so the legend has it, Snorro the Dwarf lived there.

Nobody knew where Snorro came from, or how long he had dwelt in the dark chamber inside the Dwarfie Stone. All that they knew about him was that he was a little man, with a queer, twisted, deformed body and a face of marvellous beauty, which never seemed to look any older, but was always smiling and young.

Men said that this was because Snorro's father had been a Fairy, and not a denizen of earth, who had bequeathed to his son the gift of perpetual youth, but nobody knew whether this were true or not, for the Dwarf had inhabited the Dwarfie Stone long before the oldest man or woman in Hoy had been born.

One thing was certain, however: he had inherited from his mother, whom all men agreed had been mortal, the dangerous qualities of vanity and ambition. And the longer he lived the more vain and ambitious did he become, until at last he always carried a mirror of polished steel round his neck, into which he constantly looked in order to see the reflection of his handsome face.

And he would not attend to the country people who came

to seek his help, unless they bowed themselves humbly before him and spoke to him as if he were a King.

I say that the country people sought his help, for he spent his time, or appeared to spend it, in collecting herbs and simples on the hillsides, which he carried home with him to his dark abode, and distilled medicines and potions from them, which he sold to his neighbours at wondrous high prices.

He was also the possessor of a wonderful leathern-covered book, clasped with clasps of brass, over which he would pore for hours together, and out of which he would tell the simple Islanders their fortunes, if they would.

For they feared the book almost as much as they feared Snorro himself, for it was whispered that it had once belonged to Odin, and they crossed themselves for protection as they named the mighty Enchanter.

But all the time they never guessed the real reason why Snorro chose to live in the Dwarfie Stone.

I will tell you why he did so. Not very far from the Stone there was a curious hill, shaped exactly like a wart. It was known as the Wart Hill of Hoy, and men said that somewhere in the side of it was hidden a wonderful Carbuncle, which, when it was found, would bestow on its finder marvellous magic gifts—Health, Wealth, and Happiness. Everything, in fact, that a human being could desire.

And the curious thing about this Carbuncle was, that it was said that it could be seen at certain times, if only the people who were looking for it were at the right spot at the right moment.

Now Snorro had made up his mind that he would find this wonderful stone, so, while he pretended to spend all his time in reading his great book or distilling medicines from his herbs, he was really keeping a keen look-out during his wanderings, noting every tuft of grass or piece of rock under which it might be hidden. And at night, when everyone else was asleep, he would creep out, with pickaxe and spade, to turn over the rocks or dig over the turf, in the hope of finding the long-sought-for treasure underneath them.

He was always accompanied on these occasions by an enormous grey-headed Raven, who lived in the cave along with him, and who was his bosom friend and companion. The Islanders feared this bird of ill omen as much, perhaps, as they feared its Master; for, although they went to consult Snorro in all their difficulties and perplexities, and bought medicines and love-potions from him, they always looked upon him with a certain dread, feeling that there was something weird and uncanny about him.

Now, at the time we are speaking of, Orkney was governed by two Earls, who were half-brothers. Paul, the elder, was a tall, handsome man, with dark hair, and eyes like sloes. All the country people loved him, for he was so skilled in knightly exercises, and had such a sweet and loving nature, that no one could help being fond of him. Old people's eyes would brighten at the sight of him, and the little children would run out to greet him as he rode by their mothers' doors.

And this was the more remarkable because, with all his winning manner, he had such a lack of conversation that men called him Paul the Silent, or Paul the Taciturn.

Harold, on the other hand, was as different from his brother as night is from day. He was fair-haired and blue-eyed, and he had gained for himself the name of Harold the Orator, because he was always free of speech and ready with his tongue.

But for all this he was not a favourite. For he was haughty, and jealous, and quick-tempered, and the old folks' eyes did not brighten at the sight of him, and the babes, instead of toddling out to greet him, hid their faces in their mothers' skirts when they saw him coming.

Harold could not help knowing that the people liked his silent brother best, and the knowledge made him jealous of him, so a coldness sprang up between them.

Now it chanced, one summer, that Earl Harold went on a visit to the King of Scotland, accompanied by his mother, the Countess Helga, and her sister, the Countess Fraukirk.

And while he was at Court he met a charming young Irish Maiden, the Lady Morna, who had come from Ireland to Scotland to attend upon the Scottish Queen. She was so sweet, and good, and gentle that Earl Harold's heart was won, and he made up his mind that she, and only she, should be his bride.

But although he had paid her much attention, Lady Morna had sometimes caught glimpses of his jealous temper; she had seen an evil expression in his eyes, and had heard him speak sharply to his servants, and she had no wish to marry him. So, to his great amazement, she refused the honour which he offered her, and told him that she would prefer to remain as she was.

Earl Harold ground his teeth in silent rage, but he saw that it was no use pressing his suit at that moment. So what he could not obtain by his own merits he determined to obtain by guile.

Accordingly he begged his mother to persuade the Lady Morna to go back with them on a visit, hoping that when she was alone with him in Orkney, he would be able to overcome her prejudice against him, and induce her to become his wife. And all the while he never remembered his brother Paul; or, if he did, he never thought it possible that he could be his rival.

But that was just the very thing that happened. The Lady Morna, thinking no evil, accepted the Countess Helga's invitation, and no sooner had the party arrived back in Orkney than Paul, charmed with the grace and beauty of the fair Irish Maiden, fell head over ears in love with her. And the Lady Morna, from the very first hour that she saw him, returned his love.

Of course this state of things could not long go on hidden, and when Harold realised what had happened his anger and jealousy knew no bounds. Seizing a dagger, he rushed up to the turret where his brother was sitting in his private apartments, and threatened to stab him to the heart if he did not promise to give up all thoughts of winning the lovely stranger.

But Paul met him with pleasant words.

"Calm thyself, Brother," he said. "It is true that I love the lady, but that is no proof that I shall win her. Is it likely that she will choose me, whom all men name Paul the Silent, when she hath the chance of marrying you, whose tongue moves so swiftly that to you is given the proud title of Harold the Orator?"

At these words Harold's vanity was flattered, and he thought that, after all, his step-brother was right, and that he had a very small chance, with his meagre gift of speech, of being successful in his suit. So he threw down his dagger, and, shaking hands with him, begged him to pardon his unkind thoughts, and went down the winding stair again in high good humour with himself and all the world.

By this time it was coming near to the Feast of Yule, and at that Festival it was the custom for the Earl and his Court to leave Kirkwall for some weeks, and go to the great Palace of Orphir, nine miles distant. And in order to see that everything was ready, Earl Paul took his departure some days before the others.

The evening before he left he chanced to find the Lady Morna sitting alone in one of the deep windows of the Great Hall. She had been weeping, for she was full of sadness at the thought of his departure; and at the sight of her distress the kind-hearted young Earl could no longer contain himself, but, folding her in his arms, he whispered to her how much he loved her, and begged her to promise to be his wife.

She agreed willingly. Hiding her rosy face on his shoulder, she confessed that she had loved him from the very first day that she had seen him; and ever since that moment she had determined that, if she could not wed him, she would wed no other man.

For a little time they sat together, rejoicing in their new-found happiness. Then Earl Paul sprang to his feet.

"Let us go and tell the good news to my mother and my brother," he said. "Harold may be disappointed at first, for I know, Sweetheart, he would fain have had thee for his own. But his good heart will soon overcome all that, and he will rejoice with us also."

But the Lady Morna shook her head. She knew, better than her lover, what Earl Harold's feeling would be; and she would fain put off the evil hour.

"Let us hold our peace till after Yule," she pleaded. "It will be a joy to keep our secret to ourselves for a little space; there will be time enough then to let all the world know."

Rather reluctantly, Earl Paul agreed; and next day he set off for the Palace at Orphir, leaving his ladylove behind him.

Little he guessed the danger he was in! For, all unknown to him, his step-aunt, Countess Fraukirk, had chanced to be in the Hall, the evening before, hidden behind a curtain, and she had overheard every word that the Lady Morna and he had spoken, and her heart was filled with black rage.

For she was a hard, ambitious woman, and she had always hated the young Earl, who was no blood-relation to her, and who stood in the way of his brother, her own nephew; for, if Paul were only dead, Harold would be the sole Earl of Orkney.

And now that he had stolen the heart of the Lady Morna, whom her own nephew loved, her hate and anger knew no bounds. She had hastened off to her sister's chamber as soon as the lovers had parted; and there the two women had remained talking together till the chilly dawn broke in the sky.

Next day a boat went speeding over the narrow channel of water that separates Pomona (on the mainland) from Hoy. In it sat a woman, but who she was, or what she was like, no one could say, for she was covered from head to foot with a black cloak, and her face was hidden behind a thick, dark veil.

Snorro the Dwarf knew her, even before she laid aside her trappings, for Countess Fraukirk was no stranger to him. In the course of her long life she had often had occasion to seek his aid to help her in her evil deeds, and she had always paid him well for his services in yellow gold. He therefore welcomed her gladly; but when he had heard the nature of her errand his smiling face grew grave again, and he shook his head.

"I have served thee well, Lady, in the past," he said, "but methinks that this thing goeth beyond my courage. For to compass an Earl's death is a weighty matter, especially when he is so well beloved as is the Earl Paul.

"Thou knowest why I have taken up my abode in this lonely spot—how I hope some day to light upon the Magic Carbuncle. Thou knowest also how the people fear me, and hate me too, forsooth. And if the young Earl died, and suspicion fell on me, I must needs fly the Island, for my life would not be worth a grain of sand. Then my chance of success would be gone. Nay! I cannot do it, Lady. I cannot do it."

But the wily Countess offered him much gold, and bribed him higher and higher, first with wealth, then with success, and lastly she promised to obtain for him a high post at the Court of the King of Scotland; and at that his ambition stirred within him, his determination gave way, and he consented to do what she asked.

"I will summon my magic loom," he said, "and weave a piece of cloth of finest texture and of marvellous beauty; and before I weave it I will so poison the thread with a magic potion that, when it is fashioned into a garment, whoever puts it on will die ere he hath worn it many minutes."

"Thou art a clever knave," answered the Countess, a cruel smile lighting up her evil face, "and thou shalt be rewarded. Let me have a couple of yards of this wonderful web, and I will make

a bonnie waistcoat for my fine young Earl and give it to him as a Yuletide gift. Then I reckon that he will not see the year out."

"That will he not," said Dwarf Snorro, with a malicious grin; and the two parted, after arranging that the piece of cloth should be delivered at the Palace of Orphir on the day before Christmas Eve.

Now, when the Countess Fraukirk had been away upon her wicked errand, strange things were happening at the Castle at Kirkwall. For Harold, encouraged by his brother's absence, offered his heart and hand once more to the Lady Morna. Once more she refused him, and in order to make sure that the scene should not be repeated, she told him that she had plighted her troth to his brother. When he heard that this was so, rage and fury were like to devour him. Mad with anger, he rushed from her presence, flung himself upon his horse, and rode away in the direction of the sea-shore.

While he was galloping wildly along, his eyes fell on the snow-clad hills of Hoy rising up across the strip of sea that divided the one island from the other. And his thoughts flew at once to Snorro the Dwarf, who he had had occasion, as well as his step-aunt, to visit in bygone days.

"I have it," he cried. "Stupid fool that I was not to think of it at once. I will go to Snorro, and buy from him a love potion, which will make my Lady Morna hate my precious brother and turn her thoughts kindly towards me."

So he made haste to hire a boat, and soon he was speeding over the tossing waters on his way to the Island of Hoy. When he arrived there he hurried up the lonely valley to where the Dwarfie Stone stood, and he had no difficulty in finding its uncanny occupant, for Snorro was standing at the hole that served as a door, his Raven on his shoulder, gazing placidly at the setting sun.

A curious smile crossed his face when, hearing the sound of approaching footsteps, he turned round and his eyes fell on the young noble.

"What bringeth thee here, Sir Earl?" he asked gaily, for he scented more gold.

"I come for a love potion," said Harold; and without more ado he told the whole story to the Wizard. "I will pay thee for it," he added, "if thou wilt give it to me quickly."

Snorro looked at him from head to foot. "Blind must the maiden be, Sir Orator," he said, "who needeth a love potion to make her fancy so gallant a Knight." Earl Harold laughed angrily. "It is easier to catch a sunbeam than a woman's roving fancy," he replied. "I have no time for jesting. For, hearken, old man, there is a proverb that saith, 'Time and tide wait for no man', so I need not expect the tide to wait for me. The potion I must have, and that instantly."

Snorro saw that he was in earnest, so without a word he entered his dwelling, and in a few minutes returned with a small phial in his hand, of a rosy liquid.

"Pour the contents of this into the Lady Morna's wine cup," he said, "and I warrant thee that before four-and-twenty hours have passed she will love thee better than thou lovest her now."

Then he waved his hand, as if to dismiss his visitor, and disappeared into his dwelling-place.

Earl Harold made all speed back to the Castle; but it was not until one or two days had elapsed that he found a chance to pour the love potion into the Lady Morna's wine cup. But at last, one night at supper, he found an opportunity of doing so, and, waving away the little page-boy, he handed it to her himself.

She raised it to her lips, but she only made a pretence at drinking, for she had seen the hated Earl fingering the cup, and she feared some deed of treachery. When he had gone back to his seat she managed to pour the whole of the wine on the floor, and smiled to herself at the look of satisfaction that came over Harold's face as she put down the empty cup.

His satisfaction increased, for from that moment she felt so afraid of him that she treated him with great kindness, hoping that by doing so she would keep in his good graces until the Court moved to Orphir, and her own true love could protect her.

Harold, on his side, was delighted with her graciousness, for he felt certain that the charm was beginning to work, and that his hopes would soon be fulfilled.

A week later the Court removed to the Royal Palace at Orphir, where Earl Paul had everything in readiness for the reception of his guests

Of course he was overjoyed to meet Lady Morna again, and she was overjoyed to meet him, for she felt that she was now safe from the unwelcome attentions of Earl Harold.

But to Earl Harold the sight of their joy was as gall and bitterness, and he could scarcely contain himself, although he still trusted in the efficacy of Snorro the Dwarf's love potion.

As for Countess Fraukirk and Countess Helga, they looked forward eagerly to the time when the magic web would arrive, out of which they hoped to fashion a fatal gift for Earl Paul.

At last, the day before Christmas Eve, the two wicked women were sitting in the Countess Helga's chamber talking of the time when Earl Harold would rule alone in Orkney, when a tap came to the window, and on looking round they saw Dwarf Snorro's grey-headed Raven perched on the sill, a sealed packet in its beak.

They opened the casement, and with a hoarse croak the creature let the packet drop on to the floor; then it flapped its great wings and rose slowly into the air again, its head turned in the direction of Hoy.

With fingers that trembled with excitement they broke the seals and undid the packet. It contained a piece of the most beautiful material that anyone could possibly imagine, woven in all the colours of the rainbow, and sparkling with gold and jewels.

"'Twill make a bonnie waistcoat," exclaimed Countess Fraukirk, with an unholy laugh. "The Silent Earl will be a braw man when he gets it on."

Then, without more ado, they set to work to cut out and sew the garment. All that night they worked, and all next day, till, late in the afternoon, when they were putting in the last stitches, hurried footsteps were heard ascending the winding staircase, and Earl Harold burst open the door.

His cheeks were red with passion, and his eyes were bright, for he could not but notice that, now that she was safe at Orphir under her true love's protection, the Lady Morna's manner had grown cold and distant again, and he was beginning to lose faith in Snorro's charm.

Angry and disappointed, he had sought his mother's room to pour out his story of vexation to her.

He stopped short, however, when he saw the wonderful waistcoat lying on the table, all gold and silver and shining colours. It was like a Fairy garment, and its beauty took his breath away.

"For whom hast thou purchased that?" he asked, hoping to hear that it was intended for him.

"'Tis a Christmas gift for thy brother Paul," answered his mother, and she would have gone on to tell him how deadly a thing it was, had he given her time to speak. But her words fanned his fury into madness, for it seemed to him that this hated brother of his was claiming everything.

"Everything is for Paul! I am sick of his very name," he cried. "By my troth, he shall not have this!" and he snatched the vest from the table.

It was in vain that his mother and his aunt threw themselves at his feet, begging him to lay it down, and warning him that there was not a thread in it which was not poisoned. He paid no heed to their words, but rushed from the room, and, drawing it on, ran downstairs with a reckless laugh, to show the Lady Morna how fine he was.

Alas! Alas! Scarce had he gained the Hall than he fell to the ground in great pain.

Everyone crowded round him, and the two Countesses, terrified now by what they had done, tried in vain to tear the magic vest from his body. But he felt that it was too late, the deadly poison had done its work, and, waving them aside, he turned to his brother, who, in great distress, had knelt down and taken him tenderly in his arms.

"I wronged thee, Paul," he gasped. "For thou hast ever been true and kind. Forgive me in thy thoughts, and," he added, gathering up his strength for one last effort, and pointing to the two wretched women who had wrought all this misery, "beware of those two women, for they seek to take thy life." Then his head sank back on his brother's shoulder, and, with one long sigh, he died.

When he learned what had happened, and understood where the waistcoat came from, and for what purpose it had been intended, the anger of the Silent Earl knew no bounds.

He swore a great oath that he would be avenged, not only on Snorro the Dwarf, but also on his wicked step-mother and her cruel sister.

His vengeance was baulked, however, for in the panic and confusion that followed Harold's death, the two Countesses slipped out of the Palace and fled to the coast, and took boat in haste to Scotland, where they had great possessions, and where they were much looked up to, and where no one would believe a word against them.

But retribution fell on them in the end, as it always does fall, sooner or later, on everyone who is wicked, or selfish, or cruel; for the Norsemen invaded the land, and their Castle was set on fire, and they perished miserably in the flames.

When Earl Paul found that they had escaped, he set out in hot haste for the Island of Hoy, for he was determined that the Dwarf, at least, should not escape. But when he came to the Dwarfie Stone he found it silent and deserted, all trace of its uncanny occupants having disappeared.

No one knew what had become of them; a few people were inclined to think that the Dwarf and his Raven had accompanied the Countess Fraukirk and the Countess Helga on their flight, but the greater part of the Islanders held to the belief, which I think was the true one, that the Powers of the Air spirited Snorro away, and shut him up in some unknown place as a punishment for his wickedness, and that his Raven accompanied him.

At any rate, he was never seen again by any living person, and wherever he went, he lost all chance of finding the Magic Carbuncle.

As for the Silent Earl and his Irish Sweetheart, they were married as soon as Earl Harold's funeral was over; and for hundreds of years afterwards, when the inhabitants of the Orkney Isles wanted to express great happiness, they said, "As happy as Earl Paul and the Countess Morna."

Canonbie Dick and
Thomas of Ercildoune

It chanced, long years ago, that a certain horse-dealer lived
in the South of Scotland, near the Border, not very far from
Longtown. He was known as Canonbie Dick; and as he went
up and down the country, he almost always had a long string
of horses behind him, which he bought at one fair and sold at
another, generally managing to turn a good big penny by the
transaction.

He was a very fearless man, not easily daunted; and the
people who knew him used to say that if Canonbie Dick dare
not attempt a thing, no one else need be asked to do it.

One evening, as he was returning from a fair at some
distance from his home with a pair of horses which he had
not succeeded in selling, he was riding over Bowden Moor,
which lies to the west of the Eildon Hills. These hills are, as all
men know, the scene of some of the most famous of Thomas
the Rhymer's prophecies, and also, so men say, they are the
sleeping-place of King Arthur and his Knights, who rest under
the three high peaks, waiting for the mystic call that shall
awake them.

But little recked the horse-dealer of Arthur and his Knights,
nor yet of Thomas the Rhymer. He was riding along at a snail's
pace, thinking over the bargains which he had made at the fair

that day, and wondering when he was likely to dispose of his two remaining horses.

All at once he was startled by the approach of a venerable man, with white hair and an old-world dress, who seemed almost to start out of the ground, so suddenly did he make his appearance.

When they met, the stranger stopped, and, to Canonbie Dick's great amazement, asked him for how much he would be willing to part with his horses.

The wily horse-dealer thought that he saw a chance of driving a good bargain, for the stranger looked a man of some consequence; so he named a good round sum.

The old man tried to bargain with him; but when he found that he had not much chance of succeeding—for no one ever did succeed in inducing Canonbie Dick to sell a horse for a less sum than he named for it at first—he agreed to buy the animals, and, pulling a bag of gold from the pocket of his queerly cut breeches, he began to count out the price.

As he did so, Canonbie Dick got another shock of surprise, for the gold that the stranger gave him was not the gold that was in use at the time, but was fashioned into Unicorns, and Bonnet-pieces, and other ancient coins, which would be of no use to the horse-dealer in his everyday transactions. But it was good, pure gold; and he took it gladly, for he knew that he was selling his horses at about half as much again as they were worth. "So," thought he to himself, "surely I cannot be the loser in the long run."

Then the two parted, but not before the old man had commissioned Dick to get him other good horses at the same price, the only stipulation he made being that Dick should always bring them to the same spot, after dark, and that he should always come alone.

And, as time went on, the horse-dealer found that he had indeed met a good customer.

For, whenever he came across a suitable horse, he had only to lead it over Bowden Moor after dark, and he was sure to meet the mysterious, white-headed stranger, who always paid him for the animal in old-fashioned golden pieces.

And he might have been selling horses to him yet, for aught I know, had it not been for his one failing.

Canonbie Dick was apt to get very thirsty, and his ordinary customers, knowing this, took care always to provide him with something to drink. The old man never did so; he paid down his money and led away his horses, and there was an end of the matter.

But one night, Dick, being even more thirsty than usual, and feeling sure that his mysterious friend must live somewhere in the neighbourhood, seeing that he was always wandering about the hillside when everyone else was asleep, hinted that he would be very glad to go home with him and have a little refreshment.

"He would need to be a brave man who asks to go home with me," returned the stranger, "but, if thou wilt, thou canst follow me. Only, remember this—if thy courage fail thee at that which thou wilt behold, thou wilt rue it all thy life."

Canonbie Dick laughed long and loud. "My courage hath never failed me yet," he cried. "Beshrew me if I will let it fail now. So lead on, old man, and I will follow."

Without a word the stranger turned and began to ascend a narrow path which led to a curious hillock, which from its shape, was called by the country folk "the Lucken Hare".

It was supposed to be a great haunt of Witches; and, as a rule, nobody passed that way after dark, if they could possibly help it.

Canonbie Dick was not afraid of Witches, however, so he followed his guide with a bold step up the hillside; but it must be confessed that he felt a little startled when he saw him turn down what seemed to be an entrance to a cavern, especially as he never remembered having seen any opening in the hillside there before.

He paused for a moment, looking round him in perplexity, wondering where he was being taken; and his conductor glanced at him scornfully.

"You can go back if you will," he said. "I warned thee thou wert going on a journey that would try thy courage to the uttermost." There was a jeering note in his voice that touched Dick's pride.

"Who said that I was afraid?" he retorted. "I was just taking note of where this passage stands on the hillside, so as to know it another time."

The stranger shrugged his shoulders. "Time enough to look for it when thou wouldst visit it again," he said. And then he pursued his way, with Dick following closely at his heels.

After the first yard or two they were enveloped in thick darkness, and the horse-dealer would have been sore put to it to keep near his guide had not the latter held out his hand for him to grasp. But after a little space a faint glimmering of light began to appear, which grew clearer and clearer, until at last they found themselves in an enormous cavern lit by flaming torches, which were stuck here and there in sconces in the rocky walls, and which, although they served to give light enough to see by, yet threw such ghostly shadows on the floor that they only seemed to intensify the gloom that hung over the vast apartment.

And the curious thing about this mysterious cave was that, along one side of it, ran a long row of horse stalls, just like what one would find in a stable, and in each stall stood a coal-black charger, saddled and bridled, as if ready for the fray; and on the straw, by every horse's side, lay the gallant figure of a Knight, clad from head to foot in coal-black armour, with a drawn sword in his mailed hand.

But not a horse moved, not a chain rattled. Knights and

steeds alike were silent and motionless, looking exactly as if some strange enchantment had been thrown over them, and they had been suddenly turned into black marble.

There was something so awesome in the still, cold figures and in the unearthly silence that brooded over everything that Canonbie Dick, reckless and daring though he was, felt his courage waning and his knees beginning to shake under him.

In spite of these feelings, however, he followed the old man up the Hall to the far end of it, where there was a table of ancient workmanship, on which was placed a glittering sword and a curiously wrought hunting-horn.

When they reached this table the stranger turned to him, and said, with great dignity, "Thou hast heard, good man, of Thomas of Ercildoune—Thomas the Rhymer, as men call him—he who went to dwell for a time with the Queen of Fairy-land, and from her received the Gifts of Truth and Prophecy?"

Canonbie Dick nodded; for as the wonderful Soothsayer's name fell on his ears, his heart sank within him and his tongue seemed to cleave to the roof of his mouth. If he had been brought there to parley with Thomas the Rhymer, then had he laid himself open to all the eldrich Powers of Darkness.

"I that speak to thee am he," went on the white-haired stranger. "And I have permitted thee thus to have thy desire and follow me hither in order that I may try of what stuff thou art made. Before thee lies a Horn and a Sword. He that will sound the one, or draw the other, shall, if his courage fail not, be King over the whole of Britain. I, Thomas the Rhymer, have spoken it, and, as thou knowest, my tongue cannot lie. But list ye, the outcome of it all depends on thy bravery; and it will be a light task, or a heavy, according as thou layest hand on Sword or Horn first."

Now Dick was more versed in giving blows than in making music, and his first impulse was to seize the Sword, then, come what might, he had something in his hand to defend himself with. But just as he was about to lift it the thought struck him that, if the place were full of spirits, as he felt sure that it must be, this action of his might be taken to mean defiance, and might cause them to band themselves together against him.

So, changing his mind, he picked up the Horn with a trembling hand, and blew a blast upon it, which, however, was so weak and feeble that it could scarce be heard at the other end of the Hall. The result that followed was enough to appal the stoutest heart. Thunder rolled in crashing peals through the immense Hall. The charmed Knights and their horses woke in an instant from their enchanted sleep.

The Knights sprang to their feet and seized their swords, brandishing them round their heads, while their great black chargers stamped, and snorted, and ground their bits, as if eager to escape from their stalls. And where a moment before all had been stillness and silence, there was now a scene of wild din and excitement.

Now was the time for Canonbie Dick to play the man. If he had done so all the rest of his life might have been different.

But his courage failed him, and he lost his chance. Terrified at seeing so many threatening faces turned towards him, he dropped the Horn and made one weak, undecided effort to pick up the Sword.

But, ere he could do so, a mysterious voice sounded from somewhere in the Hall, and these were the words that it uttered:

"Woe to the coward, that ever he was born,
Who did not draw the Sword before he blew the Horn."

And, before Dick knew what he was about, a perfect whirlwind of cold, raw air tore through the cavern, carrying the luckless horse-dealer along with it; and, hurrying him along the narrow passage through which he had entered, dashed him down outside on a bank of loose stones and shale. He fell right to the bottom, and was found, with little life left in him, next morning, by some shepherds, to whom he had just strength enough left to whisper the story of his weird and fearful adventure.

The Laird O' Co'

It was a fine summer morning, and the Laird o' Co' was having a dander on the green turf outside the Castle walls. His real name was the Laird o' Colzean, and his descendants today bear the proud title of Marquises of Ailsa, but all up and down Ayrshire nobody called him anything else than the Laird o' Co'; because of the Co's, or caves, which were to be found in the rock on which his Castle was built.

He was a kind man, and a courteous, always ready to be interested in the affairs of his poorer neighbours, and willing to listen to any tale of woe.

So when a little boy came across the green, carrying a small can in his hand, and, pulling his forelock, asked him if he might go to the Castle and get a little ale for his sick mother, the Laird gave his consent at once, and, patting the little fellow on the head, told him to go to the kitchen and ask for the butler, and tell him that he, the Laird, had given orders that his can was to be filled with the best ale that was in the cellar.

Away the boy went, and found the old butler, who, after listening to his message, took him down into the cellar, and proceeded to carry out his Master's orders.

There was one cask of particularly fine ale, which was kept entirely for the Laird's own use, which had been opened some time before, and which was now about half full.

"I will fill the bairn's can out o' this," thought the old man to himself. "'Tis both nourishing and light—the very thing for sick folk." So, taking the can from the child's hand, he proceeded to draw the ale.

But what was his astonishment to find that, although the ale flowed freely enough from the barrel, the little can, which could not have held more than a quarter of a gallon, remained always just half full.

The ale poured into it in a clear amber stream, until the big cask was quite empty, and still the quantity that was in the little can did not seem to increase.

The butler could not understand it. He looked at the cask, and then he looked at the can; then he looked down at the floor at his feet to see if he had not spilt any.

No, the ale had not disappeared in that way, for the cellar floor was as white, and dry, and clean, as possible.

"Plague on the can; it must be bewitched," thought the old man, and his short, stubby hair stood up like porcupine quills round his bald head, for if there was anything on earth of which he had a mortal dread, it was Warlocks, and Witches, and such like Bogles.

"I'm not going to broach another barrel," he said gruffly, handing back the half-filled can to the little lad. "So ye may just go home with what is there; the Laird's ale is too good to waste on a smatchet like thee."

But the boy stoutly held his ground. A promise was a promise, and the Laird had both promised, and sent orders to the butler that the can was to be filled, and he would not go home till it was filled.

It was in vain that the old man first argued, and then grew angry—the boy would not stir a step. The Laird had said that he was to get the ale, and the ale he must have.

At last the perturbed butler left him standing there, and hurried off to his Master to tell him he was convinced that the can was bewitched, for it had swallowed up a whole half cask of ale, and after doing so it was only half full; and to ask if he would come down himself, and order the lad off the premises.

"Not I," said the genial Laird, "for the little fellow is quite right. I promised that he should have his can full of ale to take home to his sick mother, and he shall have it if it takes all the barrels in my cellar to fill it. So haste thee to the house again, and open another cask."

The butler dare not disobey; so he reluctantly retraced his steps, but, as he went, he shook his head sadly, for it seemed to him that not only the boy with the can, but his master also, was bewitched.

When he reached the cellar he found the bairn waiting patiently where he had left him, and, without wasting further words, he took the can from his hand and broached another barrel.

If he had been astonished before, he was more astonished now. Scarce had a couple of drops fallen from the tap, than the can was full to the brim.

"Take it, laddie, and begone, with all the speed thou canst," he said, glad to get the can out of his fingers; and the boy did not wait for a second bidding. Thanking the butler most earnestly for his trouble, and paying no attention to the fact that the old man had not been so civil to him as he might have been, he departed. Nor, though the butler took pains to ask all round the countryside, could he ever hear of him again, nor of anyone who knew anything about him, or anything about his sick mother.

Years passed by, and sore trouble fell upon the House o' Co'. For the Laird went to fight in the wars in Flanders, and, chancing to be taken prisoner, he was shut up in prison, and condemned to death. Alone, in a foreign country, he had no friends to speak for him, and escape seemed hopeless.

It was the night before his execution, and he was sitting in his lonely cell, thinking sadly of his wife and children, whom he never expected to see again. At the thought of them the picture of his home rose clearly in his mind—the grand old Castle standing on its rock, and the bonnie daisy-spangled stretch of greensward which lay before its gates, where he had been wont to take a dander in the sweet summer mornings. Then, all unbidden, a vision of the little lad carrying the can, who had come to beg ale for his sick mother, and whom he had long ago forgotten, rose up before him.

The vision was so clear and distinct that he felt almost as if he were acting the scene over again, and he rubbed his eyes to get rid of it, feeling that, if he had to die tomorrow, it was time that he turned his thoughts to better things.

But as he did so the door of his cell flew noiselessly open, and there, on the threshold, stood the self-same little lad, looking not a day older, with his finger on his lip, and a mysterious smile upon his face.

> "Laird o' Co',
> Rise and go!"

he whispered, beckoning to him to follow him. Needless to say, the Laird did so, too much amazed to think of asking questions.

Through the long passages of the prison the little lad went, the Laird close at his heels; and whenever he came to a locked door, he had but to touch it, and it opened before them, so that in no long time they were safe outside the walls.

The overjoyed Laird would have overwhelmed his little deliverer with words of thanks had not the boy held up his hand to stop him. "Get on my back," he said shortly, "for thou are not safe till thou art out of this country."

The Laird did as he was bid, and, marvellous as it seems, the boy was quite able to bear his weight. As soon as he was comfortably seated the pair set off, over sea and land, and never stopped till, in almost less time than it takes to tell it, the boy set him down, in the early dawn, on the daisy-spangled green

in front of his Castle, just where he had spoken first to him so many years before.

Then he turned, and laid his little hand on the Laird's big one:

> "Ae gude turn deserves anither,
> Tak' ye that for being sae kind to my auld mither."

Having said which, he vanished.

And from that day to this he has never been seen again.

Poussie Baudrons

"Poussie, Poussie Baudrons
Where hae ye been?"
"I've been at London,
Seeing the Queen!"

"Poussie, Poussie Baudrons
What got ye there?"
"I got a guid fat mousikie,
Rinning up a stair."

"Poussie, Poussie Baudrons
What did ye do wi't?"
"I put it in my meal-poke
To eat it to my bread."

The Milk-White Doo

There was once a man who got his living by working in the fields. He had one little son, called Curly-Locks, and one little daughter, called Golden-Tresses; but his wife was dead, and, as he had to be out all day, these children were often left alone. So, as he was afraid that some evil might befall them when there was no one to look after them, he, in an ill day, married again.

I say, "in an ill day", for his second wife was a most deceitful woman, who really hated children, although she pretended, before her marriage, to love them. And she was so unkind to them, and made the house so uncomfortable with her bad temper, that her poor husband often sighed to himself, and wished that he had let well alone, and remained a widower.

But it was no use crying over spilt milk; the deed was done, and he had just to try to make the best of it. So things went on for several years, until the children were beginning to run about the doors and play by themselves.

Then one day the Goodman chanced to catch a hare, and he brought it home and gave it to his wife to cook for the dinner.

Now his wife was a very good cook, and she made the hare into a pot of delicious soup; but she was also very greedy, and while the soup was boiling she tasted it, and tasted it, till at last she discovered that it was almost gone. Then she was in a fine state of mind, for she knew that her husband would soon be coming home for his dinner, and that she would have nothing to set before him.

So what do you think the wicked woman did? She went out to the door, where her little step-son, Curly-Locks, was playing in the sun, and told him to come in and get his face washed. And while she was washing his face, she struck him on the head with a hammer and stunned him, and popped him into the pot to make soup for his father's dinner.

By and by the Goodman came in from his work, and the soup was dished up; and he, and his wife, and his little daughter, Golden-Tresses, sat down to sup it.

"Where's Curly-Locks?" asked the Goodman. "It's a pity he is not here as long as the soup is hot."

"How should I ken?" answered his wife crossly. "I have other work to do than to run about after a mischievous laddie all the morning."

The Goodman went on supping his soup in silence for some minutes; then he lifted up a little foot in his spoon.

"This is Curly-Locks' foot," he cried in horror. "There hath been ill work here."

"Hoots, havers," answered his wife, laughing, pretending to be very much amused. "What should Curly-Locks' foot be doing in the soup? 'Tis the hare's forefoot, which is very like that of a bairn."

But presently the Goodman took something else up in his spoon.

"This is Curly-Locks' hand," he said shrilly. "I ken it by the crook in its little finger."

"The man's demented," retorted his wife, "not to ken the hind foot of a hare when he sees it!"

So the poor father did not say any more, but went away out to his work, sorely perplexed in his mind; while his little daughter, Golden-Tresses, who had a shrewd suspicion of what had happened, gathered all the bones from the empty plates, and, carrying them away in her apron, buried them beneath a flat stone, close by a white rose tree that grew by the cottage door.

And, lo and behold, those poor bones, which she buried with such care:

> "Grew and grew,
> To a milk-white Doo,
> That took its wings,
> And away it flew."

And at last it lighted on a tuft of grass by a burn-side, where two women were washing clothes. It sat there cooing to itself for some time; then it sang this song softly to them:

> "Pew, pew,
> My mimmie me slew,
> My daddy me chew,
> My sister gathered my banes,
> And put them between two milk-white stanes.
> And I grew and grew
> To a milk-white Doo,
> And I took to my wings and away I flew."

The women stopped washing and looked at one another in astonishment. It was not every day that they came across a bird that could sing a song like that, and they felt that there was something not canny about it.

"Sing that song again, my bonnie bird," said one of them at last, "and we'll give thee all these clothes!"

So the bird sang its song over again, and the washerwomen gave it all the clothes, and it tucked them under its right wing, and flew on.

Presently it came to a house where all the windows were

open, and it perched on one of the window-sills, and inside it saw a man counting out a great heap of silver.

And, sitting on the window-sill, it sang its song to him:

"Pew, pew,
My mimmie me slew,
My daddy me chew,
My sister gathered my banes,
And put them between two milk-white stanes.
And I grew and grew
To a milk-white Doo,
And I took to my wings and away I flew."

The man stopped counting his silver, and listened. He felt, like the washerwomen, that there was something not canny about this Doo. When it had finished its song, he said, "Sing that song again, my bonnie bird, and I'll give thee a' this siller in a bag."

So the Doo sang its song over again, and got the bag of silver, which it tucked under its left wing. Then it flew on.

It had not flown very far, however, before it came to a mill where two millers were grinding corn. And it settled down on a sack of meal and sang its song to them.

"Pew, pew,
My mimmie me slew,
My daddy me chew,
My sister gathered my banes,
And put them between two milk-white stanes.
And I grew and grew
To a milk-white Doo,
And I took to my wings and away I flew."

The millers stopped their work, and looked at one another, scratching their heads in amazement.

"Sing that song over again, my bonnie bird!" exclaimed both of them together when the Doo had finished, "and we will give thee this millstone."

So the Doo repeated its song, and got the millstone, which it asked one of the millers to lift on its back; then it flew out of the mill, and up the valley, leaving the two men staring after it dumb with astonishment.

As you may think, the Milk-White Doo had a heavy load to carry, but it went bravely on till it came within sight of its father's cottage, and lighted down at last on the thatched roof.

Then it laid its burdens on the thatch, and flying down to the courtyard, picked up a number of little chuckie stones. With them in its beak it flew back to the roof, and began to throw them down the chimney.

By this time it was evening, and the Goodman and his wife, and his little daughter, Golden-Tresses, were sitting round the table eating their supper. And you may be sure that they were all very much startled when the stones came rattling down the chimney, bringing such a cloud of soot with them that they were like to be smothered. They all jumped up from their chairs, and ran outside to see what the matter was.

And Golden-Tresses, being the littlest, ran the fastest, and when she came out at the door the Milk-White Doo flung the bundle of clothes down at her feet.

And the father came out next, and the Milk-White Doo flung the bag of silver down at his feet.

But the wicked step-mother, being somewhat stout, came out last, and the Milk-White Doo threw the millstone right down on her head and killed her.

Then it spread its wings and flew away, and has never been seen again; but it had made the Goodman and his daughter rich for life, and it had rid them of the cruel step-mother, so that they lived in peace and plenty for the remainder of their days.

The Draiglin' Hogney

There was once a man who had three sons, and very little money to provide for them. So, when the eldest had grown into a lad, and saw that there was no means of making a livelihood at home, he went to his father and said to him:

"Father, if thou wilt give me a horse to ride on, a hound to hunt with, and a hawk to fly, I will go out into the wide world and seek my fortune."

His father gave him what he asked for; and he set out on his travels. He rode and he rode, over mountain and glen, until, just at nightfall, he came to a thick, dark wood. He entered it, thinking that he might find a path that would lead him through it; but no path was visible, and after wandering up and down for some time, he was obliged to acknowledge to himself that he was completely lost.

There seemed to be nothing for it but to tie his horse to a tree, and make a bed of leaves for himself on the ground; but just as he was about to do so he saw a light glimmering in the distance, and, riding on in the direction in which it was, he soon came to a clearing in the wood, in which stood a magnificent Castle.

The windows were all lit up, but the great door was barred; and, after he had ridden up to it, and knocked, and received no answer, the young man raised his hunting horn to his lips

146

and blew a loud blast in the hope of letting the inmates know that he was without.

Instantly the door flew open of its own accord, and the young man entered, wondering very much what this strange thing would mean. And he wondered still more when he passed from room to room, and found that, although fires were burning brightly everywhere, and there was a plentiful meal laid out on the table in the Great Hall, there did not seem to be a single person in the whole of the vast building.

However, as he was cold, and tired, and wet, he put his horse in one of the stalls of the enormous stable, and taking his hawk and hound along with him, went into the Great Hall and ate a hearty supper. After which he sat down by the side of the fire, and began to dry his clothes.

By this time it had grown late, and he was just thinking of retiring to one of the bedrooms which he had seen upstairs and going to bed, when a clock which was hanging on the wall struck twelve.

Instantly the door of the huge apartment opened, and a most awful-looking Draiglin' Hogney entered. His hair was matted and his beard was long, and his eyes shone like stars of fire from under his bushy eyebrows, and in his hands he carried a queerly shaped club.

He did not seem at all astonished to see his unbidden guest; but, coming across the Hall, he sat down upon the opposite side of the fireplace, and, resting his chin on his hands, gazed fixedly at him.

"Doth thy horse ever kick any?" he said at last, in a harsh, rough voice.

"Ay, doth he," replied the young man; for the only steed that his father had been able to give him was a wild and unbroken colt.

"I have some skill in taming horses," went on the Draiglin' Hogney, "and I will give thee something to tame thine withal.

Throw this over him." And he pulled one of the long, coarse hairs out of his head and gave it to the young man. And there was something so commanding in the Hogney's voice that he did as he was bid, and went out to the stable and threw the hair over the horse.

Then he returned to the Hall, and sat down again by the fire. The moment that he was seated the Draiglin' Hogney asked another question.

"Doth thy hound ever bite any?"

"Ay, verily," answered the youth; for his hound was so fierce-tempered that no man, save his master, dare lay a hand on him.

"I can cure the wildest tempered dog in Christendom," replied the Draiglin' Hogney. "Take that, and throw it over him." And he pulled another hair out of his head and gave it to the young man, who lost no time in flinging it over his hound.

There was still a third question to follow. "Doth ever thy hawk peck any?"

The young man laughed. "I have ever to keep a bandage over her eyes, save when she is ready to fly," said he, "else were nothing safe within her reach."

"Things will be safe now," said the Hogney, grimly. "Throw that over her." And for the third time he pulled a hair from his head and handed it to his companion. And as the other hairs had been thrown over the horse and the hound, so this one was thrown over the hawk.

Then, before the young man could draw breath, the fiercesome Draiglin' Hogney had given him such a clout on the side of his head with his queer-shaped club that he fell down in a heap on the floor.

And very soon his hawk and his hound tumbled down still and motionless beside him; and, out in the stable, his horse became stark and stiff, as if turned to stone. For the Draiglin's words had meant more than at first appeared when he said that he could make all unruly animals quiet.

Some time afterwards the second of the three sons came to his father in the old home with the same request that his brother had made. That he should be provided with a horse, a hawk, and a hound, and be allowed to go out to seek his fortune. And his father listened to him, and gave him what he asked, as he had given his brother.

And the young man set out, and in due time came to the wood, and lost himself in it, just as his brother had done; then he saw the light, and came to the Castle, and went in, and had supper, and dried his clothes, just as it all had happened before.

And the Draiglin' Hogney came in, and asked him the three questions, and he gave the same three answers, and received three hairs—one to throw over his horse, one to throw over his hound, and one to throw over his hawk; then the Hogney killed him, just as he had killed his brother.

Time passed, and the youngest son, finding that his two elder brothers never returned, asked his father for a horse, a hawk, and a hound, in order that he might go and look for them. And the poor old man, who was feeling very desolate in his old age, gladly gave them to him.

So he set out on his quest, and at nightfall he came, as the others had done, to the thick wood and the Castle. But, being a wise and cautious youth, he liked not the way in which he found things. He liked not the empty house; he liked not the spread-out feast; and, most of all, he liked not the look of the Draiglin' Hogney when he saw him. And he determined to be very careful what he said or did as long as he was in his company.

So when the Draiglin' Hogney asked him if his horse kicked, he replied that it did, in very few words; and when he got one of the Hogney's hairs to throw over him, he went out to the

So he set out on his Quest

stable, and pretended to do so, but he brought it back, hidden in his hand, and, when his unchancy companion was not looking, he threw it into the fire. It fizzled up like a tongue of flame with a little hissing sound like that of a serpent.

"What's that fizzling?" asked the Draiglin' Hogney suspiciously.

"'Tis but the sap of the green wood," replied the young man carelessly, as he turned to caress his hound.

The answer satisfied the Draiglin' Hogney, and he paid no heed to the sound which the hair that should have been thrown over the hound, or the sound which the hair that should have been thrown over the hawk, made, when the young man threw them into the fire; and they fizzled up in the same way that the first had done.

Then, thinking that he had the stranger in his power, he whisked across the hearthstone to strike him with his club, as he had struck his brothers; but the young man was on the outlook, and when he saw him coming he gave a shrill whistle. And his horse, which loved him dearly, came galloping in from the stable, and his hound sprang up from the hearthstone where he had been sleeping; and his hawk, who was sitting on his shoulder, ruffled up her feathers and screamed harshly; and they all fell on the Draiglin' Hogney at once, and he found out only too well how the horse kicked, and the hound bit, and the hawk pecked; for they kicked him, and bit him, and pecked him, till he was as dead as a door nail.

When the young man saw that the Draiglin' Hogney was dead, he took his queerly shaped club from his hand, and, armed with that, he set out to explore the Castle.

As he expected, he found that there were dark and dreary dungeons under it, and in one of them he found his two brothers, lying cold and stiff side by side. He touched them with the club, and instantly they came to life again, and sprang to their feet as well as ever.

Then he went into another dungeon; and there were the two horses, and the two hawks, and the two hounds, lying as if dead, exactly as their Masters had lain. He touched them with his magic club, and they, too, came to life again.

Then he called to his two brothers, and the three young men searched the other dungeons, and they found great stores of gold and silver hidden in them, enough to make them rich for life.

So they buried the Draiglin' Hogney, and took possession of the Castle; and two of them went home and brought their old father back with them, and they all were as prosperous and happy as they could be; and, for aught that I know, they are living there still.

The Brownie O' Ferne-Den

There have been many Brownies known in Scotland; and stories have been written about the Brownie o' Bodsbeck and the Brownie o' Blednock, but about neither of them has a prettier story been told than that which I am going to tell you about the Brownie o' Ferne-Den.

Now, Ferne-Den was a farmhouse, which got its name from the glen, or "den", on the edge of which it stood, and through which anyone who wished to reach the dwelling had to pass.

And this glen was believed to be the abode of a Brownie, who never appeared to anyone in the daytime, but who, it was said, was sometimes seen at night, stealing about like an ungainly shadow from tree to tree, trying to keep from observation, and never, by any chance, harming anybody.

Indeed, like all Brownies that are properly treated and let alone, so far was he from harming anybody that he was always on the look-out to do a good turn to those who needed his assistance. The farmer often said that he did not know what he would do without him; for if there was any work to be finished in a hurry at the farm—corn to thrash or winnow or tie up into bags, turnips to cut, clothes to wash, a kirn to be kirned, a garden to be weeded—all that the farmer and his wife had to do was to leave the door of the barn or the turnip shed or the milk house open when they went to bed, and put down a bowl of new milk on the doorstep for the Brownie's supper, and when they woke the next morning the bowl would be empty, and the job finished better than if it had been done by mortal hands.

In spite of all this, however, which might have proved to them how gentle and kindly the creature really was, everyone about the place was afraid of him, and would rather go a couple of miles round about in the dark, when they were coming home from Kirk or Market, than pass through the glen and run the risk of catching a glimpse of him.

I said that they were all afraid of him but that was not true, for the farmer's wife was so good and gentle that she was not afraid of anything on God's earth, and when the Brownie's supper had to be left outside, she always filled his bowl with the richest milk, and added a good spoonful of cream to it, for, said she, "He works so hard for us, and asks no wages, he well deserves the very best meal that we can give him."

One night this gentle lady was taken very ill, and everyone was afraid that she was going to die. Of course, her husband was greatly distressed and so were her servants, for she had been such a good Mistress to them that they loved her as if she had been their mother. But they were all young and none of them knew very much about illness, and everyone agreed that it would be better to send off for an old woman who lived about seven miles away on the other side of the river, who was known to be a very skilful nurse.

But who was to go? That was the question. For it was black midnight, and the way to the old woman's house lay straight through the glen. And whoever travelled that road ran the risk of meeting the dreaded Brownie.

The farmer would have gone only too willingly, but he dare not leave his wife alone; and the servants stood in groups about the kitchen, each one telling the other that he ought to go, yet no one offering to go themselves.

Little did they think that the cause of all their terror, a queer, wee, misshapen little man, all covered with hair, with a long beard, red-rimmed eyes, broad, flat feet, just like the feet of a paddock, and enormous long arms that touched the ground, even when he stood upright, was within a yard or two of them, listening to their talk with an anxious face, behind the kitchen door.

For he had come up as usual, from his hiding-place in the glen, to see if there were any work for him to do, and to look for his bowl of milk. And he had seen, from the open door and lit-up windows, that there was something wrong inside the farmhouse, which at that hour was wont to be dark, and still, and silent; and he had crept into the entry to try and find out what the matter was.

When he gathered from the servants' talk that the Mistress, whom he loved so dearly, and who had been so kind to him, was ill, his heart sank within him; and when he heard that the silly servants were so taken up with their own fears that they dared not set out to fetch a nurse for her, his contempt and anger knew no bounds.

"Fools, idiots, dolts!" he muttered to himself, stamping his queer, misshapen feet on the floor. "They speak as if a body were ready to take a bite off them as soon as ever he met them. If they only knew the bother it gives me to keep out of their road they wouldna be so silly. But, by my troth, if they go on like this, the bonnie lady will die amongst their fingers. So it strikes me that Brownie must e'en gang himself."

So saying, he reached up his hand, and took down a dark cloak which belonged to the farmer and was hanging on a peg on the wall, and, throwing it over his head and shoulders, as somewhat to hide his ungainly form, he hurried away to the stable, and saddled and bridled the fleetest-footed horse that stood there.

When the last buckle was fastened, he led it to the door, and scrambled on its back. "Now, if ever thou travelledst fleetly, travel fleetly now," he said; and it was as if the creature understood him, for it gave a little whinny and pricked up its ears; then it darted out into the darkness like an arrow from the bow.

In less time than the distance had ever been ridden in before, the Brownie drew rein at the old woman's cottage.

She was in bed, fast asleep; but he rapped sharply on the window, and when she rose and put her old face, framed in its white mutch, close to the pane to ask who was there, he bent forward and told her his errand.

"Thou must come with me, Goodwife, and that quickly," he commanded, in his deep, harsh voice, "if the Lady of Ferne-Den's life is to be saved; for there is no one to nurse her up-bye at the farm there, save a lot of empty-headed servant wenches."

"But how am I to get there ? Have they sent a cart for me?" asked the old woman anxiously; for, as far as she could see, there was nothing at the door save a horse and its rider.

"No, they have sent no cart," replied the Brownie, shortly. "So you must just climb up behind me on the saddle, and hang on tight to my waist, and I'll promise to land ye at Ferne-Den safe and sound."

His voice was so masterful that the old woman dare not refuse to do as she was bid; besides, she had often ridden pillion-wise when she was a lassie, so she made haste to dress herself, and when she was ready she unlocked her door, and, mounting the louping-on stane that stood beside it, she was soon seated behind the dark-cloaked stranger, with her arms clasped tightly round him.

Not a word was spoken till they approached the dreaded glen, then the old woman felt her courage giving way. "Do ye think that there will be any chance of meeting the Brownie?" she asked timidly. "I would fain not run the risk, for folk say that he is an unchancy creature."

Her companion gave a curious laugh. "Keep up your heart, and dinna talk havers," he said, "for I promise ye ye'll see naught uglier this night than the man whom ye ride behind."

"Oh, then, I'm fine and safe," replied the old woman with a sigh of relief, "for although I havena' seen your face, I warrant that ye are a true man, for the care you have taken of a poor old woman."

She relapsed into silence again till the glen was passed and the good horse had turned into the farmyard. Then the horseman slid to the ground, and, turning round, lifted her carefully down in his long, strong arms. As he did so the cloak slipped off him, revealing his short, broad body and his misshapen limbs.

"In a' the world, what kind o' man are ye?" she asked, peering into his face in the grey morning light, which was just dawning. "What makes your eyes so big? And what have ye done to your feet? They are more like paddock's webs than aught else."

The queer little man laughed again. "I've wandered many a mile in my time without a horse to help me, and I've heard it said that ower much walking makes the feet unshapely," he replied. "But waste no time in talking, good Dame. Go thy way into the house; and, hark'ee, if anyone asks thee who brought thee hither so quickly, tell them that there was a lack of men, so thou hadst e'en to be content to ride behind the BROWNIE O' FERNE-DEN."

The Witch of Fife

In the Kingdom of Fife, in the days of long ago, there lived an old man and his wife. The old man was a douce, quiet body, but the old woman was lightsome and flighty, and some of the neighbours were wont to look at her askance, and whisper to each other that they sorely feared that she was a Witch.

And her husband was afraid of it, too, for she had a curious habit of disappearing in the gloaming and staying out all night; and when she returned in the morning she looked quite white and tired, as if she had been travelling far, or working hard.

He used to try and watch her carefully, in order to find out where she went, or what she did, but he never managed to do so, for she always slipped out of the door when he was not looking, and before he could reach it to follow her, she had vanished utterly.

At last, one day, when he could stand the uncertainty no longer, he asked her to tell him straight out whether she were a Witch or no. And his blood ran cold when, without the slightest hesitation, she answered that she was; and if he would promise not to let anyone know, the next time that she went on one of her midnight expeditions she would tell him all about it.

The Goodman promised; for it seemed to him just as well that he should know all about his wife's cantrips.

He had not long to wait before he heard of them. For the very next week the moon was new, which is, as everybody knows, the time of all others when Witches like to stir abroad; and on the first night of the new moon his wife vanished. Nor did she return till daybreak next morning.

And when he asked her where she had been, she told him, in great glee, how she and four like-minded companions had met at the old Kirk on the moor and had mounted branches of the green bay tree and stalks of hemlock, which had instantly changed into horses, and how they had ridden, swift as the wind, over the country, hunting the foxes, and the weasels, and the owls; and how at last they had swam the Forth and come to the top of Ben Lomond. And how there they had dismounted from their horses, and drunk beer that had been brewed in no earthly brewery, out of horn cups that had been fashioned by no mortal hands.

And how, after that, a wee, wee man had jumped up from under a great mossy stone, with a tiny set of bagpipes under his arm, and how he had piped such wonderful music, that, at the sound of it, the very trouts jumped out of the Loch below, and the stoats crept out of their holes, and the corby crows and the herons came and sat on the trees in the darkness, to listen. And how all the Witches danced until they were so weary that, when the time came for them to mount their steeds again, if they would be home before cock-crow, they could scarce sit on them for fatigue.

The Goodman listened to this long story in silence, shaking his head meanwhile, and, when it was finished, all that he answered was, "And what the better are ye for all your dancing? Ye'd have been a deal more comfortable at home."

At the next new moon the old man's wife went off again for the night; and when she returned in the morning she told her husband how, on this occasion, she and her friends had taken cockle-shells for boats, and had sailed away over the stormy sea till they reached Norway. And there they had mounted invisible horses of wind, and had ridden and ridden, over mountains and glens, and glaciers, till they reached the land of the Lapps lying under its mantle of snow.

And here all the Elves, and Fairies, and Mermaids of the North were holding festival with Warlocks, and Brownies, and Pixies, and even the Phantom Hunters themselves, who are never looked upon by mortal eyes. And the Witches from Fife held festival with them, and danced, and feasted, and sang with them, and, what was of more consequence, they learned from them certain wonderful words, which, when they uttered them, would bear them through the air and would undo all bolts and bars, and so gain them admittance to any place soever where they wanted to be. And after that they had come home again, delighted with the knowledge which they had acquired.

"What took ye to siccan a land as that?" asked the old man, with a contemptuous grunt. "Ye would hae been a sight warmer in your bed."

But when his wife returned from her next adventure, he showed a little more interest in her doings.

For she told him how she and her friends had met in the cottage of one of their number, and how, having heard that the Lord Bishop of Carlisle had some very rare wine in his cellar, they had placed their feet on the crook from which the pot hung, and had pronounced the magic words which they had learned from the Elves of Lappland. And, lo and behold! they flew up the chimney like whiffs of smoke, and sailed through the air like little wreathes of cloud, and in less time than it takes to tell they landed at the Bishop's Palace at Carlisle.

And the bolts and the bars flew loose before them, and they went down to his cellar and sampled his wine, and were back in Fife, fine, sober, old women by cock-crow.

When he heard this, the old man started from his chair in right earnest, for he loved good wine above all things, and it was but seldom that it came his way.

"By my troth, but thou art a wife to be proud of!" he cried.

"Tell me the words, Woman, and I will e'en go and sample his Lordship's wine for myself."

But his wife shook her head. "Na, na! I cannot do that," she said, "for if I did, an' ye telled it over again, 'twould turn the whole world upside down. For everybody would be leaving their own lawful work, and flying about the world after other folk's business and other folk's dainties. So just bide content, Goodman. Ye get on fine with the knowledge ye already possess."

And although the old man tried to persuade her with all the soft words he could think of, she would not tell him her secret.

But he was a sly old man, and the thought of the Bishop's wine gave him no rest. So night after night he went and hid in the old woman's cottage, in the hope that his wife and her friends would meet there; and although for a long time it was all in vain, at last his trouble was rewarded. For one evening the whole five Witches assembled, and in low tones and with chuckles of laughter they recounted all that had befallen them in Lappland. Then, running to the fireplace, they, one after another, climbed on a chair and put their feet on the sooty crook. Then they repeated the magic words, and, hey presto, they were up the lum and away before the old man could draw his breath!

"I can do that, too," he said to himself; and he crawled out of his hiding-place and ran to the fire. He put his foot on the crook and repeated the words, and up the chimney he went, and flew through the air after his wife and her companions, as if he had been a Warlock born.

And, as Witches are not in the habit of looking over their shoulders, they never noticed that he was following them, until they reached the Bishop's Palace and went down into his cellar, then, when they found that he was among them, they were not too well pleased.

However, there was no help for it, and they settled down

to enjoy themselves. They tapped this cask of wine, and they tapped that, drinking a little of each, but not too much; for they were cautious old women, and they knew that if they wanted to get home before cock-crow it behoved them to keep their heads clear.

But the old man was not so wise, for he sipped, and he sipped, until at last he became quite drowsy, and lay down on the floor and fell fast asleep.

And his wife, seeing this, thought that she would teach him a lesson not to be so curious in the future. So, when she and her four friends thought that it was time to be gone, she departed without waking him.

He slept peacefully for some hours, until two of the Bishop's servants, coming down to the cellar to draw wine for their Master's table, almost fell over him in the darkness. Greatly astonished at his presence there, for the cellar door was fast locked, they dragged him up to the light and shook him, and cuffed him, and asked him how he came to be there.

And the poor old man was so confused at being awakened in this rough way, and his head seemed to whirl round so fast, that all he could stammer out was, "that he came from Fife, and that he had travelled on the midnight wind."

As soon as they heard that, the men servants cried out that he was a Warlock, and they dragged him before the Bishop, and, as Bishops in those days had a holy horror of Warlocks and Witches, he ordered him to be burned alive.

When the sentence was pronounced, you may be very sure that the poor old man wished with all his heart that he had stayed quietly at home in bed, and never hankered after the Bishop's wine.

But it was too late to wish that now, for the servants dragged him out into the courtyard, and put a chain round his waist, and fastened it to a great iron stake, and they piled faggots of wood round his feet and set them alight.

As the first tiny little tongue of flame crept up, the poor old man thought that his last hour had come. But when he thought that, he forgot completely that his wife was a Witch.

For, just as the little tongue of flame began to singe his breeches, there was a swish and a flutter in the air, and a great Grey Bird, with outstretched wings, appeared in the sky, and swooped down suddenly, and perched for a moment on the old man's shoulder.

And in this Grey Bird's mouth was a little red nightcap, which, to everyone's amazement, it popped onto the prisoner's head. Then it gave one fierce croak, and flew away again, but to the old man's ears that croak was the sweetest music that he had ever heard.

For to him it was the croak of no earthly bird, but the voice of his wife whispering words of magic to him. And when he heard them he jumped for joy, for he knew that they were words of deliverance, and he shouted them aloud, and his chains fell off, and he mounted in the air—up and up—while the onlookers watched him in awestruck silence.

He flew right away to the Kingdom of Fife, without as much as saying goodbye to them; and when he found himself once more safely at home, you may be very sure that he never tried to find out his wife's secrets again, but left her alone to her own devices.

Assipattle and the Mester Stoorworm

In far bygone days, in the North, there lived a well-to-do farmer, who had seven sons and one daughter. And the youngest of these seven sons bore a very curious name; for men called him Assipattle, which means, "He who grovels among the ashes".

Perhaps Assipattle deserved his name, for he was rather a lazy boy, who never did any work on the farm as his brothers did, but ran about the doors with ragged clothes and unkempt hair, and whose mind was ever filled with wondrous stories of Trolls and Giants, Elves and Goblins.

When the sun was hot in the long summer afternoons, when the bees droned drowsily and even the tiny insects seemed almost asleep, the boy was content to throw himself down on the ash-heap amongst the ashes, and lie there, lazily letting them run through his fingers, as one might play with sand on the sea-shore, basking in the sunshine and telling stories to himself.

And his brothers, working hard in the fields, would point to him with mocking fingers, and laugh, and say to each other how well the name suited him, and of how little use he was in the world.

And when they came home from their work, they would

push him about and tease him, and even his mother would make him sweep the floor, and draw water from the well, and fetch peats from the peatstack, and do all the little odd jobs that nobody else would do.

So poor Assipattle had rather a hard life of it, and he would often have been very miserable had it not been for his sister, who loved him dearly, and who would listen quite patiently to all the stories that he had to tell; who never laughed at him or told him that he was telling lies, as his brothers did.

But one day a very sad thing happened—at least, it was a sad thing for poor Assipattle.

For it chanced that the King of these parts had one only daughter, the Princess Gemdelovely, whom he loved dearly, and to whom he denied nothing. And Princess Gemdelovely was in want of a waiting-maid, and as she had seen Assipattle's sister standing by the garden gate as she was riding by one day, and had taken a fancy to her, she asked her father if she might ask her to come and live at the Castle and serve her.

Her father agreed at once, as he always did agree to any of her wishes; and sent a messenger in haste to the farmer's house to ask if his daughter would come to the Castle to be the Princess's waiting-maid.

And, of course, the farmer was very pleased at the piece of good fortune which had befallen the girl, and so was her mother, and so were her six brothers, all except poor Assipattle, who looked with wistful eyes after his sister as she rode away, proud of her new clothes and of the rivlins which her father had made her out of cowhide, which she was to wear in the Palace when she waited on the Princess, for at home she always ran barefoot.

Time passed, and one day a rider rode in hot haste through the country bearing the most terrible tidings. For the evening before, some fishermen, out in their boats, had caught sight of the Mester Stoorworm, which, as everyone knows, was the largest, and the first, and the greatest of all Sea Serpents. It was that beast which, in the Good Book is called the Leviathan, and if it had been measured in our day, its tail would have touched Iceland, while it snout rested on the North Cape.

And the fishermen had noticed that this fearsome Monster had its head turned towards the mainland and that it opened its mouth and yawned horribly, as if to show that it was hungry, and that, if it were not fed, it would kill every living thing upon the land, both man and beast, bird and creeping thing.

For 'twas well known that its breath was so poisonous that it consumed as with a burning fire everything that it lighted on. So that, if it pleased the awful creature to lift its head and put forth its breath, like noxious vapour, over the country, in a few weeks the fair land would be turned into a region of desolation.

As you may imagine, everyone was almost paralysed with terror at this awful calamity which threatened them; and the King called a solemn meeting of all his Counsellors, and asked them if they could devise any way of warding off the danger.

And for three whole days they sat in Council, these grave, bearded men, and many were the suggestions which were made, and many the words of wisdom which were spoken; but, alas, no one was wise enough to think of a way by which the Mester Stoorworm might be driven back.

At last, at the end of the third day, when everyone had given up hope of finding a remedy, the door of the Council Chamber opened and the Queen appeared.

Now the Queen was the King's second wife, and she was not a favourite in the Kingdom, for she was a proud, insolent woman, who did not behave kindly to her step-daughter, the Princess Gemdelovely, and who spent much more of her time in the company of a great Sorcerer, whom everyone feared and dreaded, than she did in that of the King, her husband.

So the sober Counsellors looked at her disapprovingly as she came boldly into the Council Chamber and stood up beside the King's Chair of State, and, speaking in a loud, clear voice, addressed them thus:

"Ye think that ye are brave men and strong, oh, ye Elders, and fit to be the Protectors of the People. And so it may be, when it is mortals that ye are called on to face. But ye be no match for the foe that now threatens our land. Before him your weapons be but as straw. 'Tis not through strength of arm, but through sorcery, that he will be overcome. So listen to my words, even though they be but those of a woman, and take counsel with the great Sorcerer, from whom nothing is hid, but who knoweth all the mysteries of the earth, and of the air, and of the sea."

Now the King and his Counsellors liked not this advice, for they hated the Sorcerer, who had, as they thought, too much influence with the Queen; but they were at their wits' end, and knew not to whom to turn for help, so they were fain to do as she said and summon the Wizard before them.

And when he obeyed the summons and appeared in their midst, they liked him none the better for his looks. For he was long, and thin, and awesome, with a beard that came down to his knee, and hair that wrapped him about like a mantle, and his face was the colour of mortar, as if he had always lived in darkness, and had been afraid to look on the sun.

But there was no help to be found in any other man, so they laid the case before him, and asked him what they should do. And he answered coldly that he would think over the matter, and come again to the Assembly the following day and give them his advice.

And his advice, when they heard it, was like to turn their hair white with horror.

For he said that the only way to satisfy the Monster, and to make it spare the land, was to feed it every Saturday with seven young maidens, who must be the fairest who could be found; and if, after this remedy had been tried once or twice, it did not succeed in mollifying the Stoorworm and inducing him to depart, there was but one other measure that he could suggest, but that was so horrible and dreadful that he would not rend their hearts by mentioning it in the meantime.

And as, although they hated him, they feared him also, the Council had e'en to abide by his words, and pronounced the awful doom.

And so it came about that, every Saturday, seven bonnie, innocent maidens were bound hand and foot and laid on a rock which ran into the sea, and the Monster stretched out his long, jagged tongue, and swept them into his mouth; while all the rest of the folk looked on from the top of a high hill—or, at least, the men looked, with cold, set faces, while the women hid theirs in their aprons and wept aloud.

"Is there no other way," they cried, "no other way than this, to save the land?"

But the men only groaned and shook their heads. "No other way," they answered, "no other way."

Then suddenly a boy's indignant voice rang out among the crowd. "Is there no grown man who would fight that Monster, and kill him, and save the lassies alive? I would do it; I am not feared for the Mester Stoorworm."

It was the boy Assipattle who spoke, and everyone looked at him in amazement as he stood staring at the great Sea Serpent, his fingers twitching with rage, and his great blue eyes glowing with pity and indignation.

"The poor bairn's mad; the sight hath turned his head," they whispered one to another; and they would have crowded round him to pet and comfort him, but his elder brother came and gave him a heavy clout on the side of his head.

"Thou fight the Stoorworm!" he cried contemptuously. "A likely story! Go home to thy ashpit, and stop speaking havers." And, taking his arm, he drew him to the place where his other brothers were waiting, and they all went home together.

But all the time Assipattle kept on saying that he meant to kill the Stoorworm; and at last his brothers became so angry at what they thought was mere bragging, that they picked up stones and pelted him so hard with them that at last he took to his heels and ran away from them.

That evening the six brothers were threshing corn in the barn, and Assipattle, as usual, was lying among the ashes thinking his own thoughts, when his mother came out and bade him run and tell the others to come in for their supper.

The boy did as he was bid, for he was a willing enough little fellow; but when he entered the barn his brothers, in revenge for his having run away from them in the afternoon, set on him and pulled him down, and piled so much straw on top of him that, had his father not come from the house to see what they were all waiting for, he would, of a surety, have been smothered.

But when, at supper-time, his mother was quarrelling with the other lads for what they had done, and saying to them that it was only cowards who set on bairns littler and younger than themselves, Assipattle looked up from the bicker of porridge which he was supping.

"Vex not thyself, Mother," he said, "for I could have fought them all if I liked; ay, and beaten them, too."

"Why didst thou not essay it then?" cried everybody at once.

"Because I knew that I would need all my strength when I go to fight the Giant Stoorworm," replied Assipattle gravely.

And, as you may fancy, the others laughed louder than before.

Time passed, and every Saturday seven lassies were thrown to the Stoorworm, until at last it was felt that this state of things could not be allowed to go on any longer; for if it did, there would soon be no maidens at all left in the country.

So the Elders met once more, and, after long consultation, it was agreed that the Sorcerer should be summoned, and asked what his other remedy was. "For, by our troth," said they, "it cannot be worse than that which we are practising now."

But, had they known it, the new remedy was even more dreadful than the old. For the cruel Queen hated her step-daughter, Gemdelovely, and the wicked Sorcerer knew that she did, and that she would not be sorry to get rid of her, and, things being as they were, he thought that he saw a way to please the Queen. So he stood up in the Council, and, pretending to be very sorry, said that the only other thing that could be done was to give the Princess Gemdelovely to the Stoorworm, then would it of a surety depart.

When they heard this sentence a terrible stillness fell upon the Council, and everyone covered his face with his hands, for no man dare look at the King.

But although his dear daughter was as the apple of his eye, he was a just and righteous Monarch, and he felt that it was not right that other fathers should have been forced to part with their daughters, in order to try and save the country, if his child was to be spared.

So, after he had had speech with the Princess, he stood up before the Elders, and declared, with trembling voice, that both he and she were ready to make the sacrifice.

"She is my only child," he said, "and the last of her race. Yet it seemeth good to both of us that she should lay down her life, if by so doing she may save the land that she loves so well."

Salt tears ran down the faces of the great bearded men as they heard their King's words, for they all knew how dear the Princess Gemdelovely was to him. But it was felt that what he said was wise and true, and that the thing was just and right; for 'twere better, surely, that one maiden should die, even although she were of Royal blood, than that bands of other maidens should go to their death week by week, and all to no purpose.

So, amid heavy sobs, the aged Lawman—he who was the

chief man of the Council—rose up to pronounce the Princess's doom. But, ere he did so, the King's Kemper—or Fighting-man—stepped forward.

"Nature teaches us that it is fitting that each beast hath a tail," he said, "and this Doom, which our Lawman is about to pronounce, is in very sooth a venomous beast. And, if I had my way, the tail which it would bear after it is this, that if the Mester Stoorworm doth not depart, and that right speedily, after he have devoured the Princess, the next thing that is offered to him be no tender young maiden, but that tough, lean old Sorcerer."

And at his words there was such a great shout of approval that the wicked Sorcerer seemed to shrink within himself, and his pale face grew paler than it was before.

Now, three weeks were allowed between the time that the Doom was pronounced upon the Princess and the time that it was carried out, so that the King might send Ambassadors to all the neighbouring Kingdoms to issue proclamations that, if any Champion would come forward who was able to drive away the Stoorworm and save the Princess, he should have her for his wife.

And with her he should have the Kingdom, as well as a very famous sword that was now in the King's possession, but which had belonged to the great god Odin, with which he had fought and vanquished all his foes.

The sword bore the name of Sickersnapper, and no man had any power against it.

The news of all these things spread over the length and breadth of the land, and everyone mourned for the fate that was like to befall the Princess Gemdelovely. And the farmer, and his wife, and their six sons mourned also—all but Assipattle, who sat amongst the ashes and said nothing.

When the King's Proclamation was made known throughout the neighbouring Kingdoms, there was a fine stir among all the young Gallants, for it seemed but a little thing to slay a Sea Monster; and a beautiful wife, a fertile Kingdom, and a trusty sword are not to be won every day.

So six-and-thirty Champions arrived at the King's Palace, each hoping to gain the prize.

But the King sent them all out to look at the Giant Stoorworm lying in the sea with its enormous mouth open, and when they saw it, twelve of them were seized with sudden illness, and twelve of them were so afraid that they took to their heels and ran, and never stopped till they reached their own countries; and so only twelve returned to the King's Palace, and as for them, they were so downcast at the thought of the task that they had undertaken that they had no spirit left in them at all.

And none of them dare try to kill the Stoorworm; so the three weeks passed slowly by, until the night before the day on which the Princess was to be sacrificed. On that night the King, feeling that he must do something to entertain his guests, made a great supper for them.

But, as you may think, it was a dreary feast, for everyone was thinking so much about the terrible thing that was to happen on the morrow, that no one could eat or drink.

And when it was all over, and everybody had retired to rest, save the King and his old Kemperman, the King returned to the Great Hall, and went slowly up to his Chair of State, high up on the dais. It was not like the Chairs of State that we know nowadays; it was nothing but a massive Kist, in which he kept all the things which he treasured most.

The old Monarch undid the iron bolts with trembling fingers, and lifted the lid, and took out the wondrous sword Sickersnapper, which had belonged to the great god Odin.

His trusty Kemperman, who had stood by him in a hundred fights, watched him with pitying eyes.

"Why lift ye out the sword," he said softly, "when thy fighting days are done? Right nobly hast thou fought thy battles in the past, oh, my Lord, when thine arm was strong and sure. But when folk's years number four score and sixteen, as thine do, 'tis time to leave such work to other and younger men."

The old King turned on him angrily, with something of the old fire in his eyes. "Wheesht," he cried, "else will I turn this sword on thee. Dost thou think that I can see my only bairn devoured by a Monster, and not lift a finger to try and save her when no other man will? I tell thee—and I will swear it with my two thumbs crossed on Sickersnapper—that both the sword and I will be destroyed before so much as one of her hairs be touched. So go, an' thou love me, my old comrade, and order my boat to be ready, with the sail set and the prow pointed out to sea. I will go myself and fight the Stoorworm; and if I do not return, I will lay it on thee to guard my cherished daughter. Peradventure, my life may redeem hers."

Now that night everybody at the farm went to bed betimes, for next morning the whole family was to set out early, to go to the top of the hill near the sea; to see the Princess eaten by the Stoorworm. All except Assipattle, who was to be left at home to herd the geese.

The lad was so vexed at this—for he had great schemes in his head—that he could not sleep. And as he lay tossing and tumbling about in his corner among the ashes, he heard his father and mother talking in the great box-bed. And, as he listened, he found that they were having an argument.

"'Tis such a long way to the hill overlooking the sea, I fear me I shall never walk it," said his mother. "I think I had better bide at home."

"Nay," replied her husband, "that would be a bonny-like thing, when all the countryside is to be there. Thou shalt ride behind me on my good mare Go-Swift."

"I do not care to trouble thee to take me behind thee," said his wife, "for methinks thou dost not love me as thou wert wont to do."

"The woman's havering," cried the Goodman of the house impatiently. "What makes thee think that I have ceased to love thee?"

"Because thou wilt no longer tell me thy secrets," answered his wife. "To go no further, think of this very horse, Go-Swift. For five long years I have been begging thee to tell me how it is that, when thou ridest her, she flies faster than the wind, while if any other man mount her, she hirples along like a broken-down nag."

The Goodman laughed. "'Twas not for lack of love, Goodwife," he said, "though it might be lack of trust. For women's tongues wag but loosely; and I did not want other folk to ken my secret. But since my silence hath vexed thy heart, I will e'en tell it thee.

"When I want Go-Swift to stand, I give her one clap on the left shoulder. When I would have her go like any other horse, I give her two claps on the right. But when I want her to fly like the wind, I whistle through the windpipe of a goose. And, as I never ken when I want her to gallop like that, I aye keep the bird's thrapple in the left-hand pocket of my coat."

"So that is how thou managest the beast," said the farmer's wife, in a satisfied tone, "and that is what becomes of all my goose thrapples. Oh, but thou art a clever fellow, Goodman! And now that I ken the way of it I may go to sleep."

Assipattle was not tumbling about in the ashes now; he was sitting up in the darkness, with glowing cheeks and sparkling eyes.

His opportunity had come at last, and he knew it.

He waited patiently till their heavy breathing told him that his parents were asleep; then he crept over to where his father's clothes were, and took the goose's windpipe out of the pocket of his coat, and slipped noiselessly out of the house. Once he was out of it, he ran like lightning to the stable. He saddled and bridled Go-Swift, and threw a halter round her neck, and led her to the stable door.

The good mare, unaccustomed to her new groom, pranced, and reared, and plunged; but Assipattle, knowing his father's secret, clapped her once on the left shoulder, and she stood as still as a stone. Then he mounted her, and gave her two claps on the right shoulder, and the good horse trotted off briskly, giving a loud neigh as she did so.

The unwonted sound, ringing out in the stillness of the night, roused the household, and the Goodman and his six sons came tumbling down the wooden stairs, shouting to one another in confusion that someone was stealing Go-Swift.

The farmer was the first to reach the door; and when he saw, in the starlight, the vanishing form of his favourite steed, he cried at the top of his voice:

> "Stop thief, ho!
> Go-Swift, whoa!"

And when Go-Swift heard that she pulled up in a moment. All seemed lost, for the farmer and his sons could run very fast indeed, and it seemed to Assipattle, sitting motionless on Go-Swift's back, that they would very soon make up on him.

But, luckily, he remembered the goose's thrapple, and he pulled it out of his pocket and whistled through it. In an instant the good mare bounded forward, swift as the wind, and was over the hill and out of reach of her pursuers before they had taken ten steps more.

Day was dawning when the lad came within sight of the sea; and there, in front of him, in the water, lay the enormous Monster whom he had come so far to slay. Anyone would have said that he was mad even to dream of making such an attempt, for he was but a slim, unarmed youth, and the Mester Stoorworm was so big that men said it would reach the fourth part round the world. And its tongue was jagged at the end like a fork, and with this fork it could sweep whatever it chose into its mouth, and devour it at its leisure.

For all this, Assipattle was not afraid, for he had the heart of a hero underneath his tattered garments.

"I must be cautious," he said to himself, "and do by my wits what I cannot do by my strength."

He climbed down from his seat on Go-Swift's back, and tethered the good steed to a tree, and walked on, looking well about him, till he came to a little cottage on the edge of a wood.

The door was not locked, so he entered, and found its occupant, an old woman, fast asleep in bed. He did not disturb her, but he took down an iron pot from the shelf, and examined it closely.

"This will serve my purpose," he said, "and surely the old Dame would not grudge it if she knew 'twas to save the Princess's life."

Then he lifted a live peat from the smouldering fire, and went his way.

Down at the water's edge he found the King's boat lying, guarded by a single boatman, with its sails set and its prow turned in the direction of the Mester Stoorworm.

"It's a cold morning," said Assipattle. "Art thou not well-nigh frozen sitting there? If thou wilt come on shore, and run about, and warm thyself, I will get into the boat and guard it till thou returnest."

"A likely story," replied the man. "And what would the King say if he were to come, as I expect every moment he will do, and find me playing myself on the sand, and his good boat left to a smatchet like thee? 'Twould be as much as my head is worth."

"As thou wilt," answered Assipattle carelessly, beginning to search among the rocks. "In the meantime, I must be looking for a wheen mussels to roast for my breakfast." And after he had gathered the mussels, he began to make a hole in the sand to put the live peat in. The boatman watched him curiously, for he, too, was beginning to feel hungry.

Presently the lad gave a wild shriek, and jumped high in the air. "Gold, gold!" he cried. "By the name of Thor, who would have looked to find gold here?"

This was too much for the boatman. Forgetting all about his head and the King, he jumped out of the boat, and, pushing Assipattle aside, began to scrape among the sand with all his might.

While he was doing so, Assipattle seized his pot, jumped into the boat, pushed her off, and was half a mile out to sea before the outwitted man, who, needless to say, could find no gold, noticed what he was about.

And, of course, he was very angry, and the old King was more angry still when he came down to the shore, attended by his Nobles and carrying the great sword Sickersnapper, in the vain hope that he, poor feeble old man that he was, might be able in some way to defeat the Monster and save his daughter.

But to make such an attempt was beyond his power now that his boat was gone. So he could only stand on the shore, along with the fast assembling crowd of his subjects, and watch what would befall.

And this was what befell!

Assipattle, sailing slowly over the sea, and watching the Mester Stoorworm intently, noticed that the terrible Monster yawned occasionally, as if longing for his weekly feast. And as it yawned a great flood of sea-water went down its throat, and came out again at its huge gills.

So the brave lad took down his sail, and pointed the prow of his boat straight at the Monster's mouth, and the next time it yawned he and his boat were sucked right in, and, like Jonah, went straight down its throat into the dark regions inside its body. On and on the boat floated; but as it went the water grew less, pouring out of the Stoorworm's gills, till at last it stuck, as it were, on dry land. And Assipattle jumped out, his pot in his hand, and began to explore.

Presently he came to the huge creature's liver, and having heard that the liver of a fish is full of oil, he made a hole in it and put in the live peat.

Woe's me! But there was a conflagration! And Assipattle just got back to his boat in time; for the Mester Stoorworm, in its convulsions, threw the boat right out of its mouth again, and it was flung up, high and dry, on the bare land.

The commotion in the sea was so terrible that the King and his daughter—who by this time had come down to the shore dressed like a bride, in white, ready to be thrown to the Monster—and all his Courtiers, and all the countryfolk, were fain to take refuge on the hill-top, out of harm's way, and stand and see what happened next.

And this was what happened next.

The poor, distressed creature—for it was now to be pitied, even although it was a great, cruel, awful Mester Stoorworm—tossed itself to and fro, twisting and writhing.

And as it tossed its awful head out of the water its tongue fell out, and struck the earth with such force that it made a great dent in it, into which the sea rushed. And that dent formed the crooked Straits which now divide Denmark from Norway and Sweden.

Then some of its teeth fell out and rested in the sea, and became the islands that we now call the Orkney Isles; and a little afterwards some more teeth dropped out, and they became what we now call the Shetland Isles.

After that the creature twisted itself into a great lump and died; and this lump became the Island of Iceland; and the fire which Assipattle had kindled with his live peat still burns on underneath it, and that is why there are mountains which throw out fire in that chilly land.

When at last it was plainly seen that the Mester Stoorworm was dead, the King could scarce contain himself with joy. He put his arms round Assipattle's neck, and kissed him, and called him his son. And he took off his own Royal Mantle and put it on the lad, and girded his good sword Sickersnapper round his waist. And he called his daughter, the Princess Gemdelovely, to him, and put her hand in his, and declared that when the right time came she should be his wife, and that he should be ruler over all the Kingdom.

Then the whole company mounted their horses again, and Assipattle rode on Go-Swift by the Princess's side; and so they returned, with great joy, to the King's Palace.

But as they were nearing the gate Assipattle's sister, she who was the Princess's maid, ran out to meet him, and signed to the Princess to bend down, and whispered something in her ear.

The Princess's face grew dark, and she turned her horse's head and rode back to where her father was, with his Nobles. She told him the words that the maiden had spoken; and when he heard them his face, too, grew as black as thunder.

For the matter was this: the cruel Queen, full of joy at the thought that she was to be rid, once for all, of her step-daughter, had been making love to the wicked Sorcerer all the morning in the old King's absence.

"He shall be killed at once," cried the Monarch. "Such behaviour cannot be overlooked."

"Thou wilt have much ado to find him, your Majesty," said the girl, "for 'tis more than an hour since he and the Queen fled together on the fleetest horses that they could find in the stables."

"But I can find him," cried Assipattle; and he went off like the wind on his good horse Go-Swift.

It was not long before he came within sight of the fugitives, and he drew his sword and shouted to them to stop.

They heard the shout, and turned round, and they both laughed aloud in derision when they saw that it was only the boy who grovelled in the ashes who pursued them.

"The insolent brat! I will cut off his head for him! I will teach him a lesson!" cried the Sorcerer; and he rode boldly back to meet Assipattle. For although he was no fighter, he knew that no ordinary weapon could harm his enchanted body; therefore he was not afraid.

But he did not count on Assipattle having Sickersnapper, the sword of the great god Odin, with which he had slain all his enemies; and before this magic weapon he was powerless. And, at one thrust, the young lad ran it through his body as easily as if he had been any ordinary man, and he fell from his horse, dead.

Then the Courtiers of the King, who had also set off in pursuit, but whose steeds were less fleet of foot than Go-Swift, came up, and seized the bridle of the Queen's horse, and led it and its rider back to the Palace.

She was brought before the Council, and judged, and condemned to be shut up in a high tower for the remainder of her life. Which thing surely came to pass.

As for Assipattle, when the proper time came he was married to the Princess Gemdelovely, with great feasting and rejoicing. And when the old King died they ruled the Kingdom for many a long year.

The Fox and the Wolf

There was once a Fox and a Wolf, who set up house together in a cave near the sea-shore. Although you may not think so, they got on very well for a time, for they went out hunting all day, and when they came back at night they were generally too tired to do anything but to eat their supper and go to bed.

They might have lived together always had it not been for the slyness and greediness of the Fox, who tried to over-reach his companion, who was not nearly so clever as he was.

And this was how it came about.

It chanced, one dark December night, that there was a dreadful storm at sea, and in the morning the beach was all strewn with wreckage. So as soon as it was daylight the two friends went down to the shore to see if they could find anything to eat.

They had the good fortune to light on a great Keg of Butter, which had been washed overboard from some ship on its way home from Ireland, where, as all the world knows, folk are famous for their butter.

The simple Wolf danced with joy when he saw it. "Marrowbones and trotters! But we will have a good supper this night," cried he, licking his lips. "Let us set to work at once and roll it up to the cave."

But the wily Fox was fond of butter, and he made up his

mind that he would have it all to himself. So he put on his wisest look, and shook his head gravely.

"Thou hast no prudence, my friend," he said reproachfully, "else wouldst thou not talk of breaking up a Keg of Butter at this time of year, when the stackyards are full of good grain, which can be had for the eating, and the farmyards are stocked with nice fat ducks and poultry No, no. It behoveth us to have foresight, and to lay it up in store for the spring, when the grain is all threshed, and the stackyards are bare, and the poultry have gone to market. So we will e'en bury the Keg, and dig it up when we have need of it."

Very reluctantly, for he was thinner and hungrier than the Fox, the Wolf agreed to this proposal. So a hole was dug, and the Keg was buried, and the two animals went off hunting as usual.

About a week passed by. Then one day the Fox came into the cave, and flung himself down on the ground as if he were very much exhausted. But if anyone had looked at him closely they would have seen a sly twinkle in his eye.

"Oh, dear, oh, dear!" he sighed. "Life is a heavy burden."

"What hath befallen thee?" asked the Wolf, who was ever kind and soft-hearted.

"Some friends of mine, who live over the hills yonder, are wanting me to go to a christening tonight. Just think of the distance that I must travel."

"But needst thou go?" asked the Wolf. "Canst thou not send an excuse?"

"I doubt that no excuse would be accepted," answered the Fox, "for they asked me to stand godfather. Therefore it behoveth me to do my duty, and pay no heed to my own feelings."

So that evening the Fox was absent, and the Wolf was alone in the cave. But it was not to a christening that the sly Fox went; it was to the Keg of Butter that was buried in the sand. About midnight he returned, looking fat and sleek, and well pleased with himself.

The Wolf had been dozing, but he looked up drowsily as his companion entered. "Well, how did they name the bairn?" he asked.

"They gave it a queer name," answered the Fox. "One of the queerest names that I ever heard."

"And what was that?" questioned the Wolf.

"Nothing less than 'Blaisean' (Let-me-taste)," replied the Fox, throwing himself down in his corner. And if the Wolf could have seen him in the darkness he would have noticed that he was laughing to himself.

Some days afterwards the same thing happened. The Fox was asked to another christening; this time at a place some twenty-five miles along the shore. And as he had grumbled before, so he grumbled again; but he declared that it was his duty to go, and he went.

At midnight he came back, smiling to himself and with no appetite for his supper. And when the Wolf asked him the name of the child, he answered that it was a more extraordinary name than the other—"Be na Inheadnon" (Be-in-its-middle).

The very next week, much to the Wolf's wonder, the Fox was asked to yet another christening. And this time the name of the child was "Sgriot an Clar" (Scrape-the-staves). After that the invitations ceased.

Time went on, and the hungry spring came, and the Fox and the Wolf had their larder bare, for food was scarce, and the weather was bleak and cold.

"Let us go and dig up the Keg of Butter," said the Wolf. "Methinks that now is the time we need it."

The Fox agreed—having made up his mind how he would act—and the two set out to the place where the Keg had been hidden. They scraped away the sand, and uncovered it; but, needless to say, they found it empty.

"This is thy work," said the Fox angrily, turning to the poor, innocent Wolf. "Thou hast crept along here while I was at the christenings, and eaten it up by stealth."

"Not I," replied the Wolf. "I have never been near the spot since the day that we buried it together."

"But I tell thee it must have been thou," insisted the Fox, "for no other creature knew it was there except ourselves. And, besides, I can see by the sleekness of thy fur that thou hast fared well of late."

Which last sentence was both unjust and untrue, for the poor Wolf looked as lean and badly nourished as he could possibly be.

So back they both went to the cave, arguing all the way. The Fox declaring that the Wolf must have been the thief, and the Wolf protesting his innocence.

"Art thou ready to swear to it?" said the Fox at last; though why he asked such a question, dear only knows.

"Yes, I am," replied the Wolf firmly; and, standing in the middle of the cave, and holding one paw up solemnly, he swore this awful oath:

"If it be that I stole the butter; if it be, if it be—
May a fateful, fell disease fall on me, fall on me."

When he was finished, he put down his paw and, turning to
the Fox, looked at him keenly; for all at once it struck him that
his fur looked sleek and fine.

"It is thy turn now," he said. "I have sworn, and thou must
do so also."

The Fox's face fell at these words, for although he was both
untruthful and dishonest now, he had been well brought up in
his youth, and he knew that it was a terrible thing to perjure
oneself and swear falsely.

So he made one excuse after another, but the Wolf, who was
getting more and more suspicious every moment, would not
listen to him.

So, as he had not courage to tell the truth, he was forced at
last to swear an oath also, and this was what he swore:

"If it be that I stole the butter; if it be, if it be—
Then let some most deadly punishment fall on me, fall on me—
Whirrum wheeckam, whirrum wheeckam,
Whirram whee, whirram whee!"

After he had heard him swear this terrible oath, the Wolf
thought that his suspicions must be groundless, and he
would have let the matter rest; but the Fox, having an uneasy
conscience, could not do so. So he suggested that as it was
clear that one of them must have eaten the Keg of Butter, they
should both stand near the fire; so that when they became hot,
the butter would ooze out of the skin of whichever of them
was guilty. And he took care that the Wolf should stand in the
hottest place.

But the fire was big and the cave was small; and while the
poor lean Wolf showed no sign of discomfort, he himself, being
nice and fat and comfortable, soon began to get unpleasantly
warm.

As this did not suit him at all, he next proposed that they

should go for a walk. "For," said he, "it is now quite plain that neither of us can have taken the butter. It must have been some stranger who hath found out our secret."

But the Wolf had seen the Fox beginning to grow greasy, and he knew now what had happened, and he determined to have his revenge. So he waited until they came to a smithy which stood at the side of the road, where a horse was waiting just outside the door to be shod.

Then, keeping at a safe distance, he said to his companion, "There is writing on that smithy door, which I cannot read, as my eyes are failing; do thou try to read it, for perchance it may be something 'twere good for us to know."

And the silly Fox, who was very vain, and did not like to confess that his eyes were no better than those of his friend, went close up to the door to try and read the writing. And he chanced to touch the horse's fetlock, and, it being a restive beast, lifted its foot and struck out at once, and killed the Fox as dead as a doornail.

And so, you see, the old saying in the Good Book came true after all: "Be sure your sin will find you out."

Katherine Crackernuts

There was once a King whose wife died, leaving him with an only daughter, whom he dearly loved. The little Princess's name was Velvet-Cheek, and she was so good and bonnie and kind-hearted that all her father's subjects loved her. But as the King was generally engaged in transacting the business of the State, the poor little maiden had rather a lonely life, and often wished that she had a sister with whom she could play, and who would be a companion to her.

The King, hearing this, made up his mind to marry a middle-aged Countess, whom he had met at a neighbouring Court, who had one daughter, named Katherine, who was just a little younger than the Princess Velvet-Cheek, and who, he thought, would make a nice playfellow for her.

He did so, and in one way the arrangement turned out very well, for the two girls loved one another dearly, and had everything in common, just as if they had really been sisters.

But in another way it turned out very badly, for the new Queen was a cruel and ambitious woman, and she wanted her own daughter to do as she had done, and make a grand marriage, and perhaps even become a Queen. And when she saw that Princess Velvet-Cheek was growing into a very beautiful young woman—more beautiful by far than her own daughter—she began to hate her, and to wish that in some way she would lose her good looks.

"For," thought she, "what suitor will heed my daughter as long as her step-sister is by her side?"

Now, among the servants and retainers at her husband's Castle there was an old Hen-wife, who, men said, was in league with the Evil Spirits of the air, and who was skilled in the knowledge of charms, and philtres, and love potions.

"Perhaps she could help me to do what I seek to do," said the wicked Queen; and one night, when it was growing dusk, she wrapped a cloak round her, and set out to this old Hen-wife's cottage.

"Send the lassie to me tomorrow morning ere she hath broken her fast," replied the old Dame when she heard what her visitor had to say. "I will find out a way to mar her beauty." And the wicked Queen went home content.

Next morning she went to the Princess's room while she was dressing, and told her to go out before breakfast and get the eggs that the Hen-wife had gathered. "And see," added she, "that thou dost not eat anything ere thou goest, for there is nothing that maketh the roses bloom on a young maiden's cheeks like going out fasting in the fresh morning air."

Princess Velvet-Cheek promised to do as she was bid, and go and fetch the eggs; but as she was not fond of going out of doors before she had had something to eat, and as, moreover, she suspected that her step-mother had some hidden reason for giving her such an unusual order, and she did not trust her step-mother's hidden reasons, she slipped into the pantry as she went downstairs and helped herself to a large slice of cake. Then, after she had eaten it, she went straight to the Hen-wife's cottage and asked for the eggs.

"Lift the lid of that pot there, your Highness, and you will see them," said the old woman, pointing to the big pot standing in the corner in which she boiled her hens' meat.

The Princess did so, and found a heap of eggs lying inside,

which she lifted into her basket, while the old woman watched her with a curious smile.

"Go home to your Lady Mother, Hinny," she said at last, "and tell her from me to keep the press door better snibbit."

The Princess went home, and gave this extraordinary message to her step-mother, wondering to herself the while what it meant.

But if she did not understand the Hen-wife's words, the Queen understood them only too well. For from them she gathered that the Princess had in some way prevented the old Witch's spell doing what she intended it to do.

So next morning, when she sent her step-daughter once more on the same errand, she accompanied her to the door of the Castle herself, so that the poor girl had no chance of paying a visit to the pantry. But as she went along the road that led to the cottage, she felt so hungry that, when she passed a party of country-folk picking peas by the roadside, she asked them to give her a handful.

They did so, and she ate the peas; and so it came about that the same thing happened that had happened yesterday.

The Hen-wife sent her to look for the eggs; but she could work no spell upon her, because she had broken her fast. So the old woman bade her go home again and give the same message to the Queen.

The Queen was very angry when she heard it, for she felt that she was being outwitted by this slip of a girl, and she determined that, although she was not fond of getting up early, she would accompany her next day herself, and make sure that she had nothing to eat as she went.

So next morning she walked with the Princess to the Hen-wife's cottage, and, as had happened twice before, the old woman sent the Royal maiden to lift the lid off the pot in the corner in order to get the eggs.

And the moment that the Princess did so, off jumped her own pretty head, and on jumped that of a sheep.

Off jumped her own pretty head
and on jumped that of a sheep

Then the wicked Queen thanked the cruel old Witch for the service that she had rendered to her, and went home quite delighted with the success of her scheme; while the poor Princess picked up her own head and put it into her basket along with the eggs, and went home crying, keeping behind the hedge all the way, for she felt so ashamed of her sheep's head that she was afraid that anyone saw her.

Now, as I told you, the Princess's step-sister Katherine loved her dearly, and when she saw what a cruel deed had been wrought on her she was so angry that she declared that she would not remain another hour in the Castle. "For," said she, "if my Lady Mother can order one such deed to be done, who can hinder her ordering another. So, methinks, 'twere better for us both to be where she cannot reach us."

So she wrapped a fine shawl round her poor step-sister's head, so that none could tell what it was like, and, putting the real head in the basket, she took her by the hand, and the two set out to seek their fortunes.

They walked and they walked, till they reached a splendid Palace, and when they came to it Katherine made as though she would go boldly up and knock at the door.

"I may perchance find work here," she explained, "and earn enough money to keep us both in comfort."

But the poor Princess would fain have pulled her back. "They will have nothing to do with thee," she whispered, "when they see that thou hast a sister with a sheep's head."

"And who is to know that thou hast a sheep's head?" asked Katherine. "If thou hold thy tongue, and keep the shawl well round thy face, and leave the rest to me."

So up she went and knocked at the kitchen door, and when the housekeeper came to answer it she asked her if there was any work that she could give her to do. "For," said she, "I have a sick sister, who is sore troubled with the migraine in her head, and I would fain find a quiet lodging for her where she could rest for the night."

"Dost thou know aught of sickness?" asked the housekeeper, who was greatly struck by Katherine's soft voice and gentle ways.

"Ay, do I," replied Katherine, "for when one's sister is

troubled with the migraine, one has to learn to go about softly and not to make a noise."

Now it chanced that the King's eldest son, the Crown Prince, was lying ill in the Palace of a strange disease, which seemed to have touched his brain. For he was so restless, especially at nights, that someone had always to be with him to watch that he did himself no harm; and this state of things had gone on so long that everyone was quite worn out.

And the old housekeeper thought that it would be a good chance to get a quiet night's sleep if this capable-looking stranger could be trusted to sit up with the Prince.

So she left her at the door, and went and consulted the King, and the King came out and spoke to Katherine and he, too, was so pleased with her voice and her appearance that he gave orders that a room should be set apart in the Palace for her sick sister and herself, and he promised that, if she would sit up that night with the Prince, and see that no harm befell him, she would have, as her reward, a bag of silver Pennies in the morning.

Katherine agreed to the bargain readily. "For," thought she, "'twill always be a night's lodging for the Princess; and, forbye that, a bag of silver Pennies is not to be got every day."

So the Princess went to bed in the comfortable chamber that was set apart for her, and Katherine went to watch by the sick Prince.

He was a handsome, comely young man, who seemed to be in some sort of fever, for his brain was not quite clear, and he tossed and tumbled from side to side, gazing anxiously in front of him, and stretching out his hands as if he were in search of something.

And at twelve o'clock at night, just when Katherine thought that he was going to fall into a refreshing sleep, what was her horror to see him rise from his bed, dress himself hastily, open the door, and slip downstairs, as if he were going to look for somebody.

"There be something strange in this," said the girl to herself. "Methinks I had better follow him and see what happens."

So she stole out of the room after the Prince and followed him safely downstairs; and what was her astonishment to find that apparently he was going some distance, for he put on his hat and riding-coat, and, unlocking the door crossed the courtyard to the stable, and began to saddle his horse.

When he had done so, he led it out, and mounted, and, whistling softly to a hound which lay asleep in a corner, he prepared to ride away.

"I must go too, and see the end of this," said Katherine bravely, "for methinks he is bewitched. These be not the actions of a sick man."

So, just as the horse was about to start, she jumped lightly on its back, and settled herself comfortably behind its rider, all unnoticed by him.

Then this strange pair rode away through the woods, and, as they went, Katherine pulled the hazelnuts that nodded in great clusters in her face. "For," said she to herself, "dear only knows where next I may get anything to eat."

On and on they rode, till they left the greenwood far behind them and came out on an open moor. Soon they reached a hillock, and here the Prince drew rein, and, stooping down, cried in a strange, uncanny whisper, "Open, open, Green Hill, and let the Prince, and his horse, and his hound enter."

"And," whispered Katherine quickly, "let his lady enter behind him."

Instantly, to her great astonishment, the top of the knowe seemed to tip up, leaving an aperture large enough for the little company to enter; then it closed gently behind them again.

They found themselves in a magnificent Hall, brilliantly lighted by hundreds of candles stuck in sconces round the walls. In the centre of this apartment was a group of the most beautiful maidens that Katherine had ever seen, all dressed in shimmering ball-gowns, with wreaths of roses and violets in their hair. And there were sprightly gallants also, who had been treading a measure with these beauteous damsels to the strains of Fairy music.

When the maidens saw the Prince, they ran to him, and led him away to join their revels. And at the touch of their hands all his languor seemed to disappear, and he became the gayest of all the throng, and laughed, and danced, and sang as if he had never known what it was to be ill.

As no one took any notice of Katherine, she sat down quietly on a bit of rock to watch what would befall. And as she watched, she became aware of a wee, wee bairnie, playing with a tiny wand, quite close to her feet.

He was a bonnie bit bairn, and she was just thinking of trying to make friends with him when one of the beautiful maidens passed, and, looking at the wand, said to her partner, in a meaning tone, "Three strokes of that wand would give Katherine's sister back her pretty face."

Here was news indeed! Katherine's breath came thick and fast; and with trembling fingers she drew some of the nuts out of her pocket, and began rolling them carelessly towards the child. Apparently he did not get nuts very often, for he dropped his little wand at once, and stretched out his tiny hands to pick them up.

This was just what she wanted; and she slipped down from her seat to the ground, and drew a little nearer to him. Then she threw one or two more nuts in his way, and, when he was picking these up, she managed to lift the wand unobserved, and to hide it under her apron. After this, she crept cautiously back to her seat again; and not a moment too soon, for just then a cock crew, and at the sound the whole of the dancers vanished—all but the Prince, who ran to mount his horse, and was in such a hurry to be gone that Katherine had much ado to get up behind him before the hillock opened, and he rode swiftly into the outer world once more.

But she managed it, and, as they rode homewards in the grey morning light, she sat and cracked her nuts and ate them as fast as she could, for her adventures had made her marvellously hungry.

When she and her strange patient had once more reached the Palace, she just waited to see him go back to bed, and begin to toss and tumble as he had done before; then she ran to her step-sister's room, and, finding her asleep, with her poor misshapen head lying peacefully on the pillow, she gave it three sharp little strokes with the Fairy wand and, lo and behold! the sheep's head vanished, and the Princess's own pretty one took its place.

In the morning the King and the old housekeeper came to inquire what kind of night the Prince had had. Katherine answered that he had had a very good night; for she was very anxious to stay with him longer, for now that she had found out that the Elfin Maidens who dwelt in the Green Knowe had thrown a spell over him, she was resolved to find out also how that spell could be loosed.

And Fortune favoured her; for the King was so pleased to think that such a suitable nurse had been found for the Prince, and he was also so charmed with the looks of her step-sister, who came out of her chamber as bright and bonnie as in the old days, declaring that her migraine was all gone, and that she was now able to do any work that the housekeeper might find for her, that he begged Katherine to stay with his son a little longer, adding that if she would do so, he would give her a bag of gold Bonnet-pieces.

So Katherine agreed readily; and that night she watched by the Prince as she had done the night before. And at twelve o'clock he rose and dressed himself, and rode to the Fairy Knowe, just as she had expected him to do, for she was quite certain that the poor young man was bewitched, and not suffering from a fever, as everyone thought he was.

And you may be sure that she accompanied him, riding

behind him all unnoticed, and filling her pockets with nuts as she rode.

When they reached the Fairy Knowe, he spoke the same words that he had spoken the night before. "Open, open, Green Hill, and let the Prince, and his horse, and his hound enter." And when the Green Hill opened, Katherine added softly, "And his lady behind him." So they all passed in together.

Katherine seated herself on a stone, and looked around her. The same revels were going on as yesternight, and the Prince was soon in the thick of them, dancing and laughing madly. The girl watched him narrowly, wondering if she would ever be able to find out what would restore him to his right mind; and, as she was watching him, the same little bairn who had played with the magic wand came up to her again. Only this time he was playing with a little bird.

And as he played, one of the dancers passed by, and, turning to her partner, said lightly, "Three bites of that birdie would lift the Prince's sickness, and make him as well as he ever was." Then she joined in the dance again, leaving Katherine sitting upright on her stone quivering with excitement.

If only she could get that bird the Prince might be cured! Very carefully she began to shake some nuts out of her pocket, and roll them across the floor towards the child.

He picked them up eagerly, letting go the bird as he did so; and, in an instant, Katherine caught it, and hid it under her apron.

In no long time after that the cock crew, and the Prince and she set out on their homeward ride. But this morning, instead of cracking nuts, she killed and plucked the bird, scattering its feathers all along the road; and the instant she gained the Prince's room, and had seen him safely into bed, she put it on a spit in front of the fire and began to roast it.

And soon it began to frizzle, and get brown, and smell deliciously, and the Prince, in his bed in the corner, opened his eyes and murmured faintly, "How I wish I had a bite of that birdie."

When she heard the words Katherine's heart jumped for joy, and as soon as the bird was roasted she cut a little piece from its breast and popped it into the Prince's mouth.

When he had eaten it his strength seemed to come back somewhat, for he rose on his elbow and looked at his nurse. "Oh, if I had but another bite of that birdie!" he said. And his voice was certainly stronger.

So Katherine gave him another piece, and when he had eaten that he sat right up in bed.

"Oh, if I had but a third bite o' that birdie!" he cried. And now the colour was coming back into his face, and his eyes were shining.

This time Katherine brought him the whole of the rest of the bird; and he ate it up greedily, picking the bones quite clean with his fingers; and when it was finished, he sprang out of bed and dressed himself, and sat down by the fire.

And when the King came in the morning, with his old housekeeper at his back, to see how the Prince was, he found him sitting cracking nuts with his nurse, for Katherine had brought home quite a lot in her apron pocket.

The King was so delighted to find his son cured that he gave all the credit to Katherine Crackernuts, as he called her, and he gave orders at once that the Prince should marry her. "For," said he, "a maiden who is such a good nurse is sure to make a good Queen."

The Prince was quite willing to do as his father bade him; and, while they were talking together, his younger brother came in, leading Princess Velvet-Cheek by the hand, whose acquaintance he had made but yesterday, declaring that he had fallen in love with her, and that he wanted to marry her immediately.

So it all fell out very well, and everybody was quite pleased; and the two weddings took place at once, and, unless they be dead since then, the young couples are living yet.

The Well O'
The World's End

There was once an old widow woman, who lived in a little cottage with her only daughter, who was such a bonnie lassie that everyone liked to look at her.

One day the old woman took a notion into her head to bake a girdleful of cakes. So she took down her bakeboard, and went to the girnel and fetched a basinful of meal; but when she went to seek a jug of water to mix the meal with, she found that there was none in the house.

So she called to her daughter, who was in the garden; and when the girl came she held out the empty jug to her, saying, "Run, like a good lassie, to the Well o' the World's End and bring me a jug of water, for I have long found that water from the Well o' the World's End makes the best cakes."

So the lassie took the jug and set out on her errand.

Now, as its name shows, it is a long road to that well, and many a weary mile had the poor maid to go ere she reached it.

But she arrived there at last; and what was her disappointment to find it dry.

She was so tired and so vexed that she sat down beside it and began to cry; for she did not know where to get any more water, and she felt that she could not go back to her mother with an empty jug.

While she was crying, a nice yellow Paddock, with very bright eyes, came jump-jump-jumping over the stones of the well, and squatted down at her feet, looking up into her face.

"And why are ye greeting, my bonnie maid?" he asked. "Is there aught that I can do to help thee?"

"I am greeting because the well is empty," she answered, "and I cannot get any water to carry home to my mother."

"Listen," said the Paddock softly. "I can get thee water in plenty, if so be thou wilt promise to be my wife."

Now the lassie had but one thought in her head, and that was to get the water for her mother's oatcakes, and she never for a moment thought that the Paddock was in earnest, so she promised gladly enough to be his wife, if he would get her a jug of water.

No sooner had the words passed her lips than the beastie jumped down the mouth of the well, and in another moment it was full to the brim with water.

The lassie filled her jug and carried it home, without troubling any more about the matter. But late that night, just as her mother and she were going to bed, something came with a faint "Thud, thud," against the cottage door, and then they heard a tiny little wee voice singing:

> "Oh, open the door, my hinnie, my heart,
>   Oh, open the door, my ain true love;
> Remember the promise that you and I made
>   Down i' the meadow, where we two met."

"Wheesht," said the old woman, raising her head. "What noise is that at the door?"

"Oh," said her daughter, who was feeling rather frightened, "it's only a yellow Paddock."

"Poor bit beastie," said the kind-hearted old mother. "Open the door and let him in. It's cold work sitting on the doorstep."

So the lassie, very unwillingly, opened the door, and the Paddock came jump-jump-jumping across the kitchen, and sat down at the fireside.

And while he sat there he began to sing this song:

> "Oh, gie me my supper, my hinnie, my heart,
> Oh, gie me my supper, my ain true love;
> Remember the promise that you and I made
> Down i' the meadow, where we two met."

"Gie the poor beast his supper," said the old woman. "He's an uncommon Paddock that can sing like that."

"Tut," replied her daughter crossly, for she was growing more and more frightened as she saw the creature's bright black eyes fixed on her face. "I'm not going to be so silly as to feed a wet, sticky Paddock."

"Don't be ill-natured and cruel," said her mother. "Who knows how far the little beastie has travelled? And I warrant that it would like a saucerful of milk."

Now, the lassie could have told her that the Paddock had travelled from the Well o' the World's End; but she held her tongue, and went ben to the milk-house, and brought back a saucerful of milk, which she set down before the strange little visitor.

> "Now chap off my head, my hinnie, my heart
> Now chap off my head, my ain true love,
> Remember the promise that you and I made
> Down i' the meadow, where we two met."

"Hout, havers, pay no heed, the creature's daft," exclaimed the old woman, running forward to stop her daughter, who was raising the axe to chop off the Paddock's head. But she was too late; down came the axe, off went the head; and lo, and behold! On the spot where the little creature had sat, stood the handsomest young Prince that had ever been seen.

He wore such a noble air, and was so richly dressed, that the astonished girl and her mother would have fallen on their knees before him had he not prevented them by a movement of his hand.

"'Tis I that should kneel to thee, sweetheart," he said, turning to the blushing girl, "for thou hast delivered me from a fearful spell, which was cast over me in my infancy by a wicked Fairy, who at the same time slew my father. For long years I have lived in that well, the Well o' the World's End, waiting for a maiden to appear, who should take pity on me, even in my loathsome disguise, and promise to be my wife, and who would also have the kindness to let me into her house, and the courage, at my bidding, to cut off my head.

"Now I can return and claim my father's Kingdom, and thou, most gracious maiden, will go with me, and be my bride, for thou well deserv'st the honour."

And this was how the lassie who went to fetch water from the Well o' the World's End became a Princess.

Farquhar MacNeill

O nce upon a time there was a young man named Farquhar
MacNeill. He had just gone to a new situation, and the
very first night after he went to it his mistress asked him if he
would go over the hill to the house of a neighbour and borrow
a sieve, for her own was all in holes, and she wanted to sift
some meal.

Farquhar agreed to do so, for he was a willing lad, and he set out
at once upon his errand, after the farmer's wife had pointed out
to him the path that he was to follow, and told him that he would
have no difficulty in finding the house, even though it was strange
to him, for he would be sure to see the light in the window.

He had not gone very far, however, before he saw what he
took to be the light from a cottage window on his left hand,
some distance from the path, and, forgetting his Mistress's
instructions that he was to follow the path right over the hill,
he left it, and walked towards the light.

It seemed to him that he had almost reached it when his foot
tripped, and he fell down, down, down, into a Fairy Parlour,
far under the ground.

It was full of Fairies, who were engaged in different
occupations.

Close by the door, or rather the hole down which he had
so unceremoniously tumbled, two little elderly women,
in black aprons and white mutches, were busily engaged in

grinding corn between two flat millstones. Other two Fairies, younger women, in blue print gowns and white kerchiefs, were gathering up the freshly ground meal, and baking it into bannocks, which they were toasting on a girdle over a peat fire, which was burning slowly in a corner.

In the centre of the large apartment a great troop of Fairies, Elves, and Sprites were dancing reels as hard as they could to the music of a tiny set of bagpipes which were being played by a brown-faced Gnome, who sat on a ledge of rock far above their heads.

They all stopped their various employments when Farquhar came suddenly down in their midst, and looked at him in alarm; but when they saw that he was not hurt, they bowed gravely and bade him be seated. Then they went on with their work and with their play as if nothing had happened.

But Farquhar, being very fond of dancing, and being in no wise anxious to be seated, thought that he would like to have a reel first, so he asked the Fairies if he might join them. And they, although they looked surprised at his request, allowed him to do so, and in a few minutes the young man was dancing away as gaily as any of them.

And as he danced a strange change came over him. He forgot his errand, he forgot his home, he forgot everything that had ever happened to him, he only knew that he wanted to remain with the Fairies all the rest of his life.

And he did remain with them—for a magic spell had been cast over him, and he became like one of themselves, and could come and go at nights without being seen, and could sip the dew from the grass and honey from the flowers as daintily and noiselessly as if he had been a Fairy born.

Time passed by, and one night he and a band of merry companions set out for a long journey through the air. They started early, for they intended to pay a visit to the Man in the Moon and be back again before cockcrow.

They Bowed Gravely

All would have gone well if Farquhar had only looked where he was going, but he did not, being deeply engaged in making love to a young Fairy Maiden by his side, so he never saw a cottage that was standing right in his way, till he struck against the chimney and stuck fast in the thatch.

His companions sped merrily on, not noticing what had befallen him, and he was left to disentangle himself as best he could.

As he was doing so he chanced to glance down the wide chimney, and in the cottage kitchen he saw a comely young woman dandling a rosy-cheeked baby.

Now, when Farquhar had been in his mortal state he had been very fond of children, and a word of blessing rose to his lips.

"God shield thee," he said, as he looked at the mother and child, little guessing what the result of his words would be.

For scarce had the Holy Name crossed his lips than the spell which had held him so long was broken, and he became as he had been before.

Instantly his thoughts flew to his friends at home, and to the new Mistress whom he had left waiting for her sieve; for he felt sure that some weeks must have elapsed since he set out to fetch it. So he made haste to go to the farm.

When he arrived in the neighbourhood everything seemed strange. There were woods where no woods used to be, and walls where no walls used to be. To his amazement, he could not find his way to the farm, and, worst of all, in the place where he expected to find his father's house he found nothing but a crop of rank green nettles.

In great distress he looked about for someone to tell him what it all meant, and at last he found an old man thatching the roof of a cottage.

This old man was so thin and grey that at first Farquhar took him for a patch of mist, but as he went nearer he saw that he was a human being, and, going close up to the wall and shouting with all his might, for he felt sure that such an ancient man would he deaf, he asked him if he could tell him where his friends had gone to, and what had happened to his father's dwelling.

The old man listened, then he shook his head. "I never heard of him," he answered slowly, "but perhaps my father might be able to tell you."

"Your father!" said Farquhar, in great surprise. "Is it possible that your father is alive?"

"Aye he is," answered the old man, with a little laugh. "If you go into the house you'll find him sitting in the armchair by the fire."

Farquhar did as he was bid and on entering the cottage found another old man, who was so thin and withered and bent that he looked as if he must at least be a hundred years old. He was feebly twisting ropes to bind the thatch on the roof.

"Can ye tell me aught of my friend, or where my father's cottage is?" asked Farquhar again, hardly expecting that this second old man would be able to answer him.

"I cannot," mumbled this ancient person, "but perhaps my father can tell you."

"Your father!" exclaimed Farquhar, more astonished than ever. "But surely he must be dead long ago.'

The old man shook his head with a weird grimace.

'Look there," he said, and pointed with a twisted finger, to a leathern purse, or sporran, which was hanging to one of the posts of a wooden bedstead in the corner.

Farquhar approached it, and was almost frightened out of his wits by seeing a tiny shrivelled face crowned by a red nightcap, looking over the edge of the sporran.

"Tak' him out; he'll no touch ye," chuckled the old man by the fire.

So Farquhar took the little creature out carefully between his finger and thumb, and set him on the palm of his left hand. He was so shrivelled with age that he looked just like a mummy.

"Dost know anything of my friends, or where my father's cottage is gone to?" asked Farquhar for the third time, hardly expecting to get an answer.

"They were all dead long before I was born," piped out the tiny figure. "I never saw any of them, but I have heard my father speak of them."

"Then I must be older than you!" cried Farquhar, in great dismay. And he got such a shock at the thought that his bones suddenly dissolved into dust, and he fell, a heap of grey ashes, on the floor.

Peerifool

There was once a King and a Queen in Rousay who had three daughters. When the young Princesses were just grown up, the King died, and the Crown passed to a distant cousin, who had always hated him, and who paid no heed to the widowed Queen and her daughters.

So they were left very badly off, and they went to live in a tiny cottage, and did all the housework themselves. They had a kailyard in front of the cottage, and a little field behind it, and they had a cow that grazed in the field, and which they fed with the cabbages that grew in the kailyard. For everyone knows that to feed cows with cabbages makes them give a larger quantity of milk.

But they soon discovered that some one was coming at night and stealing the cabbages, and, of course, this annoyed them very much. For they knew that if they had not cabbages to give to the cow, they would not have enough milk to sell.

So the eldest Princess said she would take out a three-legged stool, and wrap herself in a blanket, and sit in the kailyard all night to see if she could catch the thief. And, although it was very cold and very dark, she did so.

At first it seemed as if all her trouble would be in vain, for hour after hour passed and nothing happened. But in the small hours of the morning, just as the clock was striking two, she heard a stealthy trampling in the field behind, as if some very heavy person were trying to tread very softly, and presently a mighty Giant stepped right over the wall into the kailyard.

He carried an enormous creel on his arm, and a large, sharp knife in his hand; and he began to cut the cabbages, and to throw them into the creel as fast as he could.

Now the Princess was no coward, so, although she had not expected to face a Giant, she gathered up her courage, and cried out sharply, "Who gave thee liberty to cut our cabbages? Leave off this minute, and go away."

The Giant paid no heed, but went on steadily with what he was doing.

"Dost thou not hear me?" cried the girl indignantly; for she was the Princess Royal, and had always been accustomed to be obeyed.

"If thou be not quiet, I will take thee too," said the Giant grimly, pressing the cabbages down into the creel .

"I should like to see thee try," retorted the Princess, rising from her stool and stamping her foot for she felt so angry that she forgot for a moment that she was only a weak maiden and he was a great and powerful Giant.

And, as if to show her how strong he was, he seized her by her arm and her leg, and put her in his creel on the top of the cabbages, and carried her away bodily.

When he reached his home, which was in a great square house on a lonely moor, he took her out, and set her down roughly on the floor.

"Thou wilt be my servant now," he said, "and keep my house, and do my errands for me. I have a cow, which thou must drive out every day to the hillside; and see, here is a bag of wool, when thou hast taken out the cow, thou must come back and settle thyself at home, as a good housewife should, and comb, and card it, and spin it into yarn, with which to weave a good thick cloth for my raiment. I am out most of the day, but when

I come home I shall expect to find all this done, and a great bicker of porridge boiled besides for my supper."

The poor Princess was very dismayed when she heard these words, for she had never been accustomed to work hard, and she had always had her sisters to help her; but the Giant took no notice of her distress, but went out as soon as it was daylight, leaving her alone in the house to begin her work.

As soon as he had gone she drove the cow to the pasture, as he had told her to do; but she had a good long walk over the moor before she reached the hill, and by the time that she got back to the house she felt very tired.

So she thought that she would put on the porridge pot, and make herself some porridge before she began to card and comb the wool. She did so, and just as she was sitting down to sup them the door opened, and a crowd of wee, wee Peerie Folk came in.

They were the tiniest men and women that the Princess had ever seen; not one of them would have reached halfway to her knee; and they were dressed in dresses fashioned out of all the colours of the rainbow—scarlet and blue, green and yellow, orange and violet; and the funny thing was, that every one of them had a shock of straw-coloured yellow hair.

They were all talking and laughing with one another; and they hopped up, first on stools, then on chairs, till at last they reached the top of the table, where they clustered round the bowl, out of which the Princess was eating her porridge.

"We be hungry, we be hungry," they cried, in their tiny shrill voices. "Spare a little porridge for the Peerie Folk."

But the Princess was hungry also; and, besides being hungry, she was both tired and cross; so she shook her head and waved them impatiently away with her spoon.

> "Little for one, and less for two,
> And never a grain have I for you."

she said sharply, and, to her great delight, for she did not feel quite comfortable with all the Peerie Folk standing on the table looking at her, they vanished in a moment.

After this she finished her porridge in peace, then she took the wool out of the bag, and she set to work to comb and card it. But it seemed as if it were bewitched; it curled and twisted and coiled itself round her fingers so that, try as she would, she could not do anything with it. And when the Giant came home he found her sitting in despair with it all in confusion round her, and the porridge, which she had left for him in the pot, burned to a cinder.

As you may imagine, he was very angry, and raged, and stamped, and used the most dreadful words; and at last he took her by the heels, and beat her until all her back was skinned and bleeding; then he carried her out to the byre, and threw her up on the joists among the hens. And, although she was not dead, she was so stunned and bruised that she could only lie there motionless, looking down on the backs of the cows.

Time went on, and in the kailyard at home the cabbages were disappearing as fast as ever. So the second Princess said that she would do as her sister had done, and wrap herself in a blanket, and go and sit on a three-legged stool all night, to see what was becoming of them.

She did so, and exactly the same fate befell her that had befallen her elder sister. The Giant appeared with his creel, and he carried her off, and set her to mind the cow and the house, and to make his porridge and to spin; and the little yellow-headed Peerie Folk appeared and asked her for some supper, and she refused to give it to them; and after that, she could not comb or card her wool, and the Giant was angry, and he scolded her, and beat her, and threw her up, half-dead, on the joists beside her sister and the hens.

Then the youngest Princess determined to sit out in the kailyard all night, not so much to see what was becoming of the cabbages, as to discover what had happened to her sisters.

And when the Giant came and carried her off, she was not at all sorry, but very glad, for she was a brave and loving little maiden; and now she felt that she had a chance of finding out where they were, and whether they were dead or alive.

So she was quite cheerful and happy, for she felt certain that she was clever enough to outwit the Giant, if only she were watchful and patient; so she lay quite quietly in her creel above the cabbages, but she kept her eyes very wide open to see by which road he was carrying her off.

And when he set her down in his kitchen, and told her all that he expected her to do, she did not look downcast like her sisters, but nodded her head brightly, and said that she felt sure that she could do it.

And she sang to herself as she drove the cow over the moor to pasture, and she ran the whole way back, so that she should have a good long afternoon to work at the wool, and, although she would not have told the Giant this, to search the house.

Before she set to work, however, she made herself some porridge, just as her sisters had done; and, just as she was going to sup her porridge, all the little yellow-haired Peerie Folk trooped in, and climbed up on the table, and stood and stared at her.

"We be hungry, we be hungry," they cried. "Spare a little porridge for the Peerie Folk."

"With all my heart," replied the good-natured Princess. "If you can find dishes little enough for you to sup out of, I will fill them for you. But, methinks, if I were to give you all porringers, you would smother yourselves among the porridge."

At her words the Peerie Folk shouted with laughter, till their straw-coloured hair tumbled right over their faces; then they hopped onto the floor and ran out of the house, and presently they came trooping back holding cups of bluebells, and foxgloves, and saucers of primroses and anemones in their hands; and the Princess put a tiny spoonful of porridge into each saucer, and a tiny drop of milk into each cup, and they ate it all up as daintily as possible with neat little grass spoons, which they had brought with them in their pockets.

When they had finished they all cried out, "Thank you! Thank you!" and ran out of the kitchen again, leaving the Princess alone. And, being alone, she went all over the house to look for her sisters, but, of course, she could not find them.

"Never mind, I will find them soon," she said to herself. "Tomorrow I will search the byre and the outhouses; in the meantime, I had better get on with my work." So she went back to the kitchen, and took out the bag of wool, which the Giant had told her to make into cloth.

But just as she was doing so the door opened once more, and a Yellow-Haired Peerie Boy entered. He was exactly like the other Peerie Folk who had eaten the Princess's porridge, only he was bigger, and he wore a very rich dress of grass-green velvet. He walked boldly into the middle of the kitchen and looked round him.

"Hast thou any work for me to do?" he asked. "I ken grand how to handle wool and turn it into fine thick cloth."

"I have plenty of work for anybody who asks it," replied the Princess. "But I have no money to pay for it, and there are but few folk in this world who will work without wages."

"All the wages that I ask is that thou wilt take the trouble to find out my name, for few folk ken it, and few folk care to ken. But if by any chance thou canst not find it out, then must thou pay toll of half of thy cloth." The Princess thought that it would be quite an easy thing to find out the Boy's name, so she agreed to the bargain, and, putting all the wool back into the bag, she gave it to him, and he swung it over his shoulder and departed.

She ran to the door to see where he went, for she had made up her mind that she would follow him secretly to his home, and find out from the neighbours what his name was.

But, to her great dismay, though she looked this way and that, he had vanished completely, and she began to wonder what she should do if the Giant came back and found that she had allowed someone, whose name she did not even know, to carry off all the wool.

And, as the afternoon wore on, and she could think of no way of finding out who the boy was, or where he came from, she felt that she had made a great mistake, and she began to grow very frightened.

Just as the gloaming was beginning to fall a knock came at the door, and, when she opened it, she found an old woman standing outside, who begged for a night's lodging.

Now, as I have told you, the Princess was very kind-hearted, and she would fain have granted the poor old Dame's request, but she dared not, for she did not know what the Giant would say. So she told the old woman that she could not take her in for the night, as she was only a servant, and not the mistress of the house; but she made her sit down on a bench beside the door, and brought her out some bread and milk, and gave her some water to bathe her poor, tired feet.

She was so bonnie, and gentle, and kind, and she looked so sorry when she told her that she would need to turn her away, that the old woman gave her her blessing, and told her not to vex herself, as it was a fine, dry night, and now that she had had a meal she could easily sit down somewhere and sleep in the shelter of the outhouses.

And, when she had finished her bread and milk, she went and laid down by the side of a green knowe, which rose out of the moor not very far from the byre door.

And, strange to say, as she lay there she felt the earth beneath her getting warmer and warmer, until she was so hot that she was fain to crawl up the side of the hillock, in the hope of getting a mouthful of fresh air.

And as she got near the top she heard a voice, which seemed to come from somewhere beneath her, saying, "TEASE, TEASENS, TEASE; CARD, CARDENS, CARD; SPIN, SPINNENS, SPIN; for PEERIFOOL, PEERIFOOL, PEERIFOOL is what men call me." And when she got to the very top, she found that there was a crack in the earth, through which rays of light were coming; and when she put her eye to the crack, what should she see down below her but a brilliantly lighted chamber, in which all the Peerie Folk were sitting in a circle, working away as hard as they could.

Some of them were carding wool, some of them were combing it, some of them were spinning it, constantly wetting their fingers with their lips, in order to twist the yarn fine as they drew it from the distaff, and some of them were spinning the yarn into cloth.

While round and round the circle, cracking a little whip, and urging them to work faster, was a Yellow-Haired Peerie Boy.

"This is a strange thing, and these be queer ongoings," said the old woman to herself, creeping hastily down to the bottom of the hillock again. "I must e'en go and tell the bonnie lassie in the house yonder. Maybe the knowledge of what I have seen will stand her in good stead some day. When there be Peerie Folk about, it is well to be on one's guard."

So she went back to the house and told the Princess all that she had seen and heard, and the Princess was so delighted with what she had told her that she risked the Giant's wrath and allowed her to go and sleep in the hayloft.

It was not very long after the old woman had gone to rest before the door opened, and the Peerie Boy appeared once more with a number of webs of cloth upon his shoulder. "Here is thy cloth," he said, with a sly smile, "and I will put it on the shelf for thee the moment that thou tellest me what my name is."

Then the Princess, who was a merry maiden, thought that she would tease the little fellow for a time ere she let him know that she had found out his secret.

So she mentioned first one name and then another, always pretending to think that she had hit upon the right one; and all the time the Peerie Boy jumped from side to side with delight, for he thought that she would never find out the right name, and that half of the cloth would be his.

But at last the Princess grew tired of joking, and she cried out, with a little laugh of triumph, "Dost thou by any chance ken anyone called PEERIFOOL, little Mannikin?"

Then he knew that in some way she had found out what men called him, and he was so angry and disappointed that he flung the webs of cloth down in a heap on the floor, and ran out at the door, slamming it behind him.

Meanwhile the Giant was coming down the hill in the darkening, and, to his astonishment, he met a troop of little Peerie Folk toiling up it, looking as if they were so tired that they could hardly get along. Their eyes were dim and listless, their heads were hanging on their breasts, and their lips were so long and twisted that the poor little people looked quite hideous.

The Giant asked how this was, and they told him that they had to work so hard all day, spinning for their Master, that they were quite exhausted; and that the reason why their lips were so distorted was that they used them constantly to wet their fingers, so that they might pull the wool in very fine strands from the distaff.

"I always thought a great deal of women who could spin," said the Giant, "and I looked out for a housewife that could do so. But after this I will be more careful, for the housewife that I have now is a bonnie little woman, and I would be loth to have her spoil her face in that manner."

And he hurried home in a great state of mind in case he should find that his new servant's pretty red lips had grown long and ugly in his absence.

Great was his relief to see her standing by the table, bonnie and winsome as ever, with all the webs of cloth in a pile in front of her.

"By my troth, thou art an industrious maiden," he said, in high good humour, "and, as a reward for working so diligently, I will restore thy sisters to thee." And he went out to the byre, and lifted the two other Princesses down from the rafters, and brought them in and laid them on the settle.

Their little sister nearly screamed aloud when she saw how ill they looked and how bruised their backs were, but, like a prudent maiden, she held her tongue, and busied herself with applying a cooling ointment to their wounds, and binding them up, and by and by her sisters revived, and, after the Giant had gone to bed, they told her all that had befallen them.

"I will be avenged on him for his cruelty," said the little Princess firmly; and when she spoke like that her sisters knew that she meant what she said.

So next morning, before the Giant was up, she fetched his creel, and put her eldest sister into it, and covered her with all the fine silken hangings and tapestry that she could find, and on the top of all she put a handful of grass, and when the Giant came downstairs she asked him, in her sweetest tone, if he would do her a favour.

And the Giant, who was very pleased with her because of the quantity of cloth which she had spun, said that he would.

"Then carry that creelful of grass home to my mother's cottage for her cow to eat," said the Princess. "'Twill help to make up for all the cabbages which thou hast stolen from her kailyard."

And, wonderful to relate, the Giant did as he was bid, and carried the creel to the cottage.

Next morning she put her second sister into another creel, and covered her with all the fine napery she could find in the house, and put an armful of grass on the top of it, and at her bidding the Giant, who was really getting very fond of her, carried it also home to her mother.

The next morning the little Princess told him that she thought that she would go for a long walk after she had done her housework, and that she might not be in when he came home at night, but that she would have another creel of grass ready for him, if he would carry it to the cottage as he had done on the two previous evenings. He promised to do so; then, as usual, he went out for the day.

In the afternoon the clever little maiden went through the house, gathering together all the lace, and silver, and jewellery that she could find, and brought them and placed them beside the creel. Then she went out and cut an armful of grass, and brought it in and laid it beside them.

Then she crept into the creel herself, and pulled all the fine things in above her, and then she covered everything up with the grass, which was a very difficult thing to do, seeing she herself was at the bottom of the basket. Then she lay quite still and waited.

Presently the Giant came in, and, obedient to his promise, he lifted the creel and carried it off to the old Queen's cottage.

No one seemed to be at home, so he set it down in the entry, and turned to go away. But the little Princess had told her sisters what to do, and they had a great can of boiling water ready in one of the rooms upstairs, and when they heard his steps coming round that side of the house, they threw open the window and emptied it all over his head; and that was the end of him.

The Battle of the Birds

I will tell you a story about the Wren. There was once a farmer who was seeking a servant, and the Wren met him and said, "What are you seeking?"

"I am seeking a servant," said the farmer to the Wren.

"Will you take me?" said the Wren.

"You, you poor creature, what good would you do?"

"Try me," said the Wren.

So he engaged him, and the first work he set him to do was threshing in the barn. The Wren threshed (what did he thresh with? Why a flail to be sure), and he knocked off one grain. A mouse came out and she eats that.

"I'll trouble you not to do that again," said the Wren.

He struck again, and he struck off two grains. Out came the mouse and she eats them. So they arranged a contest to see who was strongest, and the Wren brings his twelve birds, and the mouse her tribe.

"You have your tribe with you," said the Wren.

"As well as yourself," said the mouse, and she struck out her leg proudly. But the Wren broke it with his flail, and there was a pitched battle on a set day.

When every creature and bird was gathering to battle, the son of the King of Tethertown said that he would go to see the battle, and that he would bring sure word home to his father the King, who would be King of the Creatures this year. The battle was over before he arrived all but one fight, between a great black Raven and a snake. The snake was twined about the Raven's neck, and the Raven held the snake's throat in his beak, and it seemed as if the snake would get the victory over the raven. When the King's son saw this he helped the Raven, and with one blow takes the head off the snake. When the Raven had taken breath, and saw that the snake was dead, he said, "For thy kindness to me this day, I will give thee a sight. Come up now on the root of my two wings." The King's son put his hands about the Raven before his wings, and before he stopped, he took him over nine Bens, and nine Glens, and nine Mountain Moors.

"Now," said the Raven, "see you that house yonder? Go now to it. It is a sister of mine that makes her dwelling in it; and I will go bail that you are welcome. And if she asks you, 'Were you at the Battle of the Birds?' say you were. And if she asks, 'Did you see any one like me?' say you did, but be sure that you meet me tomorrow morning here, in this place." The King's son got good and right good treatment that night. Meat of each meat, drink of each drink, warm water to his feet, and a soft bed for his limbs.

On the next day the Raven gave him the same sight over six Bens, and six Glens, and six Mountain Moors. They saw a bothy far off, but, though far off, they were soon there. He got good treatment this night, as before—plenty of meat and drink, and warm water to his feet, and a soft bed to his limbs—and on the next day it was the same thing, over three Bens and three Glens, and three Mountain Moors.

On the third morning, instead of seeing the Raven as at the other times, who should meet him but the handsomest lad he ever saw, with gold rings in his hair, with a bundle in his hand. The King's son asked this lad if he had seen a big black Raven.

Said the lad to him, "You will never see the Raven again, for I am that Raven. I was put under spells by a bad Druid;

it was meeting you that loosed me, and for that you shall get this bundle. Now," said the lad, "you must turn back on the self-same steps, and lie a night in each house as before; but you must not loose the bundle which I gave ye, till in the place where you would most wish to dwell."

The King's son turned his back to the lad, and his face to his father's house; and he got lodging from the Raven's sisters, just as he got it when going forward. When he was nearing his father's house he was going through a close wood. It seemed to him that the bundle was growing heavy, and he thought he would look what was in it.

When he loosed the bundle he was astonished. In a twinkling he sees the very grandest place he ever saw. A great Castle, and an orchard about the Castle, in which was every kind of fruit and herb. He stood full of wonder and regret for having loosed the bundle—for it was not in his power to put it back again—and he would have wished this pretty place to be in the pretty little green hollow that was opposite his father's house; but he looked up and saw a great Giant coming towards him.

"Bad's the place where you have built the house, King's son," says the Giant.

"Yes, but it is not here I would wish it to be, though it happens to be here by mishap," says the King's son.

"What's the reward for putting it back in the bundle as it was before?"

"What's the reward you would ask?" says the King's son.

"That you will give me the first son you have when he is seven years of age," says the Giant.

"If I have a son you shall have him," said the King's son.

In a twinkling the Giant put each garden, and orchard, and Castle in the bundle as they were before.

"Now," says the Giant, "take your own road, and I will take mine; but mind your promise, and if you forget I will remember."

The King's son took to the road, and at the end of a few days he reached the place he was fondest of. He loosed the bundle, and the Castle was just as it was before. And when he opened the Castle door he sees the handsomest maiden he ever cast eye upon.

"Advance, King's son," said the pretty maid, "everything is in order for you, if you will marry me this very day."

"It's I that am willing," said the King's son. And on the same day they married.

But at the end of a day and seven years, who should be seen coming to the Castle but the Giant. The King's son was reminded of his promise to the Giant, and till now he had not told his promise to the Queen.

"Leave the matter between me and the Giant," says the Queen.

"Turn out your son," says the Giant. "Mind your promise."

"You shall have him," says the King, "when his mother puts him in order for his journey."

The Queen dressed up the cook's son, and she gave him to the Giant by the hand. The Giant went away with him; but he had not gone far when he put a rod in the hand of the little laddie. The Giant asked him, "If thy father had that rod what would he do with it?"

"If my father had that rod he would beat the dogs and the cats, so that they shouldn't be going near the King's meat," said the little laddie.

"Thou'rt the cook's son," said the Giant. He catches him by the two small ankles and knocks him against the stone that was beside him. The Giant turned back to the Castle in rage and madness, and he said that if they did not send out the King's son to him, the highest stone of the Castle would be the lowest.

Said the Queen to the King, "We'll try it yet; the butler's son is of the same age as our son."

She dressed up the butler's son, and she gives him to the Giant by the hand. The Giant had not gone far when he put the rod in his hand.

"If thy father had that rod," says the Giant, "what would he do with it?"

"He would beat the dogs and the cats when they would be coming near the King's bottles and glasses."

"Thou art the son of the butler," says the Giant and dashed his brains out too. The Giant returned in a very great rage and anger. The earth shook under the soles of his feet, and the Castle shook and all that was in it.

"OUT HERE WITH THY SON," says the Giant, "or in a twinkling the stone that is highest in the dwelling will be the lowest." So they had to give the King's son to the Giant.

When they were gone a little bit from the earth, the Giant showed him the rod that was in his hand and said, "What would thy father do with this rod if he had it?"

The King's son said, "My father has a braver rod than that."

And the Giant asked him, "Where is thy father when he has that brave rod?"

And the king's son said, "He will be sitting in his kingly chair."

Then the Giant understood that he had the right one.

The Giant took him to his own house, and he reared him as his own son. On a day of days when the Giant was from home, the lad heard the sweetest music he ever heard in a room at the top of the Giant's house. At a glance he saw the finest face he had ever seen. She beckoned to him to come a bit nearer to her, and she said her name was Auburn Mary but she told him to go this time, but to be sure to be at the same place about that dead midnight.

And as he promised he did. The Giant's daughter was at his side in a twinkling, and she said, "Tomorrow you will get the choice of my two sisters to marry; but say that you will not take either, but me. My father wants me to marry the son of the King of the Green City, but I don't like him." On the morrow the Giant took out his three daughters, and he said, "Now, son of the King of Tethertown, thou hast not lost by living with me so long. Thou wilt get to wife one of the two eldest of my daughters, and with her leave to go home with her the day after the wedding."

"If you will give me this pretty little one," says the King's son, "I will take you at your word."

The Giant's wrath kindled, and he said, "Before thou gett'st her thou must do the three things that I ask thee to do."

"Say on," says the King's son.

The Giant took him to the byre.

"Now," says the Giant, "a hundred cattle are stabled here, and it has not been cleansed for seven years. I am going from home today, and if this be not cleaned before night comes, so clean that a golden apple will run from end to end of it, not only thou shalt not get my daughter, but 'tis only a drink of thy fresh, goodly, beautiful blood that will quench my thirst this night."

The King's son begins cleaning the byre, but he might just as well to keep baling the great ocean. After midday when sweat was blinding him, the Giant's youngest daughter came where he was, and she said to him, "You are being punished, King's son."

"I am that," says the King's son.

"Come over," says Auburn Mary, "and lay down your weariness."

"I will do that," says he, "there is but death awaiting me, at any rate." He sat down near her. He was so tired that he fell asleep beside her. When he awoke, the Giant's daughter was not to be seen, but the byre was so well cleaned that a golden apple would run from end to end of it and raise no stain. In comes the Giant, and he said, "Hast thou cleaned the byre, King's son?"

"I have cleaned it," says he.

"Somebody cleaned it," says the Giant.

"You did not clean it, at all events," said the King's son.

"Well, well!" says the Giant. "Since thou wert so active today, thou wilt get to this time tomorrow to thatch this byre with birds' down, from birds with no two feathers of one colour."

The King's son was on foot before the sun; he caught up his bow and his quiver of arrows to kill the birds. He took to the moors, but if he did, the birds were not so easy to take. He was running after them till the sweat was blinding him. About midday who should come but Auburn Mary.

"You are exhausting yourself, King's son," says she.

"I am," said he. "There fell but these two Blackbirds, and both of one colour."

"Come over and lay down your weariness on this pretty hillock," says the Giant's daughter.

"It's I am willing," said he.

He thought she would aid him this time, too, and he sat down near her, and he was not long there till he fell asleep.

When he awoke, Auburn Mary was gone. He thought he would go back to the house, and he sees the byre thatched with feathers. When the Giant came home, he said, "Hast thou thatched the byre, King's son?"

"I thatched it," says he.

"Somebody thatched it," says the Giant.

"You did not thatch it," says the King's son.

"Yes, yes!" says the Giant. "Now there is a fir tree beside that loch down there, and there is a Magpie's nest in its top. The eggs thou wilt find in the nest. I must have them for my first meal. Not one must be burst or broken, and there are five in the nest."

Early in the morning the King's son went where the tree was, and that tree was not hard to hit upon. Its match was not in the whole wood. From the foot to the first branch was five

The Giant's Daughter

Bids the Birds thatch her Father's Byre.

hundred feet. The King's son was going all round the tree. She came who was always bringing help to him.

"You are losing the skin of your hands and feet."

"Ach! I am," says he. "I am no sooner up than down."

"This is no time for stopping," says the Giant's daughter. "Now you must kill me, strip the flesh from my bones, take all those bones apart, and use them as steps for climbing the tree. When you are climbing the tree, they will stick to the grass as if they had grown out of it; but when you are coming down, and have put your foot on each one, they will drop into your hand when you touch them. Be sure and stand on each bone, leave none untouched; if you do, it will stay behind. Put all my flesh into this clean cloth by the side of the spring at the roots of the tree. When you come to the earth, arrange my bones together, put the flesh over them, sprinkle it with water from the spring, and I shall be alive before you. But don't forget a bone of me on the tree."

"How could I kill you," asked the King's son, "after what you have done for me?"

"If you won't obey, you and I are done for," said Auburn Mary. "You must climb the tree, or we are lost; and to climb the tree you must do as I say."

The King's son obeyed. He killed Auburn Mary, cut the flesh from her body, and unjointed the bones, as she had told him.

As he went up, the King's son put the bones of Auburn Mary's body against the side of the tree, using them as steps, till he came under the nest and stood on the last bone.

Then he took the eggs, and coming down, put his foot on every bone, then took it with him, till he came to the last bone, which was so near the ground that he failed to touch it with his foot.

He now placed all the bones of Auburn Mary in order again at the side of the spring, put the flesh on them, sprinkled it with water from the spring. She rose up before him, and said, "Didn't I tell you not to leave a bone of my body without stepping on it? Now I am lame for life! You left my little finger on the tree without touching it, and I have but nine fingers."

"Now," says she, "go home with the eggs quickly, and you will get me to marry tonight if you can know me. I and my two sisters will be arrayed in the same garments, and made like each other, but look at me when my father says, 'Go to thy wife, King's son' and you will see a hand without a little finger."

He gave the eggs to the Giant.

"Yes, yes!" says the Giant. "Be making ready for your marriage."

Then, indeed, there was a wedding, and it was a wedding! Giants and gentlemen, and the son of the King of the Green City was in the midst of them. They were married, and the dancing began, that was a dance! The Giant's house was shaking from top to bottom.

But bedtime came, and the Giant said, "It is time for thee to go to rest, son of the King of Tethertown; choose thy bride to take with thee from amidst those."

Auburn Mary put out the hand off which the little finger was, and he caught her by the hand.

"Thou hast aimed well this time too; but there is no knowing but we may meet thee another way," said the Giant.

But to rest they went. "Now," says she, "sleep not, or else you are a dead man. We must fly, quick, quick, or for certain my father will kill you."

Out they went, and on the blue-grey filly in the stable they mounted. "Stop a while," says she, "and I will play a trick to the old hero." She jumped in, and cut an apple into nine shares, and she put two shares at the head of the bed, and two shares at the foot of the bed, and two shares at the door of the kitchen, and two shares at the big door, and one outside the house.

The Giant awoke and called, "Are you asleep?"

"Not yet," said the apple that was at the head of the bed.

At the end of a while he called again.

"Not yet," said the apple that was at the foot of the bed.

A while after this he called again, "Are you asleep?"

"Not yet," said the apple at the kitchen door.

The Giant called again.

The apple that was at the big door answered.

"You are now going far from me," says the Giant.

"Not yet," says the apple that was outside the house.

"You are flying," says the Giant. The Giant jumped on his feet, and to the bed he went, but it was cold—empty.

"My own daughter's tricks are trying me," said the Giant. "Here's after them," says he.

At the mouth of day, the Giant's daughter said that her father's breath was burning her back.

"Put your hand, quick," said she, "in the ear of the grey filly, and whatever you find in it, throw it behind us."

"There is a twig of sloe tree," said he.

"Throw it behind us," said she.

No sooner did he that, than there were twenty miles of blackthorn wood, so thick that scarce a weasel could go through it.

The Giant came headlong, and there he is fleecing his head and neck in the thorns.

"My own daughter's tricks are here as before," said the Giant, "but if I had my own big axe and wood-knife here, I would not be long making a way through this."

He went home for the big axe and the wood-knife, and sure he was not long on his journey, and he was the boy behind the big axe. He was not long making a way through the blackthorn.

"I will leave the axe and the wood-knife here till I return," says he.

"If you leave 'em, leave 'em," said a Hoodie Crow that was in a tree, "we'll steal 'em, steal 'em."

"If you will do that," says the Giant, "I must take them home." He returned home and left them at the house.

At the heat of day the Giant's daughter felt her father's breath burning her back.

"Put your finger in the filly's ear, and throw behind whatever you find in it."

He got a splinter of grey stone, and in a twinkling there were twenty miles, by breadth and height, of great grey rock behind them.

The Giant came full pelt, but past the rock he could not go.

"The tricks of my own daughter are the hardest things that ever met me," says the Giant, "but if I had my lever and my mighty mattock, I would not be long in making my way through this rock also."

There was no help for it, but to turn the chase for them; and he was the boy to split the stones. He was not long in making a road through the rock.

"I will leave the tools here, and I will return no more."

"If you leave 'em, leave 'em," says the Hoodie, "we will steal 'em, steal 'em."

"Do that if you will; there is no time to go back."

At the time of breaking the watch, the Giant's daughter said that she felt her father's breath burning her back.

"Look in the filly's ear, King's son, or else we are lost.

He did so, and it was a bladder of water that was in her ear this time. He threw it behind him and there was a fresh-water loch, twenty miles in length and breadth, behind them.

The Giant came on, but with the speed he had on him, he was in the middle of the loch, and he went under, and he rose no more.

On the next day the young companions were come in sight of his father's house. "Now," says she, "my father is drowned, and he won't trouble us any more; but before we go further, King's son," says she, "go you to your father's house, and tell that you have the likes of me; but let neither man nor creature kiss you, for if you do, you will not remember that you have ever seen me.

Every one he met gave the King's son welcome and luck, and he charged his father and mother not to kiss him; but as mishap was to be, an old greyhound was indoors, and she knew him, and jumped up to his mouth, and after that he did not remember the Giant's daughter.

She was sitting at the well's side as he left her, but the King's son was not coming. In the mouth of night she climbed up into a tree of oak that was beside the well, and she lay in the fork of that tree all night. A shoemaker had a house near the well, and about midday on the morrow, the shoemaker asked his wife to go for a drink for him out of the well. When the shoemaker's wife reached the well, and when she saw the shadow of her that was in the tree, thinking it was her own shadow—and she never thought till now that she was so handsome—she gave a cast to the dish that was in her hand, and it was broken on the ground, and she took herself to the house without vessel or water.

"Where is the water, wife?" said the shoemaker.

"You shambling, contemptible old carle, without grace, I have stayed too long your water and wood thrall."

"I think, wife, that you have turned crazy. Go you, daughter, quickly, and fetch a drink for your father."

His daughter went, and in the same way so it happened to her. She never thought till now that she was so lovable, and she took herself home.

"Up with the drink," said her father.

"You homespun shoe carle, do you think I am fit to be your thrall?"

The poor shoemaker thought that they had taken a turn in their understandings, and he went himself to the well. He saw the shadow of the maiden in the well, and he looked up to the tree, and he sees the finest woman he ever saw.

"Your seat is wavering, but your face is fair," said the shoemaker. "Come down, for there is need of you for a short while at my house."

The shoemaker understood that this was the shadow that had driven his people mad. The shoemaker took her to his house, and he said that he had but a poor bothy, but that she should get a share of all that was in it.

One day, the shoemaker had shoes ready, for on that very day the King's son was to be married. The shoemaker was going to the Castle with the shoes of the young people, and the girl said to the shoemaker, "I would like to get a sight of the King's son before he marries."

"Come with me," says the shoemaker, "I am well acquainted with the servants at the Castle, and you shall get a sight of the King's son and all the company."

And when the Gentles saw the pretty woman that was here they took her to the wedding-room, and they filled for her a glass of wine. When she was going to drink what is in it, a flame went up out of the glass, and a Golden Pigeon and a Silver Pigeon sprang out of it. They were flying about when three grains of barley fell on the floor. The Silver Pigeon sprung, and ate that up.

Said the Golden Pigeon to him, "If you remembered when I cleaned the byre, you would not eat that without giving me a share."

Again there fell three other grains of barley, and the Silver Pigeon sprung, and ate that up as before.

"If you remembered when I thatched the byre, you would not eat that without giving me my share," says the Golden Pigeon.

Three other grains fall, and the Silver Pigeon sprung, and ate that up.

"If you remembered when I harried the Magpie's nest, you would not eat that without giving me my share," says the Golden Pigeon. "I lost my little finger bringing it down, and I want it still."

The King's son minded, and he knew who it was that was before him.

"Well," said the King's son to the guests at the feast, "when I was a little younger than I am now, I lost the key of a casket that I had. I had a new key made, but after it was brought to me I found the old one. Now, I'll leave it to any one here to tell me what I am to do. Which of the keys should I keep?"

"My advice to you," said one of the guests, "is to keep the old key, for it fits the lock better and you're more used to it."

Then the King's son stood up and said, "I thank you for a wise advice and an honest word. This is my bride—the daughter of the Giant who saved my life at the risk of her own. I'll have her and no other woman."

So the King's son married Auburn Mary and the wedding lasted long and all were happy. But all I got was butter on a live coal, porridge in a basket, and paper shoes for my feet, and they sent me for water to the stream, and the paper shoes came to an end.

The Sea-Maiden

There was once a poor old fisherman, and one year he was not getting much fish. On a day of days, while he was fishing, there rose a sea-maiden at the side of his boat, and she asked him, "Are you getting much fish?" The old man answered and said, "Not I."

"What reward would you give me for sending plenty of fish to you?"

"Ach!" said the old man, "I have not much to spare."

"Will you give me the first son you have?" said she.

"I would give ye that, were I to have a son," said he.

"Then go home, and remember me when your son is twenty years of age, and you yourself will get plenty of fish after this."

Everything happened as the sea-maiden said, and he himself got plenty of fish; but when the end of the twenty years was nearing, the old man was growing more and more sorrowful and heavy hearted, while he counted each day as it came.

He had rest neither day nor night. The son asked his father one day, "Is any one troubling you?" The old man said, "Some one is, but that's nought to do with you nor anyone else." The lad said, "I must know what it is." His father told him at last how the matter was with him and the sea-maiden. "Let not that put you in any trouble," said the son, "I will not oppose you."

"You shall not; you shall not go, my son, though I never get fish any more."

"If you will not let me go with you, go to the smithy, and let the smith make me a great strong sword, and I will go seek my fortune," said the son.

His father went to the smithy, and the smith made a doughty sword for him. His father came home with the sword. The lad grasped it and gave it a shake or two, and it flew into a hundred splinters. He asked his father to go to the smithy and get him another sword in which there should be twice as much weight; and so his father did, and so likewise it happened to the next sword—it broke in two halves. Back went the old fisherman to the smithy; and the smith made a great sword, its like he never made before. "There's thy sword for thee," said the smith, "and the fist must be good that plays this blade." The old man gave the sword to his son who gave it a shake or two. "This will do," said he. "It's high time now to travel on my way."

On the next morning he put a saddle on a black horse that his father had, and he took the world for his pillow. When he went on a bit, he fell in with the carcass of a sheep beside the road. And there were a great black dog, a falcon, and an otter, and they were quarrelling over the spoil. So they asked him to divide it for them. He came down off the horse, and he divided the carcass amongst the three. Three shares to the dog, two shares to the otter, and a share to the falcon. "For this," said the dog, "if swiftness of foot or sharpness of tooth will give thee aid, mind me, and I will be at thy side." Said the otter, "If the swimming of foot on the ground of a pool will loose thee, mind me, and I will be at thy side." Said the falcon, "If hardship comes on thee, where swiftness of wing or crook of a claw will do good, mind me, and I will be at thy side."

On this he went onward till he reached a King's house, and he took service to be a herd, and his wages were to be according to the milk of the cattle. He went away with the cattle, and the grazing was but bare. In the evening when he took them home they had not much milk, the place was so bare, and his meat and drink was but spare that night.

On the next day he went on further with them; and at last he came to a place exceedingly grassy, in a green glen, of which he never saw the like.

But about the time when he should drive the cattle homewards, who should he see coming but a great Giant with his sword in his hand. "HI! HO! !HOGARACH!" says the Giant. "Those cattle are mine; they are on my land, and a dead man art thou."

"I say not that," says the herd, "there is no knowing, but that may be easier to say than to do."

He drew the great clean-sweeping sword, and he neared the Giant. The herd drew back his sword, and the head was off the Giant in a twinkling. He leaped on the black horse, and he went to look for the Giant's house. In went the herd, and that's the place where there was money in plenty, and dresses of each kind in the wardrobe with gold and silver, and each thing finer than the other. At the mouth of night he took himself to the King's house, but he took not a thing from the Giant's house. And when the cattle were milked this night there was milk. He got good feeding this night, meat and drink without stint, and the King was hugely pleased that he had caught such a herd. He went on for a time in this way, but at last the glen grew bare of grass, and the grazing was not so good.

So he thought he would go a little further forward in on the Giant's land; and he sees a great park of grass. He returned for the cattle, and he put them into the park.

They were but a short time grazing in the park when a great wild Giant came full of rage and "HI! HAW! HOGARAICH!" said the Giant. "It is a drink of thy blood that I will this night."

"There is no knowing," said the herd, "but that's easier to say than to do." And at each other went the men. There was shaking of blades! At length and at last it seemed as if the Giant would get the victory over the herd. Then the herd called on the dog, and with one spring the black dog caught the Giant by the neck, and swiftly the herd struck off his head.

He went home very tired this night but it's a wonder if the King's cattle had not milk. The whole family was delighted that they had got such a herd.

Next day he betakes himself to the Castle. When he reached the door, a little flattering Witch met him standing in the door.

"All hail and good luck to thee, fisher's son; 'tis I myself am pleased to see thee; great is the honour for this kingdom, for they like to be come into it—thy coming in is fame for this little bothy; go in first; honour to the Gentles; go on, and take breath."

"In before me, thou crone; I like not flattery out of doors; go in and let's hear thy speech." In went the crone, and when her back was to him he drew his sword and whips her head off; but the sword flew out of his hand. And swift the crone gripped her head with both hands, and puts it on her neck as it was before. The dog sprung on the crone, and she struck the generous dog with the club of magic; and there he lay. But the herd struggled for a hold of the club of magic, and with one blow on the top of the head she was on earth in the twinkling of an eye. He went forward, up a little, and there was spoil! Gold and silver, and each thing more precious than another, in the crone's Castle. He went back to the King's house, and then there was rejoicing.

He followed herding in this way for a time; but one night after he came home, instead of getting "All hail" and "Good luck" from the dairymaid, all were at crying and woe.

He asked what cause of woe there was that night. The dairymaid said, "There is a great beast with three heads in the loch, and it must get someone every year, and the lot had come this year on the King's daughter, and at midday tomorrow she is to meet the Laidly Beast at the upper end of the loch, but there is a great suitor yonder who is going to rescue her."

"What suitor is that?" said the herd. "Oh, he is a great General of arms," said the dairymaid, "and when he kills the beast, he will marry the King's daughter, for the King has said that he who could save his daughter should get her to marry."

But on the morrow, when the time grew near, the King's daughter and this hero of arms went to give a meeting to the beast, and they reached the black rock, at the upper end of the loch. They were but a short time there when the beast stirred in the midst of the loch; but when the General saw this terror of a beast with three heads, he took fright, and he slunk away, and he hid himself. And the King's daughter was under fear and under trembling, with no one at all to save her. Suddenly she sees a doughty handsome youth, riding a black horse, and coming where she was. He was marvellously arrayed and full armed, and his black dog moved after him. "There is gloom on your face, girl," said the youth. "What do you here?"

"Oh, that's no matter!" said the King's daughter. "It's not long I'll be here, at all events."

"I say not that," said he.

"A champion fled as likely as you, and not long since," said she.

"He is a champion who stands the war," said the youth. And to meet the Laidly Beast he went with his sword and his dog. But there was a spluttering and a splashing between himself and the beast! The dog kept doing all he might, and the King's daughter was palsied by fear of the noise of the beast! One of them would now be under, and now above. But at last he cut one of the heads off it. It gave one roar, and the son of earth, echo of the rocks, called to its screech, and it drove the loch in spindrift from end to end, and in a twinkling it went out of sight.

"Good luck and victory follow you, lad!" said the King's

daughter. "I am, safe for one night, but the beast will come again and again, until the other two heads come off it." He caught the beast's head, and he drew a knot through it, and he told her to bring it with her there tomorrow. She gave him a gold ring, and went home with the head on her shoulder, and the herd betook himself to the cows.

But she had not gone far when the great General saw her, and he said to her, "I will kill you if you do not say that 'twas I took the head off the beast." "Oh!" says she. "'Tis I will say it; who else took the head off the beast but you!" They reached the King's house, and the head was on the General's shoulder. But here was rejoicing, that she should come home alive and whole, and this great General with the Laidly Beast's head full of blood in his hand. On the morrow they went away, and there was no question at all but that this hero would save the King's daughter.

They reached the same place, and they were not long there when the fearful Laidly Beast stirred in the midst of the loch, and the General slunk away as he did on yesterday, but it was not long after this when the man of the black horse came, with another dress on. No matter; she knew that it was the very same lad. "It is I am pleased to see you," said she. "I am in hopes you will handle your great sword today as you did yesterday. Come up and take breath." But they were not long there when they saw the beast steaming in the midst of the loch.

At once he went to meet the beast, but here was Cloopersteich and Claperstich, spluttering, splashing, raving, and roaring on the beast! They kept at it thus for a long time, and about the mouth of night he cut another head off the beast. He put it on the knot and gave it to her. She gave him one of her earrings, and he leaped on the black horse, and he betook himself to the herding. The King's daughter went home with the two heads. The General met her, and took the heads from her, and he said to her, that she must tell that it was he who took the head off the beast this time also. "Who else took the head off the beast but you?" said she. They reached the King's house with the head. Then there was joy and gladness.

About the same time on the morrow, the two went away. The General hid himself as he usually did. The King's daughter betook herself to the bank of the loch. The hero of the black horse came, and if roaring and raving were on the beast on the days that were passed, this day it was horrible. But no matter, he took the third head off the beast, and drew it through the knot, and gave it to her. She gave him her other earring, and then she went home with the heads as before. When they reached the King's house, all were full of smiles, and the General was to marry the King's daughter the next day. The wedding was going on, and every one about the Castle longing till the priest should come. But when the priest came, she would marry only the one who could take the three heads of the Laidly Beast off the knot without cutting it.

"Who should take the heads off the knot but the man that put the heads on?" said the King.

The General tried them, but he could not loose them and at last there was no one about the house but had tried to take the heads off the knot, but they could not. The King asked if there were anyone else about the house that would try to take the heads off the knot. They said that the herd had not tried them yet. Word went for the herd; and he was not long throwing them hither and thither.

"But stop a bit, my lad," said the King's daughter, "the man that took the heads off the beast, he has my ring and my two earrings." The herd put his hand in his pocket, and he threw them on the board. "Thou art my man," said the King's daughter. The King was not so pleased when he saw that it was a herd who was to marry his daughter, but he ordered that he should be put in a better dress; but his daughter spoke, and she said that he had a dress as fine as any that ever was in his Castle; and thus it happened. The herd put on the Giant's golden dress, and they married that same day.

They were now married, and everything went on well. But one day, and it was the namesake of the day when his father had promised him to the sea-maiden, they were sauntering by the side of the loch, and lo and behold, she came and took him away to the loch without leave or asking. The King's daughter was now mournful, tearful, blind-sorrowful for her married man; she was always with her eye on the loch. An old soothsayer met her, and she told how it had befallen her married mate. Then he told her the thing to do to save her mate, and that she did.

She took her harp to the sea-shore, and sat and played; and the sea-maiden came up to listen, for sea-maidens are fonder of music than all other creatures. But when the wife saw the sea-maiden she stopped. The sea-maiden said, "Play on!" but the princess said, "No, not till I see my man again." So the sea-maiden put up her man's head out of the loch. Then the princess played again, and stopped till the sea-maiden put him up to the waist. Then the princess played and stopped again, and this time the sea-maiden put him all out of the loch, and he called on the falcon and became one and flew on shore. But the sea-maiden took the princess, his wife.

Sorrowful was each one that was in the town on this night. Her man was mournful, tearful, wandering down and up about the banks of the loch, by day and night. The old soothsayer met him. The soothsayer told him that there was no way of killing the sea-maiden but the one way, and this is it: "In the island that is in the midst of the loch is the whitefooted hind of the slenderest legs and the swiftest step, and though she be caught, there will spring a hoodie out of her, and though the hoodie should be caught, there will spring a trout out of her, but there is an egg in the mouth of the trout, and the soul of the sea-maiden is in the egg, and if the egg breaks, she is dead."

Now, there was no way of getting to this island, for the sea-maiden would sink each boat and raft that would go on the loch. He thought he would try to leap the strait with the black horse, and even so he did. The black horse leaped the strait. He saw the hind, and he let the black dog after her, but when he was on one side of the island, the hind would be on the other side. "Oh, would the black dog of the carcass of flesh were here!" No sooner spoke he the word than the grateful dog was at his side; and after the hind he went, and they were not long in bringing her to earth.

But he no sooner caught her than a hoodie sprang out of her. "Would that the falcon grey, of sharpest eye and swiftest wing, were here!" No sooner said he this than the falcon was after the hoodie, and she was not long putting her to earth; and as the hoodie fell on the bank of the loch, out of her jumps the trout.

"Oh, otter, that thou wert by me now!" No sooner said than the otter was at his side, and out on the loch she leaped, and brings the trout from the midst of the loch; but no sooner was the otter on shore with the trout than the egg came from his mouth. He sprang and he put his foot on it. 'Twas then the sea-maiden appeared, and she said, "Break not the egg, and you shall get all you ask."

"Deliver to me my wife!" In the wink of an eye she was by his side. When he got hold of her hands in both his hands, he let his foot down on the egg and the sea-maiden died.

Rashin-Coatie

Once, a long time ago, there was a gentleman had two lassies. The oldest was ugly and ill-natured, but the youngest was a bonnie lassie and good; but the ugly one was the favourite with her father and mother. So they ill-used the youngest in every way, and they sent her into the woods to herd cattle, and all the food she got was a little porridge and whey.

Well, amongst the cattle was a red calf, and one day it said to the lassie, "Gee that porridge and whey to the doggie, and come wi' me."

So the lassie followed the calf through the wood, and they came to a bonnie hoosie, where there was a nice dinner ready for them; and after they had feasted on everything nice they went back to the herding.

Every day the calf took the lassie away, and feasted her on dainties; and every day she grew bonnier. This disappointed the father and mother and the ugly sister. They expected that the rough usage she was getting would take away her beauty; and they watched and watched until they saw the calf take the lassie away to the feast. So they resolved to kill the calf; and not only that, but the lassie was to be compelled to kill him with an axe. Her ugly sister was to hold his head, and the lassie who loved him had to give the blow and kill him.

She could do nothing but greet; but the calf told her not to greet, but to do as he bade her, and his plan was that instead of coming down on his head she was to come down on the lassie's head who was holding him, and then she was to jump on his back and they would run off. Well, the day came for the calf to be killed and everything was ready—the ugly lassie holding his head, and the bonnie lassie armed with the axe. So she raised the axe, and came down on the ugly sister's head; and in the confusion that took place she got on the calf's back and they ran away. And they ran and better ran till they came to a meadow where grew a great lot of rashes; and, as the lassie had not on many clothes, they pu'ed rashes, and made a coatie for her. And they set off again and travelled, and travelled, till they came to the King's house. They went in, and asked if they wanted a servant. The mistress said she wanted a kitchen lassie, and she would take Rashin-coatie. So Rashin-coatie said she would stop, if they keepit the calf too. They were willing to do that. So the lassie and the calf stoppit in the King's house, and everybody was well pleased with her; and when Yule came, they said she was to stop at home and make the dinner, while all the rest went to the kirk. After they were away the calf asked if she would like to go. She said she would, but she had no clothes, and she could not leave the dinner. The calf said he would give her clothes, and make the dinner too. He went out, and came back with a grand dress, all silk and satin, and such a nice pair of slippers. The lassie put on the dress, and before she left she said:

> "Ilka peat gar anither burn,
> An' ilka spit gar anither turn,
> An' ilka pot gar anither play,
> Till I come frae the kirk on gude Yule day."

So she went to the kirk, and nobody kent it was Rashin-coatie. They wondered who the bonnie lady could be; and, so soon as the young Prince saw her, he fell in love with her, and resolved he would find out who she was, before she got home; but Rashin-coatie left before the rest, so that she might get home in time to take off her dress, and look after the dinner.

When the Prince saw her leaving, he made for the door to stop her; but she jumped past him, and in the hurry lost one of her shoes. The Prince kept the shoe, and Rashin-coatie got home all right, and the folk said the dinner was very nice.

Now the Prince was resolved to find out who the bonnie lady was, and he sent a servant through all the land with the shoe. Every lady was to try it on, and the Prince promised to marry the one it would fit. That servant went to a great many houses, but could not find a lady that the shoe would go on, it was so little and neat. At last he came to a Hen-wife's house, and her daughter had little feet. At first the shoe would not go on, but she paret her feet, and clippit her toes, until the shoes went on. Now the Prince was very angry. He knew it was not the lady that he wanted; but, because he had promised to marry whoever the shoe fitted, he had to keep his promise.

The marriage day came, and, as they were all riding to the kirk, a little bird flew through the air, and it sang:

"Clippit feet an' paret taes is on the saidle set;
But bonnie feet an' braw feet sits in the kitchen neuk."

"What's that ye say?" said the Prince. "Oh," says the Hen-wife, "would ye mind what a feel bird says?" But the Prince said "Sing that again, bonnie birdie." So the bird sings:

"Clippit feet an' paret taes is on the saidle set;
But bonnie feet an' braw feet sits in the kitchen neuk."

The Prince turned his horse and rode home, and went straight to his father's kitchen, and there sat Rashin-coatie. He kent her at once, she was so bonnie; and when she tried on the shoe it fitted her, and so the Prince married Rashin-coatie, and they lived happy, and built a house for the red calf, who had been so kind to her.

The Fox Outwitted

One day the Fox succeeded in catching a fine fat Goose asleep by the side of a loch; he held her by the wing, and making a joke of her cackling, hissing, and fears, he said:

"Now, if you had me in your mouth as I have you, tell me what you would do?"

"Why," said the Goose, "that is an easy question. I would fold my hands, shut my eyes, say a grace, and then eat you."

"Just what I mean to do," said the Fox; and folding his hands, and looking very demure, he said a pious grace with his eyes shut.

But while he did this the Goose had spread her wings, and she was now halfway over the loch; so the Fox was left to lick his lips for supper.

"I will make a rule of this," he said in disgust, "never in all my life to say a grace again till after I feel the meat warm in my belly."

How the Wolf Lost his Tail

One day the Wolf and the Fox were out together, and they stole a dish of crowdie. Now the Wolf was the biggest beast of the two, and he had a long tail like a greyhound, and great teeth.

The Fox was afraid of him, and did not dare to say a word when the Wolf ate the most of the crowdie, and left only a little at the bottom of the dish for him, but he determined to punish him for it; so the next night when they were out together the Fox said:

"I smell a very nice cheese, and"—pointing to the moonshine on the ice—"there it is too."

"And how will you get it?" said the Wolf.

"Well, stop you here till I see if the farmer is asleep, and if you keep your tail on it, nobody will see you or know that it is there. Keep it steady. I may be some time coming back."

So the Wolf lay down and laid his tail on the moonshine in the ice, and kept it for an hour till it was fast. Then the Fox, who had been watching him, ran in to the farmer and said, "The Wolf is there; he will eat up the children. The Wolf! The Wolf!"

Then the farmer and his wife came out with sticks to kill the Wolf, but the Wolf ran off leaving his tail behind him, and that's why the Wolf is stumpy-tailed to this day, though the Fox has a long brush.

The Worme of Linton

Crossing the Border into Roxburghshire, we approach the haunts of the Worme of Linton, and very romantic they are. There is the mountain stream of the Kale, bursting in brightness from the Cheviot Hills, and hurrying into the plain below, where it pauses, ere it wends its way to join the Teviot; there is the low, irregular mound, marking where stood the Tower of Linton, the stronghold of the Somervilles; there is the old village church, standing on its remarkable knoll of sand; there are the stately woods of Clifton, and, above all, the lofty heights of Cheviot crowning the distance.

Such is the fair scene which tradition avers was once laid waste by a fierce and voracious monster, the Worme of Linton. His den, still named the "Worm's Hole", lay in a hollow to the east of the Hill of Linton; and small need had he to leave it, for from this retreat he could with his sweeping and venomous breath draw the neighbouring flocks and herds within reach of his fangs. Still he did occasionally emerge and coil himself round an eminence of some height, at no great distance, still bearing the name of Wormington or Wormiston. Liberal guerdons were offered to any champion who would rid the country of such a scourge, but in vain—such was the dread inspired by the monster's poisonous breath. Not only were the neighbouring villagers beside themselves with terror, but the inhabitants of Jedburgh, full ten miles off, were struck with such a panic that they were ready to desert their town.

At last, however, the Laird of Lariston, a man of reckless bravery, came forward to the rescue of this distressed district; and, as the Linton cottagers testify to this day, having once failed in an attack with ordinary weapons, he resorted to the expedient of thrusting down the Worme's throat a peat dipped in scalding pitch and fixed on his lance. The device proved perfectly successful. The aromatic quality of the burning pitch, while it suffocated and choked the monster, preserved the champion from the effects of its poison-laden breath. While dying, the Worme is said to have contracted its folds with such violent muscular energy that the sides of Wormington Hill are still marked with their spiral impressions. In requital of his service, the Laird of Lariston received the gift of extensive lands in the neighbourhood.

The Legend of Linton Church

There is another legend connected with Linton of exceeding interest. It is sometimes interwoven with that of the Worme, but I am informed that in its more correct form it stands alone. The church is built on a little knoll of fine compact sand, without any admixture of stone, or even pebbles, and widely differing from the soil of the neighbouring heights. The sand has nowhere hardened into stone, yet the particles are so coherent, that the sides of newly opened graves appear smooth as a wall, and this to the depth of fifteen feet. This singular phenomenon is thus accounted for on the spot:

Many ages ago a young man killed a priest in this place, and was condemned to suffer death for murder and sacrilege. His doom seemed inevitable, but powerful intercession was made for him, especially by his two sisters, who were fondly attached to their brother. At last his life was granted him, on condition that the sisters should sift as much sand as would form a mound on which to build a church. The maidens joyfully undertook the task, and their patience did not fail. They completed it, and the church was built, though it is added that one of the sisters died immediately after her brother's liberation, either from the effects of past fatigue or overpowering joy. Such is the version of the legend, deemed the correct one at Linton. The villagers point to the sandy knoll in confirmation of its truth, and show a hollow place, a short distance to the westward, as that from which the sand was taken.

Michael Scott

In the early part of Michael Scott's life he was in the habit of emigrating annually to the Scottish metropolis, for the purpose of being employed in his capacity of mason. One time as he and two companions were journeying to the place of their destination for a similar object, they had occasion to pass over a high hill, the name of which is not mentioned, but which is supposed to have been one of the Grampians, and being fatigued with climbing, they sat down to rest themselves. They had no sooner done so than they were warned to take to their heels by the hissing of a large serpent, which they observed revolving itself towards them with great velocity. Terrified at the sight, Michael's two companions fled, while he, on the contrary, resolved to encounter the reptile. The appalling monster approached Michael Scott with distended mouth and forked tongue; and, throwing itself into a coil at his feet, was raising its head to inflict a mortal sting, when Michael, with one stroke of his stick, severed its body into three pieces. Having rejoined his affrighted comrades, they resumed their journey; and on arriving at the next public house, it being late, and the travellers being weary, they took up their quarters at it for the night. In the course of the night's conversation, reference was naturally made to Michael's recent exploit with the serpent, when the landlady of the house, who was remarkable for her "arts", happened to be present. Her curiosity appeared much excited by the conversation; and, after making some inquiries regarding the colour of the serpent, which she was told was white, she offered any of them that would procure her the middle piece such a tempting reward, as induced one of the party instantly to go for it. The distance was not very great; and on reaching the spot, he found the middle and tail piece in the place where Michael left them, but the head piece was gone.

The landlady on receiving the piece, which still vibrated with life, seemed highly gratified at her acquisition; and, over and above the promised reward, regaled her lodgers very plentifully with the choicest dainties in her house. Fired with curiosity to know the purpose for which the serpent was intended, the wily Michael Scott was immediately seized with a severe fit of indisposition, which caused him to prefer the request that he might be allowed to sleep beside the fire, the warmth of which, he affirmed, was in the highest degree beneficial to him.

Never suspecting Michael Scott's hypocrisy, and naturally supposing that a person so severely indisposed would feel very little curiosity about the contents of any cooking utensils which might lie around the fire, the landlady allowed his request. As soon as the other inmates of the house were retired to bed, the landlady resorted to her darling occupation; and, in his feigned state of indisposition, Michael had a favourable opportunity of watching most scrupulously all her actions through the keyhole of a door leading to the next apartment where she was. He could see the rites and ceremonies with which the serpent was put into the oven, along with many mysterious ingredients. After which the unsuspicious landlady placed the dish by the fireside, where lay the distressed traveller, to stove till the morning.

Once or twice in the course of the night the landlady under the pretence of inquiring for her sick lodger, and administering to him some renovating cordials, the beneficial effects of which he gratefully acknowledged, took occasion to dip her finger in her saucepan, upon which the cock, perched on his roost, crowed aloud. All Michael's sickness could not prevent him considering very inquisitively the landlady's cantrips, and particularly the influence of the sauce upon the crowing of the cock. Nor could he dissipate some inward desires he felt to follow her example. At the same time, he suspected that Satan had a hand in the pie, yet he thought he would like very much to be at the bottom of the concern; and thus his reason and his curiosity clashed against each other for a space of several hours. At length passion, as is too often the case, became the conqueror. Michael, too, dipped his finger in the sauce, and applied it to the tip of his tongue, and immediately the cock perched on the spardan announced the circumstance in a mournful clarion. Instantly his mind received anew light to which he was formerly a stranger, and the astonished dupe of the landlady now found it in her interest to admit her sagacious lodger into a knowledge of the remainder of her secrets.

Endowed with the knowledge of "good and evil", Michael left his lodgings in the morning with the philosopher's stone in his pocket. By daily perfecting his supernatural attainments, by new series of discoveries, he became more than a match for Satan himself. Having seduced some thousands of Satan's best workmen into his employment, he trained them up so successfully to the architective business, and inspired them with such industrious habits, that he was more than sufficient for all the architectural work of the empire. To establish this assertion, we need only refer to some remains of his workmanship still existing north of the Grampians, some of them, stupendous bridges built by him in one short night, with no other visible agents than two or three workmen.

On one occasion work was getting scarce, as might have been naturally expected, and his workmen, as they were wont, flocked to his doors, perpetually exclaiming, "Work! Work! Work!" Continually annoyed by their incessant entreaties, he called out to them in derision to go and make a dry road from Fortrose to Arderseir, over the Moray Firth. Immediately their cry ceased, and as Scott supposed it wholly impossible for them to execute his order, he retired to rest, laughing most heartily at the chimerical sort of employment he had given to his industrious workmen. Early in the morning, however, he got up and took a walk at the break of day down to the shore to divert himself at the fruitless labours of his zealous workmen. But on reaching the spot, what was his astonishment to find the formidable piece of work allotted to them only a few hours before already nearly finished. Seeing the great damage the commercial class of the community would sustain from the operation, he ordered the workmen to demolish the most part of their work; leaving, however, the point of Fortrose to show the traveller to this day the wonderful exploit of Michael Scott's Fairies.

On being thus again thrown out of employment, their former clamour was resumed, nor could Michael Scott, with all his sagacity, devise a plan to keep them in innocent employment. He at length discovered one. "Go," says he, "and manufacture me ropes that will carry me to the back of the moon, of these materials—miller's sudds and sea-sand." Michael Scott here obtained rest from his active operators; for, when other work failed them, he always dispatched them to their rope manufactory. But though these agents could never make proper ropes of those materials, their efforts to that effect are far from being contemptible, for some of their ropes are seen by the seaside to this day.

In consequence of a violent quarrel which Michael Scott once had with a person whom he conceived to have caused him some injury, he resolved, as the highest punishment he could inflict upon him, to send his adversary to that evil place designed only for Satan and his evil companions.

He accordingly, by means of his supernatural machinations,

sent the poor unfortunate man thither; and had he been sent by any other means than those of Michael Scott, he would no doubt have met with a warm reception. Out of pure spite to Michael, however, when Satan learned who was his billet-master, he would no more receive him than he would receive the Wife of Beth; and instead of treating the unfortunate man with the harshness characteristic of him, he showed him considerable civilities. Introducing him to his "Ben Taigh", he directed her to show the stranger any curiosities he might wish to see, hinting very significantly that he had provided some accommodation for their mutual friend, Michael Scott, the sight of which might afford him some gratification. The polite housekeeper accordingly conducted the stranger through the principal apartments in the house, where he saw fearful sights. But the bed of Michael Scott! His greatest enemy could not but feel satiated with revenge at the sight of it. It was a place too horrid to be described, filled promiscuously with all the awful brutes imaginable. Toads and lions, lizards and leeches, and, amongst the rest, not the least conspicuous, a large serpent gaping for Michael Scott, with its mouth wide open. This last sight having satisfied the stranger's curiosity, he was led to the outer gate, and came away. He reached his friends, and, among other pieces of news touching his travels, he was not backward in relating the entertainment that awaited his friend Michael Scott, as soon as he would "stretch his foot" for the other world. But Michael did not at all appear disconcerted at his friend's intelligence. He affirmed that he would disappoint all his enemies in their expectations—in proof of which he gave the following signs: "When I am just dead," says he, "open my breast and extract my heart. Carry it to some place where the public may see the result. You will then transfix it upon a long pole, and if Satan will have my soul, he will come in the likeness of a black raven and carry it off; and if my soul will be saved it will be carried off by a white dove."

His friends faithfully obeyed his instructions. Having exhibited his heart in the manner directed, a large black raven was observed to come from the east with great fleetness, while a white dove came from the west with equal velocity. The raven made a furious dash at the heart, missing which, it was unable to curb its force, till it was considerably past it; and the dove, reaching the spot at the same time, carried off the heart amidst the rejoicing and ejaculations of the spectators.

The Tale of
Sir James Ramsay o' Bamff

"Well, ye see, I dinna mind the beginning o' the story. But the Sir James Ramsay o' Bamff of that time was said to be ane o' the conspirators, and his lands were forfaulted, and himsel' banished the country, and a price set upon his head if he came back.

He gaed to France or Spain, I'm no sure which, and was very ill off. Ae day that he was walking in a wood, he met an oldish man wi' a lang beard, weel dressed and respectable looking. This man lookit hard at Sir James and then said to him that he lookit ill and distressed like; that he himsel' was a doctor, and if Sir James would tell his complaints, maybe he might be able to do him good.

Syne Sir James said he was not ill but for want o' food, and that all the medicine he needed was some way to earn his living as a gentleman. The auld doctor said to him he would take him as an apprentice if he liked; that he should live in his house and at his table, and learn his profession. So Sir James went hame wi' him, and was very kindly tret. After he had been wi' him a while, his master said to him ae day that he kend how to make the best and most wonderful medicine in the world—a medicine that would make baith their fortunes, and a' that belanged to them—but that it was a difficult business to get the materials that the medicine was made of. They could only be gotten frae the river that ran through the county of — , in Scotland, and at a particular part of the river, which he described; and that it would need to be some canny person, that kend that pairt o' the country weel, to gang wi' ony chance o' success. Sir James said naebody kend that pairt o' the country better than himsel', for it was on his ain estate o' Bamff, and that he was very willing to run the risk o' going hame for his master's sake, that had been sae kind to him, and for the sake o' seeing his ain place again.

Then the doctor gied him strict directions what he was to do, and how he was to make sure o' getting the beast that he was to make the medicine o'. He was to gang to a pairt o' the river where there was a deep pool o' water, and he was to hide himsel' behind some big trees that come down to the water-side for the three nights that the moon was at the full. He would see a white serpent come out o' the water, and go up to a big stane, and creep under it. He maun watch till it came out again, and catch it on its way back to the water, and kill it, and bring it awa' wi' him.

Weel, Sir James did a' that he was bidden. He put on a disguise, and gaed back to Scotland and to Bamff, and got there without onybody kenning him. He hid himsel' behind the trees at the water-side, and watched night after night. He saw the white serpent come out the first twa nights, and creep under the stane; but it aye got back to the water afore he could catch it; but the third night he did catch it, and killed it, and brought it awa' wi' him to Spain to his master. His master was very glad to get it, but he wasna sae kind after to Sir James as he used to be. He told him, now that they had got the serpent, the next thing to do was to cook it, and he maun do that too. He was to go down to a vault, and there stew the serpent till it was turned into oil. If ony body saw him at the wark, or if he tasted food till it was done, the charm would be spoiled; and if by ony chance he was to taste the medicine, it would kill him at ance, unless he had the proper remedy. Sae Sir James gaed down to the vault, and prepared the medicine just as he had been ordered; but when he was pouring it out o' the pan into the box where it was to be keepit, he let some drops fa' on his fingers that brunt them; and in the pain and hurry he forgot his master's order, and put his fingers into his mouth to suck out the pain. He did not die, but he found that his een were opened, and that he could see through everything. And when his master came down at the appointed time to speer if the medicine was ready, he found he could see into his master's insides and could tell a' that was going on there. But he keepit his ain secret, and never let on to his master what had happened; and it was very lucky, for he soon found out that his master was a bad man, and would have killed him if he had kend that he had got the secret o' the medicine. He had only been kind to him because he kend that Sir James was the best man to catch the serpent. However, Sir James learnt to be a skilfu' doctor under him; and at last he managed to get awa' frae him, and syne he travelled over the warld as a doctor, doing mony wonders, because he could clearly see what was wrang in folk's insides. But he wearied sair to get back to Scotland, and he thought that naebody would ken him as a doctor. Sae he ventured to gae back; and when he arrived, he tand that the King was very ill, and no man could find out what was the matter wi' him. He had tried a' the doctors in Scotland, and a' that came to him frae far and near, but he was nane the better; and at last he published a proclamation, that the would gie the Princess, his daughter, in marriage to ony man that would cure him. Sae Sir James gaed to the Court, and askit leave to try his skill. As soon as he came into the King's presence, and looked at him, he saw there was ball o' hair in his inside, and that no medicine could touch it. But he said if the King would trust to him, he would cure him; and the King having consented, he put him sae fast asleep, that he cuttit the ball o' hair out of his inside without his ever wakening When he did waken, he was free from illness, only weak a little frae the loss o' blood; and he was sae pleased wi' his doctor, that Sir James kneeled down and tell't him what he was, and the King pardoned him, and gied him back a' his lands, and gied him the Princess, his daughter, in marriage.

The Lee Penny

The following adventure is said to have befallen Sir Simon Lockhart, whilst fighting against the Saracens in the Holy Land. He made prisoner in battle an Emir of wealth and note. The aged mother of his captive came to the Christian camp to redeem her son from this captivity. Lockhart fixed the price at which his prisoner should ransom himself; and the lady, pulling out a large embroidered purse, proceeded to tell down the amount. In this operation, a pebble inserted in a coin, some say of the lower empire, fell out of the purse, and the Saracen matron testified so much haste to recover it as to give the Scottish knight a high idea of its value. "I will not consent," he said, "to grant your son's liberty unless the amulet be added to the ransom." The lady not only consented to this, but explained to Sir Simon the mode in which the talisman was to be used. The water in which it was dipped operated either as a styptic, or as a febrifuge, and the amulet besides possessed several other properties as a medical talisman.

Sir Simon Lockhart, after much experience of the wonders which it wrought, brought it to his own country, and left it to his heirs, by whom, and by Clydeside in general, it was, and is still, distinguished by the name of the Lee Penny, from the name of his native seat of Lee.

The virtues were brought into operation by dropping the stone into water given to the diseased to drink, washing at the same time the part affected. No words were used in dipping the stone, or money permitted to be taken by the servants of Lee. People came from all parts of Scotland, and many places in England, to carry away water to give to their cattle.

The amulet is a stone of a deep-red colour and triangular shape—each side being about half an inch in length—set in a piece of silver coin.

The Craig Liath Mhor

At the foot of Glen Errochdie, on the road between Struan and Rannoch, stand the ruins of the ancient farmhouse of Blairfettie. The present building is comparatively a modern structure, but the one I refer to is situated across the river, immediately opposite the present one. It is now a complete ruin, and, in fact, its site is almost obliterated. At the foot of a birch plantation, and in close proximity to the River Errochdie, it formerly commanded an extensive view of the glen. Towards the latter end of the seventeenth century, it was the property of a certain Laird of Muirlaggan, Rannoch, who resided there along with his eleven sons, all but one of whom were manly and stalwart Highlanders.

Their mother having died when giving birth to the youngest— a fair-haired, sickly looking child—the sons resolved to remain at home to support and comfort their venerable father in his declining years.

Being muscular and powerful fellows, their sole delight was in fishing and hunting, and exerting and testing their strength at feats of valour and skill. Their aged father they honoured with unbounded respect, always consulting him before engaging in any contemplated hunting or deer stalking expedition.

The youngest brother, who was at the period of my tale only about sixteen years of age, would never consent to join his bigger bothers in their games, as his disposition was perfectly opposite to theirs, he preferring to roam amongst the woods and down the river's side in quest of blaeberries and wild flowers.

He was his father's favourite, which, together with his girlish manners, and his utter distaste for manly sports, made him disliked by his brethren.

One morning, towards the fall of the year, the brothers decided on going on a deer stalking expedition. The place chosen for the chase was the Hill of Tulloch, now part of the Auchlecks estate. Accompanied by their youngest brother, whom they had with some difficulty induced to join them, and taking with them a few couples of staghounds, which they held in leashes, they started on their journey, striding along gaily and enlivening the way with merry banter and chat, whilst teasing and tormenting their youngest brother on his unsportsmanlike appearance.

Attaining the summit of the hill, they at once engaged in the hunt, which was continued up to midday, when they decided to rest and partake of their oatmeal bannocks, and usquebaugh. The spot where they rested is called the "Craig Liath Mhor", which, literally translated, means the "Big Grey Crag".

Having partaken of their meal, they engaged in conversation, to while the time away before again resuming the chase.

During the course of their talk, the staghounds suddenly commenced to quarrel and fight, and would upon no account be separated, although various measures were resorted to to quell and subdue them. All attempts at pacification proving futile, the company in the last resort resolved to let the outrageous animals fight it out, and thereupon sat down to witness the result. Wagers were freely engaged in, and out of one of these wagers there arose a quarrel between two of the brothers. Like the dogs, they were determined to fight it out, and agreed to settle the dispute at the point of the dirk.

The rest of the bothers, unwilling that any such affair should disgrace their family, strove their utmost to separate the two combatants; but, instead of quelling the dispute, they only succeeded in adding fuel to the fire.

Without further ado lots were cast, and a general and equal-sided fight then began.

Fierce and bloody was the fray, and melancholy the result; for not a single man of the brothers remained alive at the end of it, except the youngest, who had taken no active part in the combat.

He returned to his father with the sad and terrible tidings of what had occurred; upon hearing which the wretched man was heartbroken, and within a few days succumbed to his grief. What became of the survivor I cannot tell, as all traces of him seem to have been lost.

On the summit of the "Craig Liath Mhor" may be seen to this day ten cairns, which mark the last resting place of the brothers. A few stones roughly piled one above the other are all that mark the spot where the fatal struggle took place.

Fiddler's Well

The path rises by a kind of natural stair to the top of the precipices, and continues to ascend till it reaches a spring of limpid water, which comes gushing out of the side of a bank covered with moss and daisies, and which for more than a century has been known to the townspeople by the name of Fiddler's Well. Its waters are said to be medicinal, and there is a pretty tradition still extant of the circumstance through which their virtues were first discovered, and to which the spring owes its name.

Two young men of Cromarty, who were much attached to each other, were seized at nearly the same time by consumption. In one the progress of the disease was rapid—he died two short months after he was attacked by it; while the other, though wasted almost to a shadow, had yet strength enough left to follow the corpse of his companion to the grave. The name of the survivor was Fiddler—a name still common among the seafaring men of the town. On the evening of the interment he felt oppressed and unhappy; his imagination was haunted by a thousand feverish shapes of open graves with bones mouldering round their edges, and of coffins with the lids displaced; and after he had fallen asleep, the images, which were still the same, became more ghastly and horrible. Towards morning, however, they had all vanished; and he dreamed that he was walking alone by the sea-shore in a clear and beautiful day of summer.

Suddenly, as he thought, some person stepped up behind, and

whispered in his ear, in the voice of his deceased companion, "Go on, Willie; I shall meet you at Stormy." There is a rock in the neighbourhood of Fiddler's Well, so called, from the violence with which the sea beats against it when the wind blows strongly from the east. On hearing the voice he turned round, and seeing no one, he went on, as he thought, to the place named, in the hope of meeting his friend, and sat down on a bank to wait his coming; but he waited long—lonely and dejected. And then remembering that he for whom he waited was dead, he burst into tears. At this moment a large field-bee came humming from the west, and began to fly round his head. He raised his hand to brush it away; it widened its circle, and then came humming into his ear as before. He raised his hand a second time, but the bee would not be scared off; it hummed ceaselessly round and round him, until at length its ' murmurings seemed to be fashioned into words, articulated in the voice of his deceased companion. "Dig, Willie, and drink!" it said. "Dig, Willie, and drink!"

He accordingly set himself to dig, and no sooner had he torn a sod out of the bank than a spring of clear water gushed from the hollow; and the bee, taking a wider circle, and humming in a voice of triumph that seemed to emulate the sound of a distant trumpet, flew away. He looked after it, but as he looked the images of his dream began to mingle with those of the waking world; the scenery of the hill seemed obscured by a dark cloud, in the centre of which there glimmered a faint light; the rocks, the sea, the long declivity faded into the cloud; and turning round he saw only a dark apartment, and the faint beams of morning shining in at a window. He rose, and, after digging the well, drank of the water and recovered. And its virtues are still celebrated; for though the water be only simple water, it must be drunk in the morning, and as it gushes from the bank; and with pure air, exercise, and early rising for its auxiliaries, it continues to work cures.

The Fairies of Scotland

The Fairies of Scotland are represented as a diminutive race of beings, of a mixed, or rather dubious nature, capricious in their dispositions, and mischievous in their resentment. They inhabit the interior of green hills, chiefly those of a conical form, in Gaelic termed Sighan, on which they lead their dances by moonlight; impressing upon the surface the marks of circles, which sometimes appear yellow and blasted, sometimes of a deep green hue; and within which it is dangerous to sleep, or to be found after sunset. The removal of those large portions of turf, which thunderbolts sometimes scoop out of the ground with singular regularity, is also ascribed to their agency. Cattle, which are suddenly seized with the cramp, or some similar disorder, are said to be Elf-shot; and the approved cure is, to chafe the parts affected with a blue bonnet, which, it may be readily believed, often restores the circulation. The triangular flints, frequently found in Scotland, with which the ancient inhabitants probably barbed their shafts, are supposed to be the weapons of Fairy resentment, and are termed Elf arrow-heads. The rude brazen battle-axes of the ancients, commonly called Celts, are also ascribed to their manufacture. But, like the Gothic Duergar, of Dwarf, their skill is not confined to the fabrication of arms; for they are heard sedulously hammering in linns, precipices, and rocky or cavernous situations, where, like the Dwarfs of the mines, mentioned by Georg. Agricola, they busy themselves in imitating the actions of the various employments of men. The Brook of Beaumont, for example, which passes, in its course, by numerous linns and caverns, is notorious for being haunted by the Fairies; and the perforated and rounded stones which are formed by trituration in its channel, are termed, by the vulgar, Fairy cups and dishes.

It is sometimes accounted unlucky to pass such places, without performing some ceremony to avert the displeasure of the elves. There is, upon the top of Minchmuir, a mountain in Peeblesshire, a spring called the Cheese Well, because, anciently, those who passed that way were wont to throw into it a piece of cheese, as an offering to the Fairies, to whom it was consecrated.

The usual dress of the Fairies is green; though on the moors they have been sometimes observed in heath-brown, or in weeds dyed with the stoneraw, or lichen. They often ride in invisible procession, when their presence is discovered by the shrill ringing of their bridles. On these occasions they sometimes borrow mortal steeds; and when such are found at morning, panting and fatigued in their stalls, with their manes and tails dishevelled and entangled, the grooms, I presume, often find this a convenient excuse for their situation; as the common belief of the Elves quaffing the choicest liquors in the cellars of the rich might occasionally cloak the delinquencies of an unfaithful butler.

The Fairy and
the Miller's Wife

One day as a mother was sitting rocking her baby to sleep, she was surprised, on looking up, to see a lady of elegant and courtly demeanour, so unlike anyone she had ever seen in that part of the country, standing in the middle of the room. She had not heard anyone enter, therefore you may judge it was with no little surprise, not unmingled with curiosity, that she rose to welcome her strange visitor. She handed her a chair, but the visitor very politely declined to be seated. She was very magnificently attired; her dress was of the richest green, embroidered round with spangles of gold, and on her head was a small coronet of pearls.

The mother was still more surprised at the lady's strange request. She asked, in a rich musical voice, if she would oblige her with a basin of oatmeal. A basin full to overflowing was immediately handed to her, for the woman's husband, being both a farmer and miller, had plenty of meal at command. The lady promised to return it, and named the day she would do so. One of the children put out her hand to get hold of the grand lady's spangles, but told her mother afterwards that she felt nothing. The mother was afraid the child would lose the use of her hands, but no such calamity ensued. It would have been very ungrateful in her Fairy majesty if she had struck the child powerless for touching her dress, if indeed such power were hers.

But to return to our story. The very day mentioned the oatmeal was returned, not by the same lady, but by a curious little figure with a yelping voice; she was likewise dressed in green. After handing the meal, she yelped out, "Braw meal; it's the top pickle of the sin corn." It was excellent; and what was very strange, all the family were advised to partake of it but one servant lad, who spurned the Fairy's meal; and he dying shortly after, the miller and his wife firmly believed it was because he refused to eat of the meal. They also firmly believed their first visitor was no less a personage than the Queen of the Fairies, who, having dismissed her court, had not one maid of honour in waiting to obey her commands.

A few nights after this strange visit, as the miller was going to bed, a gentle tap was heard at the door, and on its being opened by him, with a light in his hand, there stood a little figure dressed in green, who, in a shrill voice, but very polite manner, requested him to let on the water and set the mill in order, for she was going to grind some corn. The miller did not dare to refuse, so did as she desired him. She told him to go to bed again, and he would find all as he had left it. He found everything in the morning as she said he would. So much for the honesty of Fairies.

Water Fairies

The Dracae are a sort of water-spirit who inveigle women and children into the recesses which they inhabit, beneath lakes and rivers, by floating past them, on the surface of the water, in the shape of gold rings or cups. The women thus seized are employed as nurses, and after seven years are permitted to revisit earth.

Gervase of Tilbury mentions one woman in particular who had been allured by observing a wooden dish, or cup, float by her, while she was washing clothes in the river. Being seized as soon as she reached the depths, she was conducted into one of the subterranean recesses, which she described as very magnificent, and employed as nurse to one of the brood of the hag who had allured her. During her residence in this capacity, having accidentally touched one of her eyes with an ointment of serpent's grease, she perceived, at her return to the world, that she had acquired the faculty of seeing the Dracae, when they intermingle themselves with men. Of this power she was, however, deprived by the touch of her ghostly mistress, whom she had one day incautiously addressed. It is a curious fact that this story, in almost all its parts, is current in both the Highlands and Lowlands of Scotland, with no other variation than the substitution of Fairies for Dracae, and the cavern of a hill for that of a river. Indeed many of the vulgar account it extremely dangerous to touch anything which they may happen to find without saining (blessing) it, the snares of the enemy being notorious and well attested.

A poor woman of Teviotdale having been fortunate enough, as she thought herself, to find a wooden beetle, at the very time when she needed such an implement, seized it without pronouncing a proper blessing, and, carrying it home, laid it above her bed to be ready for employment in the morning. At midnight the window of her cottage opened, and a loud voice was heard calling up someone within by a strange and uncouth name. The terrified cottager ejaculated a prayer, which, we may suppose, ensured her personal safety; while the enchanted implement of housewifery, tumbling from the bedstead, departed by the window with no small noise and precipitation.

Fairy Transportation

The power of the Fairies was not confined to unchristened children alone; it was supposed frequently to be extended to full-grown persons, especially such as in an unlucky hour were devoted to the devil by the execration of parents and of masters; or those who were found asleep under a rock, or on a green hill, belonging to the Fairies, after sunset, or, finally to those who unwarily joined their orgies.

A tradition existed, during the seventeenth century, concerning an ancestor of the noble family of Duffus, who, walking abroad in the fields, near to his own house, was suddenly carried away, and found the next day at Paris, in the French King's cellar, with a silver cup in his hand. Being brought into the King's presence, and questioned by him who he was, and how he came thither, he told his name, his country, and the place of his residence and that on such a day of the month, which proved to be the day immediately preceding, being in the fields, he heard the noise of a whirlwind, and of voices, crying "Horse and Hattock!" (these are the words which the fairies are said to use when they remove from any place), whereupon he cried "Horse and Hattock", also, and was immediately caught up and transported through the air by the Fairies, to that place, where, after he had drunk heartily, he fell asleep, and before he woke, the rest of the company were gone, and had left him in the posture wherein he was found. It is said the King gave him the cup which was found in his hand, and dismissed him.

The narrator affirms "that the cup was still preserved, and known by the name of the Fairy Cup." He adds that Mr. Steward, tutor to the then Lord Duffus, had informed him that when a boy at the school of Forres, he and his school-fellows were upon a time whipping their tops in the churchyard, before the door of the church, when, though the day was calm, they heard a noise of a wind, and at some distance saw the small dust begin to rise and turn round, which motion continued advancing till it came to the place where they were, whereupon they began to bless themselves; but one of their number being, it seems, a little more bold and confident than his companions, said, "Horse and Hattock with my top," and immediately they all saw the top lifted up from the ground, but could not see which way it was carried, by reason of a cloud of dust which was raised at the same time. They sought for the top all about the place where it was taken up, but in vain; and it was found afterwards in the churchyard, on the other side of the church.

The Fairy Boy of Leith

The worthy Captain George Burton communicated to Richard Bovet, gentleman author of the interesting work entitled *Pandæmonium*, or *The Devil's Cloister Opened*, the following singular account of a lad called the Fairy Boy of Leith, who, it seems, acted as a drummer to the Elves, who weekly held rendezvous in the Calton Hill, near Edinburgh.

"About fifteen years since, having business that detained me for some time at Leith, which is near Edinburgh, in the kingdom of Scotland, I often met some of my acquaintance at a certain house there, where we used to drink a glass of wine for our refection; the woman who kept the house was of honest reputation among the neighbours, which made me give the more attention to what she told me one day about a Fairy boy (as they called him), who lived about that town. She had given me so strange an account of him that I desired her I might see him the first opportunity, which she promised; and not long after, passing that way, she told me there was the Fairy boy but a little before I came by; and, casting her eye into the street, said, 'Look you, sir, yonder he is at play with those other boys.' And designing him to me, I went, and, by smooth words, and a piece of money, got him to come into the house with me; where, in the presence of divers people, I demanded of him several astrological questions, which he answered with great subtilty; and, through all his discourse, carried it with a cunning much above his years, which seemed not to exceed ten or eleven.

"He seemed to make a motion like drumming upon the table with his fingers, upon which I asked him whether he could beat a drum. To which he replied, 'Yes, sir, as well as any man in Scotland; for every Thursday night I beat all points to a sort of people that used to meet under yonder hill' (pointing to the great hill between Edenborough and Leith). 'How, boy? quoth I. 'What company have you there?' 'There are, sir,' said he, 'a great company both of men and women, and they are entertained with many sorts of musick, besides my drum; they have, besides, plenty of variety of meats and wine, and many times we are carried into France or Holland in a night, and return again, and whilst we are there we enjoy all the pleasures the country doth afford.'

I demanded of him how they got under that hill. To which he replied that there was a great pair of gates that opened to them, though they were invisible to others; and that within there were brave large rooms, as well accommodated as most in Scotland. I then asked him how I should know what he said to be true. Upon which he told me he would read my fortune, saying I should have two wives, and that he saw the forms of them sitting on my shoulders; that both would be very handsome women. As he was thus speaking, a woman of the neighbourhood, coming into the room, demanded of him what her fortune should be. He told her that she had two bastards before she was married, which put her in such a rage that she desired not to hear the rest.

"The woman of the house told me that all the people in Scotland could not keep him from the rendezvous on Thursday night; upon which, by promising him some more money, I got a promise of him to meet me at the same place, in the afternoon, the Thursday following, and so dismist him at that time. The boy came again, at the place and time appointed, and I had prevailed with some friends to continue with me, if possible, to prevent his moving that night. He was placed between us, and answered many questions, until, about eleven of the clock, he was got away unperceived by the company; but I suddenly missing him, hasted to the door, and took hold of him, and so returned him into the same room; we all watched him, and, of a sudden, he was again got out of doors; I followed him close, and he made a noise in the street, as if he had been set upon; but from that time I could never see him." (George Burton)

The Smith and the Fairies

Years ago there lived in Crossbrig a smith of the name of MacEachern. This man had an only child, a boy of about thirteen or fourteen years of age, cheerful, strong, and healthy. All of a sudden he fell ill, took to his bed, and moped whole days away. No one could tell what was the matter with him and the boy himself could not, or would not, tell how he felt. He was wasting away fast; getting thin, old, and yellow; and his father and all his friends were afraid that he would die.

At last one day, after the boy had been lying in this condition for a long time, getting neither better nor worse, always confined to bed, but with an extraordinary appetite, one day, while sadly revolving these things, and standing idly at his forge, with no heart to work, the smith was agreeably surprised to see an old man, well known to him for his sagacity and knowledge of out-of-the-way things, walk into his workshop. Forthwith he told him the occurrence which had clouded his life.

The old man looked grave as he listened; and, after sitting a long time pondering over all he had heard, he gave his opinion thus: "It is not your son you have got. The boy has been carried away by the 'Daoine Sith,' and they have left a Sibhreach in his place." "Alas! And what then am I to do?" said the smith. "How am I ever to see my own son again?" "I will tell you how," answered the old man. "But, first, to make sure that it is not your own son you have got, take as many empty eggshells as you can get, go with them into the room, spread them out carefully before his sight, then proceed to draw water with them, carrying them two and two in your hands as if they were a great weight, and arrange when full, with every sort of earnestness, round the fire." The smith accordingly gathered as many broken eggshells as he could get, went into the room, and proceeded to carry out all the old man's instructions.

He had not been long at work before there arose from the bed a shout of laughter, and the voice of the seeming sick boy exclaimed, "I am now 800 years of age, and I have never seen the like of that before."

The smith returned and told the old man. "Well, now," said the sage to him, "did I not tell you that it was not your son you had. Your son is in Brorra-cheill in a digh there (that is, a round green hill frequented by Fairies). Get rid as soon as possible of this intruder, and I think I may promise you your son.

"You must light a very large and bright fire before the bed on which this stranger is lying. He will ask you, 'What is the use of such a fire as that?' Answer him at once, 'You will see that presently!' and then seize him, and throw him into the middle of it. If it is your own son you have got, he will call out to save him; but if not, this thing will fly through the roof."

The smith again followed the old man's advice; kindled a large fire, answered the question put to him as he had been directed to do, and seizing the child flung him in without hesitation. The "Sibhreach" gave an awful yell, and sprung through the roof, where a hole was left to let the smoke out.

On a certain night the old man told him the green round hill, where the Fairies kept the boy, would be open. And on that night the smith, having provided himself with a Bible, a dirk, and a crowing cock, was to proceed to the hill. He would hear singing and dancing and much merriment going on, but he was to advance boldly; the Bible he carried would be a certain safeguard to him against any danger from the Fairies.

On entering the hill he was to stick the dirk in the threshold, to prevent the hill from closing upon him. "And then," continued the old man, "on entering you will see a spacious apartment before you, beautifully clean, and there, standing far within, working at a forge, you will also see your own son. When you are questioned, say you come to seek him, and will not go without him."

Not long after this the time came round, and the smith sallied forth, prepared as instructed. Sure enough, as he approached the hill, there was a light where light was seldom seen before. Soon after a sound of piping, dancing, and joyous merriment reached the anxious father on the night wind.

Overcoming every impulse to fear, the smith approached the threshold steadily, stuck the dirk into it as directed and entered. Protected by the Bible he carried on his breast, the Fairies could not touch him; but they asked him, with a good deal of displeasure, what he wanted there. He answered, "I want my son, whom I see down there, and I will not go without him."

Upon hearing this the whole company before him gave a loud laugh, which wakened up the cock he carried dozing in his arms, who at once leaped up on his shoulders, clapped his wings lustily, and crowed loud and long.

The Fairies, incensed, seized the smith and his son, and throwing them out of the hill, flung the dirk after them, and in an instant all was dark.

For a year and a day the boy never did a turn of work, and hardly ever spoke a word; but at last one day, sitting by his father and watching him finishing a sword he was making for some chief, and which he was very particular about, he suddenly exclaimed, "That is not the way to do it," and, taking the tools from his father's hands, he set to work himself in his place, and soon fashioned a sword the like of which was never seen in the country before.

From that day the young man wrought constantly with his

father, and became the inventor of a peculiarly fine and well-tempered weapon, the making of which kept the two smiths, father and son, in constant employment, spread their fame far and wide, and gave them the means in abundance, as they before had the disposition, to live content with all the world and very happily with one another.

Redemption from Fairy-land

Near the town of Aberdeen, in Scotland, lived James Campbell, who had one daughter, named Mary, who was married to John Nelson, a young man of that neighbourhood. Shortly after their marriage, they being a young couple, they went to live in the town of Aberdeen, where he followed his trade, being a goldsmith. They lived loving and agreeable together until the time of her lying-in, when there were female attendants prepared suitable to her situation; near the hour of twelve at night they were alarmed with a dreadful noise, at which of a sudden the candles went out, which drove the attendants in the utmost confusion; soon as the women regained their half-lost senses, they called in their neighbours, who, after striking up lights, and looking towards the lying-in woman, found her a corpse, which caused great confusion in the family. There was no grief could exceed that of her husband, who, next morning, prepared ornaments for her funeral; people of all sects came to her wake. Amongst others came the Rev. Mr. Dodd, who, at first sight of the corpse said, "It's not the body of any Christian." He said that Mrs. Nelson was taken away by the Fairies, and what they took for her was only some substance left in her place. He was not believed, so he refused attending her funeral; they kept her in the following night, and the next day she was interred.

Her husband, one evening after sunset, being riding in his

own field, heard a most pleasant concert of music, and soon after espied a woman coming towards him dressed in white; she being veiled, he could not observe her face, yet he rode near her, and asked very friendly who she was that chose to walk alone so late in the evening. At which she unveiled her face, and burst into tears, saying, "I am not permitted to tell you who I am." He knowing her to be his wife, asked her in the name of God, what disturbed her, or what occasioned her to appear at that hour. She said her appearing at any hour was of no consequence. "For though you believe me to be dead and buried, I am not, but was taken away by the Fairies the night of my delivery; you only buried a piece of wood in my place; I can be recovered if you take proper means; as for my child, it has three nurses to attend it, but I fear it cannot be brought home; the greatest dependence I have on any person is my brother Robert who is a captain of a merchant ship, and will be home in ten days hence."

Her husband asked her what means he should take to win her. She told him he should find a letter the Sunday morning following, on the desk in his own room, directed to her brother, wherein there would be directions for winning her. "Since my being taken from you," she said, "I have had the attendance of a Queen or Empress, and if you look over my right shoulder you will see several of my companions." He then did as she desired, when, at a small distance, he saw a King and Queen sitting, beside a moat, or knoll, on a throne, in splendour.

She then desired him to look right and left, which he did, and observed other kings on each side of the King and Queen, well guarded. He said, "I fear it is an impossibility to win you from such a place."

"No," says she, "were my brother Robert here in your place, he would bring me home; but let it not encourage you to attempt the like, for that could occasion the loss of me for ever; there is now severe punishment threatened to me for speaking to you; but, to prevent that, do you ride up to the moat, where (suppose you will see no person) all you now see will be near you, and do you threaten to burn all the old thorns and brambles that is round the moat, if you do not get a firm promise that I shall get no punishment; I shall be forgiven." Which he promised. She then disappeared, and he lost sight of all he had seen; he then rode very resolutely up to the moat, and went round it, vowing he would burn all about it if he would not get a promise that his wife should get no hurt. A voice desired him to cast away a book that was in his pocket, and then demand his request; he answered he would not part with his book, but grant his request, or they should find the effect of his rage. The voice answered, that upon honour she should be forgave her fault, but for him to suffer no prejudice to come to the moat, which he promised to fulfil, at which he heard most pleasant music.

He then returned home, and sent for the Rev. Mr. Dodd, and related to him what he had seen; Mr. Dodd stayed with him till Sunday morning following, when as Mr. Nelson looked on the desk in his room, he espied a letter, which he took up, it being directed to his wife's brother, who in a few days came home; on his receiving the letter he opened it, wherein he found the following:

"Dear Brother,-

My husband can relate to you my present circumstances. I request that you will (the first night after you see this) come to the moat where I parted from my husband: let nothing daunt you, but stand in the centre of the moat at the hour of twelve at night, and call me, when I, with several others, will surround you; I shall have on the whitest dress of any in company. Then take hold of me, and do not forsake me; all the frightful methods they shall use let it not surprise you, but keep your hold, suppose they continue till cock crow, when they shall vanish all of a sudden, and I shall be safe, when I will return home and live with my husband. If you succeed in your attempt, you will gain applause from all your friends, and have the blessing of your ever-loving and affectionate sister,

Mary Nelson

No sooner had he read the letter than he vowed to win his sister and her child, or perish in the attempt. He returned to the ship, and related to his sailors the contents of the letter; he delayed till ten at night, when his loyal sailors offered to go with him, which he refused, thinking it best to go alone. As he left his ship a frightful lion came roaring towards him; he drew his sword and struck at the lion, which he observed was of no substance, it being only the appearance of one, to terrify him in his attempt. It only encouraged him, so that he proceeded to the moat, in the centre of which he observed a white handkerchief spread; on which he was surrounded with a number of women, the cries of whom were the most frightful he ever heard. His sister being in the whitest dress of any round him, he seized her by the right hand, and said "With the help of God, I will preserve you from all infernal imps." When of a sudden, the moat seemed to be on fire around him. He likewise heard the most dreadful thunder could be imagined; frightful birds and beasts seemed to make towards him out of the fire, which he knew was not real; nothing daunted his courage; he kept hold of his sister for the space of an hour and three-quarters, when the cocks began to crow; then the fire disappeared, and all the frightful imps vanished. He held her in his arms, and fell on his knees, and gave God thanks for his proceedings that night. He, believing her clothing to be light, put his outside coat on her; she then embraced him, saying she was now safe, as he put any of his clothing on her; he then brought her home to her husband, which occasioned great rejoicing.

Her husband and her brother began to conclude to destroy the moat in revenge of the child they had away, when instantly they heard a voice, which said. You shall have your son safe, and well, on condition that you will not till the ground within three perches of the moat, nor damage bushes or brambles round that place." Which they agreed to, and, in a few minutes, the child was left on his mother's knee, which caused them to kneel and return thanks to God.

The circumstance of this terrifying affair was occasioned by leaving Mrs. Nelson, the night of her lying-in, in the care of women who were mostly intoxicated with liquor!

Thom and Willie

Thom and Willie, two young fisher-mates of Lunna, in Shetland, were rivals for the hand of the fair Osla, daughter of Jarm.

Now it so happened that one October afternoon, they took their hand-lines and went out fishing together in their boat. Towards dusk the wind rose, and it soon blew so hard as to compel the young men to run for the nearest shelter—a haven in the islet of Linga in Whalsay Sound, which they happily reached in safety. The islet was uninhabited, and the fishermen had with them neither food nor the means of kindling a fire. They had, however, a roof over their heads; for there was a hut, or lodge, on the island, used by fishermen in the fair weather season, but deserted since the close of that period. For two days the storm raged without ceasing, and at last the situation of the castaways began to grow very serious. However, on the morning of the third day, a little before daybreak, Willie, who was awake before his companion, discovered that the weather had faired, and that the wind blew in a favouring direction. Upon this, without rousing Thom, he proceeded to the boat, which lay safely hauled up upon the shore, and by dint of great exertion managed to launch her single-handed.

Meantime Thom had awoke; and, at last, as Willie did not come back, he followed him to the noust, or place where boats are drawn up. And here a sight met his view which filled him with dismay. The yawl had disappeared from her place; but, raising his eyes, he beheld her already far out at sea and speeding before the breeze in the direction of Lunna. At this sight poor Thom gave way to despair. He realised that his comrade had basely and heartlessly deserted him; he knew that it was not likely that the islet would be visited until the fishing-season should have come round again; and he had small hopes of help from any exertions on his behalf which might be made by his friends, seeing that they would be in ignorance where to look for him. Amid melancholy thoughts and forebodings the day passed slowly, and at nightfall he betook himself to his shake-down of straw within the lodge. Darkness closed in, and he slept.

But, towards the small hours of the morning, he was suddenly awakened; when great was his astonishment to see that the hut was lighted up with a strange illumination, whilst a queer inhuman hum and chatter, accompanied by the patter of many pairs of little feet and the jingle of gold and silver vessels, smote upon his ear. A Fairy banquet was, in fact, in course of preparation in the lodge. Thom raised himself noiselessly upon his elbow, and watched the proceedings. With infinite bustle and clatter, the table was at last laid. Then there entered a party of Trows, who bore between them in a chair, or litter, a female Fairy, to whom all appeared to pay honour. The company took seats, and the banquet was on the point of commencing, when in a moment the scene of festivity was changed to one of wild alarm and confusion. A moment more, and Thom learnt to his cost the cause of the sudden change. The presence of a human being had been detected, and at a word from their Queen the "Grey People", swarming together, were about to rush upon the intruder. But in this trying juncture Thom did not lose his presence of mind. His loaded fowling-piece lay by his side, and, as the Fairies rushed upon him, he raised it to his shoulder and fired. In an instant the light was extinguished, and all was darkness, silence, and solitude.

Let us now return to the perfidious Willie. Reaching Lunna in safety, he related a tragic tale (which he had invented on the voyage), to account for the absence of his comrade; and, finding that his story was believed, he began anew, without much loss of time, to urge his suit with the fair Osla. Her father, Jarm, regarded him with favour; but the maiden herself turned a deaf ear to all his entreaties. She felt that she could not love him; and, besides, she was haunted by a suspicion that Thom, in whose welfare she felt a tender interest, had been the victim of foul play. Pressure was, however, put upon her, and in spite of her objections, an early day was fixed for the wedding.

The poor girl was in great distress. However, one night, when she had cried herself to sleep, she dreamed a dream, the result of which was that next morning she proceeded to the house of Thom's parents, and begged them to join her in a search for their missing son. This, notwithstanding their love for him, they were somewhat reluctant to do; arguing that, even supposing him to have been abandoned, as she divined, upon one of the rocky islets of the coast, he must ere now have perished from exposure and starvation. But the girl persisted in her entreaties, which at last prevailed. A boat was manned, and by Osla's direction was steered towards Linga, upon approaching which, sure enough, as the girl had predicted, it was discovered that the islet had a human tenant. Thom met his friends on the beach, and when the first eager greetings had passed, surprise was expressed at the freshness and robustness of his appearance. But this surprise increased tenfold when, in recounting his adventures, he explained that, during the latter days of his isolation, he had supported life upon the remains of the scarcely-tasted Fairy banquet, adding that never in his life before had he fared so delicately.

On their return to Lunna, the party were received with rejoicings; and it is scarcely necessary to add that Thom and Osla were soon made man and wife. From that time forward

Willie prospered no more. The loss of his health and fortune followed that of his good name, and he sank ere long into an early and unregretted grave.

The Scottish Brownie

The Scottish Brownie formed a class of beings distinct in habit and disposition from the freakish and mischievous Elves. He was meagre, shaggy, and wild in his appearance. In the daytime he lurked in remote recesses of the old houses which he delighted to haunt; and in the night sedulously employed himself in discharging any laborious task which he thought might be acceptable to the family to whose service he had devoted himself. But the Brownie does not drudge from the hope of recompense. On the contrary, so delicate is his attachment that the offer of reward, but particularly of food, infallibly occasions his disappearance for ever.

It is told of a Brownie, who haunted a Border family now extinct, that the lady having fallen unexpectedly in labour, and the servant, who was ordered to ride to Jedburgh for the sage femme, showing no great alertness in setting out, the familiar spirit slipt on the great-coat of the lingering domestic, rode to the town on the laird's best horse, and returned with the midwife en croupe. During the short space of his absence, the River Tweed, which they must necessarily ford, rose to a dangerous height. Brownie, who transported his charge with all rapidity, was not to be stopped by this obstacle. He plunged in with the terrified old lady, and landed her in safety where her services were wanted. Having put the horse into the stable (where it was afterwards found in a woeful plight), he proceeded to the room of the servant whose duty he had discharged, and, finding him just in the act of drawing on his boots, administered to him a most merciless drubbing with his own horsewhip. Such an important service excited the gratitude of the Laird, who, understanding the Brownie had been heard to express a wish to have a green coat, ordered a vestment of that colour to be made and left in his haunts. Brownie took away the green coat, but was never seen more. We may suppose that, tired of his domestic drudgery, he went in his new livery to join the Fairies.

The Brownie of Bodsbeck

The Brownie of the farmhouse of Bodsbeck, in Moffatdale, left his employment upwards of a century ago, on a similar account. He had exerted himself so much in the farm-labour, both in and out of doors, that Bodsbeck became the most prosperous farm in the district. He always took his meat as it pleased himself, usually in very moderate quantities, and of the most humble description. During a time of very hard labour, perhaps harvest, when a little better fare than ordinary might have been judged acceptable, the goodman took the liberty of leaving out a mess of bread and milk, thinking it but fair that at a time when some improvement, both in quantity and quality, was made upon the fare of the human servants, the useful Brownie should obtain a share in the blessing. He, however, found his error, for the result was that the Brownie left the house for ever exclaiming:

"Ca', Brownie, ca'
A' the luck o' Bodsbeck away to Leithenha'."

The luck of Bodsbeck accordingly departed with its Brownie, and settled in the neighbouring farmhouse called Leithenhall, whither the Brownie transferred his friendship and services.

The Bogle

This a freakish spirit, who delights rather to perplex and frighten mankind than either to serve or seriously to hurt them. Shellycoat, a spirit who resides in the waters, and has given his name to many a rock and stone upon the Scottish coast, belongs to the class of Bogles. When he appeared, he seemed to be decked with marine productions, and in particular with shells, whose clattering announced his approach. From this circumstance he derived his name. One of his pranks is thus narrated

Two men, on a very dark night, approaching the banks of the Ettrick, heard a doleful voice from its waves repeatedly exclaim, "Lost! Lost!" They followed the sound, which seemed to be the voice of a drowning person, and, to their infinite astonishment, they found that it ascended the river. Still they continued, during a long and tempestuous night, to follow the cry of the malicious sprite; and arriving, before morning's dawn, at the very sources of the river, the voice was now heard descending the opposite side of the mountain in which they arise. The fatigued and deluded travellers now relinquished the pursuit, and had no sooner done so than they heard Shellycoat applauding, in loud bursts of laughter, his successful roguery. The spirit was supposed particularly to haunt the old house of Gorinberry, situated on the River Hermitage, in Liddesdale.

The Doomed Rider

The Conan is as bonny a river as we hae in a' the north country. There's mony a sweet sunny spot on its banks, an' mony a time an' aft hae I waded through its shallows, whan a boy, to set my little scauting-line for the trouts an' the eels, or to gather the big pearl-mussels that lie sae thick in the fords. But its bonny wooded banks are places for enjoying the day in—no for passing the nicht. I kenna how it is; it's nane o' your wild streams that wander desolate through a desert country, like the Aven, or that come rushing down in foam and thunder, ower broken rocks, like the Foyers, or that wallow in darkness, deep, deep in the bowels o' the earth, like the fearfu' Auldgraunt; an' yet no ane o' these rivers has mair or frightfuller stories connected wi' it than the Conan. Ane can hardly saunter ower half-a-mile in its course frae where it leaves Contin till where it enters the sea, without passing ower the scene o' some frightful auld legend o' the Kelpie or the Waterwraith. And ane o' the most frightful looking o' these places is to be found among the woods of Conan House. Ye enter a swampy meadow that waves wi' flags an' rushes like a cornfield in harvest, an' see a hillock covered wi' willows rising like an island in the midst. There are thick mirk-woods on ilka side; the river, dark an' awesome, an' whirling round an' round in mossy eddies, sweeps away behind it; an' there is an auld burying-ground, wi' the broken ruins o' an auld Papist kirk, on the tap. Ane can see amang the rougher stanes the rose-wrought mullions of an arched window, an' the trough that ance held the holy water. About twa hunder years ago—a wee mair maybe, or a wee less, for ane canna be very sure o' the date o' thae old stories—the building was entire; an' a spot near it, whar the wood now grows thickest, was laid out in a cornfield. The marks o' the furrows may still be seen amang the trees.

A party o' Highlanders were busily engaged, ae day in harvest, in cutting down the corn o' that field; an' just aboot noon, when the sun shone brightest an' they were busiest in the work, they heard a voice frae the river exclaim, "The hour but not the man has come.' Sure enough, on looking round, there was the Kelpie stan'in' in what they ca' a fause ford, just fornent the auld kirk. There is a deep black pool baith above an' below, but i' the ford there's a bonny ripple, that shows, as ane might think, but little depth o' water; an' just i' the middle o' that, in a place where a horse might swim, stood the Kelpie. An' it again repeated its words, "The hour but not the man has come," an' then flashing though the water like a drake, it disappeared in the lower pool.

When the folk stood wondering what the creature might mean, they saw a man on horseback come spurring down the hill in hot haste, making straight for the fause ford. They could then understand her words at ance; an' four o' the stoutest o' them sprang oot frae amang the corn to warn him o' his danger, an' keep him back. An' sae they tauld him what they had seen an' heard, an' urged him either to turn back an' tak' anither road, or stay for an hour or sae where he was. But he just wadna hear them, for he was baith unbelieving an' in haste, an' wauld hae taen the ford for a' they could say, hadna the Highlanders, determined on saving him whether he would or no, gathered round him an' pulled him frae his horse, an' then, to mak' sure of him, locked him up in the auld kirk. Weel, when the hour had gone by—the fatal hour o' the Kelpie—they flung open the door, an' cried to him that he might noo gang on his journey. Ah, but there was nae answer, though; an' sae they cried a second time, an' there was nae answer still; and then they went in, an' found him lying stiff an' cauld on the floor, wi' his face buried in the water o' the very stone trough that we may still see amang the ruins. His hour had come, an' he had fallen in a fit, as twould seem, head-foremost amang the water o' the trough, where he had ben smothered—an' sae ye see, the prophecy o' the Kelpie availed naething."

Nuckelavee

Nuckelavee was a monster of unmixed malignity, never willingly resting from doing evil to mankind. He was a spirit in flesh. His home was the sea; and whatever his means of transit were in that element, when he moved on land he rode a horse as terrible in aspect as himself. Some thought that rider and horse were really one, and that this was the shape of the monster. Nuckelavee's head was like a man's, only ten times larger, and his mouth projected like that of a pig, and was enormously wide. There was not a hair on the monster's body, for the very good reason that he had no skin.

If crops were blighted by sea-gust or mildew, if livestock fell over high rocks that skirt the shores, or if an epidemic raged among men, or among the lower animals, Nuckelavee was the cause of all. His breath was venom, falling like blight on vegetable, and with deadly disease on animal life. He was also blamed for long-continued droughts; for some unknown reason he had serious objections to fresh water, and was never known to visit the land during rain.

I knew an old man who was credited with having once encountered Nuckelavee, and with having made a narrow escape from the monster's clutches. This man was very reticent on the subject. However, after much higgling and persuasion, the following narrative was extracted:

Tammie, like his namesake Tam o' Shanter, was out late one

night. It was, though moonless, a fine starlit night. Tammie's road lay close by the sea-shore, and as he entered a part of the road that was hemmed in on one side by the sea, and on the other by a deep freshwater loch, he saw some huge object in front of, and moving towards him. What was he to do? He was sure it was no earthly thing that was steadily coming towards him. He could not go to either side, and to turn his back to an evil thing he had heard was the most dangerous position of all; so Tammie said to himself, "The Lord be aboot me, an' tak' care o' me, as I am oot on no evil intent this night!" Tammie was always regarded as rough and foolhardy. Anyway, he determined, as the best of two evils, to face the foe, and so walked resolutely yet slowly forward.

He soon discovered to his horror that the gruesome creature approaching him was no other than the dreaded Nuckelavee. The lower part of this terrible monster, as seen by Tammie, was like a great horse with flappers like fins about his legs, with a mouth as wide as a whale's, from whence came breath like steam from a brewing-kettle. He had but one eye, and that as red as fire. On him sat, or rather seemed to grow from his back, a huge man with no legs, and arms that reached nearly to the ground. His head was as big as a clue of simmons (a clue of straw ropes, generally about three feet in diameter), and this huge head kept rolling from one shoulder to the other as if it meant to tumble off. But what to Tammie appeared most horrible of all, was that the monster was skinless—this utter want of skin adding much to the terrific appearance of the creature's naked body— the whole surface of it showing only red raw flesh, in which Tammie saw blood, black as tar, running through yellow veins, and great white sinews, thick as horse tethers, twisting, stretching, and contracting as the monster moved.

Tammie went slowly on in mortal terror, his hair on end, a cold sensation like a film of ice between his scalp and his skull, and a cold sweat bursting from every pore. But he knew it was useless to flee, and he said, if he had to die, he would rather see who killed him than die with his back to the foe. In all his terror Tammie remembered what he had heard of Nuckelavee's dislike of fresh water, and, therefore, took that side of the road nearest to the loch. The awful moment came when the lower part of the head of the monster got abreast of Tammie. The mouth of the monster yawned like a bottomless pit. Tammie found its hot breath like fire on his face; the long arms were stretched out to seize the unhappy man. To avoid, if possible, the monster's clutch, Tammie swerved as near as he could to the loch, splashing up some water on the foreleg of the monster, whereat the horse gave a snort like thunder and shied over to the other side of the road, and Tammie felt the wind of Nuckelavee's clutches as he narrowly escaped the monster's grip.

Tammie saw his opportunity, and ran with all his might; and sore need had he to run, for Nuckelavee had turned and was galloping after him, and bellowing with a sound like the roaring of the sea. In front of Tammie lay a rivulet, through which the surplus water of the loch found its way to the sea, and Tammie knew, if he could only cross the running water, he was safe; so he strained every nerve. As he reached the near bank another clutch was made at him by the long arms. Tammie made a desperate spring and reached the other side, leaving his bonnet in the monster's clutches. Nuckelavee gave a wild unearthly yell of disappointed rage as Tammie fell senseless on the safe side of the water.

The Witch of Laggan

The same day, another hero, celebrated for his hatred of witchcraft, was warming himself in his hunting hut, in the Forest of Gaick, in Badenoch. His faithful hounds, fatigued with the morning chase, lay stretched on the turf by his side; his gun, that would not miss, reclined in the neuk of the bothy; the skian dhu of the sharp edge hung by his side, and these alone constituted his company. As the hunter sat listening to the howling storm as it whistled by, there entered at the door an apparently poor weatherbeaten cat, shivering with cold, and drenched to the skin. On observing her, the hairs of the dogs became erected bristles, and they immediately rose to attack the pitiable cat, which stood trembling at the door

"Great hunter of the hills," exclaims the poor-looking trembling cat, "I claim your protection. I know your hatred to my craft, and perhaps it is just. Still spare, oh spare a poor jaded wretch, who thus flies to you for protection from the cruelty and oppression of her sisterhood."

Moved to compassion by her eloquent address, and disdaining to take advantage of his greatest enemy in such a seemingly forlorn situation, he pacified his infuriated dogs, and desired her to come forward to the fire and warm herself. "Nay," says she, "in the first place, you will please bind with this long hair those two furious hounds of yours, for I am afraid they will tear my poor hams to pieces. I pray you, therefore, my dear sir, that you would have the goodness to bind them together by the necks with this long hair." But the curious nature of the hair induced the hunter to dissemble a little. Instead of having bound his dogs with it, as he pretended, he threw it across a beam of wood which connected the couple of the bothy. The Witch then, supposing the dogs securely bound, approached the fire, and squatted herself down as if to dry herself. She had not sitten many minutes, when the hunter could easily discover a striking increase in her size, which he could not forbear remarking in a jocular manner to herself.

"A bad death to you, you nasty beast," says the hunter, "you are getting very large."

"Ay, ay," replied the cat equally jocosely, "as my hairs imbibe the heat, they naturally expand."

These jokes, however, were but a prelude to a more serious conversation. The cat, still continuing her growth, had at length attained a most extraordinary size, when, in the twinkling of an eye, she transformed herself into her proper likeness of the Goodwife of Laggan, and thus addressed him:

"Hunter of the Hills, your hour of reckoning is arrived. Behold me before you, the avowed champion of my devoted sisterhood, of whom Macgillichallum of Razay and you were always the most relentless enemies. But Razay is no more. His last breath is fled. He lies a lifeless corpse on the bottom of the main; and now, Hunter of the Hills, it is your turn."

With these words, assuming a most hideous and terrific appearance, she made a spring at the hunter. The two dogs, which she supposed securely bound by the infernal hair, sprung at her in her turn, and a most furious conflict ensued. The Witch, thus unexpectedly attacked by the dogs, now began to repent of her temerity. "Fasten, hair, fasten," she perpetually exclaimed, supposing the dogs to have been bound by the hair; and so effectually did the hair fasten, according to her order, that it at last snapt the beam in twain. At length, finding herself completely overpowered, she attempted a retreat, but so closely were the hounds fastened in her breasts, that it was with no small difficulty she could get herself disengaged from them.

Screaming and shrieking, the Wife of Laggan dragged herself out of the house, trailing after the dogs, which were fastened in her so closely that they never loosed their hold until she demolished every tooth in their heads. Then metamorphosing herself into the likeness of a raven she fled over the mountains in the direction of her home. The two faithful dogs, bleeding and exhausted, returned to their master, and, in the act of caressing his hand, both fell down and expired at his feet. Regretting their loss with a sorrow only known to the parent who weeps over the remains of departed children, he buried his devoted dogs, and returned home to his family.

His wife was not in the house when he arrived, but she soon made her appearance. "Where have you been, my love?" inquired the husband. "Indeed," replies she, "I have been seeing the Goodwife of Laggan, who has been just seized with so severe an illness that she is not expected to live for any time." "Ay! ay!" says he, "what is the matter with the worthy woman?" "She was all day absent in the moss at her peats," replies the wife, "and was seized with a sudden colic, in consequence of getting wet feet; and now all her friends and neighbours are expecting her demission." "Poor woman," says the husband, "I am sorry for her. Get me some dinner; it will be right that I should go and see her also."

Dinner being provided and despatched, the hunter immediately proceeded to the house of Laggan, where he found a great assemblage of neighbours mourning, with great sincerity, the approaching decease of a woman whom they all had hitherto esteemed virtuous. The hunter, walking up to the sick woman's bed in a rage, proportioned to the greatness of its cause, stripped the sick woman of all her coverings. A shriek from the now exposed Witch brought all the company around her. "Behold," says he, "the object of your solicitude, who is nothing less than an infernal Witch. Today, she informs me, she was present at the death of the Laird of Razay, and only a few hours have elapsed since she attempted to make me share his fate. This night, however, she shall expiate her crime by the forfeiture of her horrid life." Relating to the company the whole circumstances of her attack upon him, which were too well corroborated by the conclusive marks she bore on her person, the whole company were perfectly convinced of her criminality; and the customary punishment was about to be inflicted on her, when the miserable wretch addressed them as follows:

"My ill-requited friends, spare an old acquaintance, already in the agonies of death, from any further mortal degradation. My crimes and my folly now stare me in the face, in their true colours; while my vile and perfidious seducer, the enemy of your temporal and spiritual interests, only laughs at me in my distress; and, as a reward for my fidelity to his interest, in seducing everything that was amiable, and in destroying everything that was good, he is now about to consign my soul to eternal misery. Let my example be a warning to all the people of the earth to shun the fatal rock on which I have split; and as a strong inducement for them to do so I shall atone for my iniquity to the utmost of my ability by detailing to you the awful history of my life."

Here the Wife of Laggan detailed at full length the way she was seduced into the service of the Evil One,-all the criminal adventures in which she had been engaged, and ended with a particular account of the death of Macgillichallum of Razay, and her attack upon the hunter, and then she expired.

Meanwhile a neighbour of the Wife of Laggan was returning home late at night from Strathdearn, where he had been upon some business, and had just entered the dreary forest of Monalea, in Badenoch, when he met a woman dressed in black, who ran with great speed, and inquired of the traveller, with great agitation, how far she was distant from the churchyard of Dalarossie, and if she could be there by twelve o'clock. The traveller told her she might, if she continued to go at the same pace that she did then. She then fled alongst the road, uttering the most desponding lamentations, and the traveller continued his road to Badenoch. He had not, however, walked many miles when he met a large black dog, which travelled past him with much velocity, as if upon the scent of a track of footsteps; and soon after he met another large black dog sweeping along in the same manner. The last dog, however, was scarcely past, when he met a stout black man on a fine fleet black courser, prancing along in the same direction after the dogs. "Pray," says the rider to the traveller, "did you meet a woman as you came along the hill?" The traveller replied in the affirmative. "And did you meet a dog soon after?" rejoined the rider. The traveller replied he did. "And," added the rider, "do you think the dog will overtake her ere she can reach the church of Dalarossie?" "He will, at any rate, be very close upon her heels," answered the traveller. Each then took his own way. But before the traveller had got the length of Glenbanchar, the rider overtook him on his return with the foresaid woman before him across the bow of his saddle, and one of the dogs fixed in her breast, and another in her thigh. "Where did you overtake the woman?" inquired the traveller. "Just as she was entering the churchyard of Dalarossie," was his reply. On the traveller's return home, he heard of the fate of the unfortunate Wife of Laggan, which soon explained the nature of the company he had met on the road. It was, no doubt, the spirit of the Wife of Laggan flying for protection from the infernal spirits (to whom she had sold herself), to the churchyard of Dalarossie, which is so sacred a place that a Witch is immediately dissolved from all her ties with Satan on making a pilgrimage to it, either dead or alive. But it seems the unhappy Wife of Laggan was a stage too late.

The Blacksmith's
Wife of Yarrowfoot

Some years back, the blacksmith of Yarrowfoot had for apprentices two brothers, both steady lads, and, when bound to him, fine healthy fellows. After a few months, however, the younger of the two began to grow pale and lean, lose his appetite, and show other marks of declining health. His brother, much concerned, often questioned him as to what ailed him, but to no purpose. At last, however, the poor lad burst into an agony of tears, and confessed that he was quite worn-out, and should soon be brought to the grave through the ill-usage of his mistress, who was in truth a Witch, though none suspected it.

"Every night," he sobbed out, "she comes to my bedside, puts a magic bridle on me, and changes me into a horse. Then, seated on my back, she urges me on for many a mile to the wild moors, where she and I know not what other vile creatures hold their hideous feasts. There she keeps me all night, and at early morning I carry her home. She takes off my bridle, and there I am, but so weary I can ill stand. And thus I pass my nights while you are soundly sleeping."

The elder brother at once declared he would take his chance of a night among the Witches, so he put the younger one in his own place next the wall, and lay awake himself till the usual time of the Witch-woman's arrival. She came, bridle in hand, and flinging it over the elder brother's head, up sprang a fine hunting horse. The lady leaped on his back, and started for the trysting-place, which on this occasion, as it chanced, was the cellar of a neighbouring laird.

While she and the rest of the vile crew were regaling themselves with claret and sack, the hunter, who was left in a spare stall of the stable, rubbed and rubbed his head against the wall till he loosened the bridle, and finally got it off, on which he recovered his human form. Holding the bridle firmly in his hand, he concealed himself at the back of the stall till his mistress came within reach, when in an instant he flung the magic bridle over her head, and, behold, a fine grey mare! He mounted her and dashed off, riding through hedge and ditch, till, looking down, he perceived she had lost a shoe from one of her forefeet. He took her to the first smithy that was open, had the shoe replaced, and a new one put on the other forefoot, and then rode her up and down a ploughed field till she was nearly worn out. At last he took her home, and pulled the bridle off just in time for her to creep into bed before her husband awoke, and got up for his day's work.

The honest blacksmith arose, little thinking what had been going on all night; but his wife complained of being very ill, almost dying, and begged him to send for a doctor. He accordingly aroused his apprentices; the elder one went out, and soon returned with one whom he had chanced to meet already abroad. The doctor wished to feel his patient's pulse, but she resolutely hid her hands, and refused to show them. The village Esculapius was perplexed; but the husband, impatient at her obstinacy, pulled off the bedclothes, and found, to his horror, the horseshoes were tightly nailed to both hands! On further examination, her sides appeared galled with kicks, the same that the apprentice had given her during his ride up and down the ploughed field.

The brothers now came forward, and related all that had passed. On the following day the Witch was tried by the magistrates of Selkirk, and. condemned to be burned to death on a stone at the Bullsheugh, a sentence which was promptly carried into effect. It is added that the younger apprentice was at last restored to health by eating butter made from the milk of cows fed in kirkyards, a sovereign remedy for consumption brought on through being Witch-ridden.

The Missing Web of Linen

"Some time since, when calling at the house of one of my oldest parishioners, who had been a hand-loom weaver, he fell to speak of other days; and, amongst other things, he told me of the disappearance, some years back, on a fine summer's evening, of a web of linen which had been laid to bleach by the riverside at the foot of the glebe. The fishermen, it seems, were "burning the water" in the Skerry, and the man who had charge of the web went off to see the salmon "leistered", and on his return the web was gone. Of course there was a sensation. The story was soon in everybody's mouth, with abundant suspicions of as many persons as there were yards in the web of linen.

The web belonged to a very important personage, no less than the Howdie, or old village midwife, who was not disposed to sit down quietly under her loss. So she called in the aid of a wise man from Leitholm, and next day told her friend the weaver, my informant, that she had found the thief, for the wise man had turned the key. The weaver being anxious to see something of diablerie, the Howdie brought the wise man to his house; and the door being locked on all within (four in number), the magician proceeded as follows. He took a small key, and attached it to a string, which he tied into the family Bible at a particular place, leaving the key hanging out. Next he read two chapters from the Bible, one of which was the history of Saul and the Witch of Endor; he then directed the Howdie and another person to support the key between them, on the tips of their forefingers, and in that attitude the former was told to repeat the names of all the suspected parties.

Many persons were named, but the key still hung between the fingers, when the wise man cried out, "Why don't you say Jock Wilsop?" This was accordingly done, and immediately the key dropped, i.e., turned off the finger-ends. So the news spread far and wide that the thief was discovered, for the key had been turned and Jock Wilson was the man! He proved, however, not to be the man to stand such imputations, and being without doubt an honest fellow, he declared "he wudna be made a thief by the deevil." So he went to consult a lawyer, but after many long discussions the matter died away; and my authority, the weaver, says it was believed the lawyer was bribed, "for he aye likit a dram."

The Witches of Delnabo

In the time of my grandmother, the farm of Delnabo was proportionally divided between three tenants. At first equally comfortable in their circumstances, it was in the course of some time remarked by all, and by none more forcibly than by one of the said three portioners, that, although superior in point of industry and talent of his two fellow-portioners, one of the tenants was daily lapsing into poverty, while his two neighbours were daily improving in estate. Amazed and grieved at the adverse fortune which thus attended his family, compared to the prosperous condition of his neighbours, the wife of the poor man was in the habit of expressing her astonishment at the circumstance, not only to her own particular friends, but likewise to the wives of her neighbours themselves.

On one of these occasions, the other two wives asked her what would she do to ameliorate her condition, if it were in her power? She answered them she would do anything whatever. (Here the other wives thought they had got a gudgeon that would snap at any bait, and immediately resolved to make her their confidante.) "Well, then," says one of the other two wives, "if you agree to keep our communications strictly secret, and implicitly obey our instructions, neither poverty nor want shall ever assail you more." This speech of the other wife immediately impressed the poor man's wife with a strong suspicion of their real character. Dissembling all surprise at the circumstance, she promised to agree to all their conditions. She was then directed, when she went to bed that night, to carry along with her the floor broom, well known for its magical properties, which she was to leave by her husband's side in the course of the night, and which would represent her so exactly that the husband could not distinguish the difference in the morning. They at the same time enjoined her to discard all fears of detection, as their own husbands had been satisfied with those lovely substitutes (the brooms) for a great number of years. Matters being thus arranged, she was desired to join them at the hour of midnight, in order to accompany them to that scene which was to realise her future happiness.

Promising to attend to their instructions, the poor man's wife took leave of her neighbours, full of those sensations of horror which the discovery of such depravity was calculated to produce in a virtuous mind. Hastening home to her husband, she thought it no crime to break her promise to her wicked neighbours, and, like a dutiful and prudent wife, to reveal to the husband of her bosom the whole particulars of their interview. The husband greatly commended his wife's fidelity, and immediately entered into a collusion with her, which displays no ordinary degree of ingenuity. It was agreed that the husband should exchange apparel with the wife, and that he should, in this disguise, accompany the wives to the place appointed, to see what cantrips they intended to perform.

He accordingly arrayed himself in his wife's habiliments, and, at the the hour of midnight, joined the party at the place appointed. The "bride", as they called him, was most cordially received by the two Ladies of the Broom who warmly congratulated the bride upon her good fortune, and the speedy consummation of her happiness. He was then presented with a fir torch, a broom, and a riddle, articles with which they themselves were furnished. They directed their course along the banks of the rolling Avon, until they reached Craic-polnain, or the Craig of the Birds Pool. Here, in consequence of the steepness of the craig, they found it convenient to pass to the other side of the river. This passage they effected without the use of the navy, the river being fordable at the place. They then came in sight of Polnain, and lo, what human eye ever witnessed such a scene before! The pool appeared as if actually enveloped in a flame of fire. A hundred torches blazed aloft, reflecting their beams on the towering woods of Loynchork. And what ear ever heard such shrieks and yells as proceeded from the horrid crew engaged at their hellish orgies on Pol-nain? Those cried were, however, sweet music to the two Wives of Delnabo. Every yell produced from them a burst of unrestrained pleasure, and away they frisked, leaving the amiable bride a considerable way behind.

For the fact is, that he was in no hurry to reach the scene, and when he did reach it, it was with a determination to be only a spectator, and not a participator in the night's performance. On reaching the pool's side he saw what was going on—he saw abundance of hags steering themselves to and fro in their riddles, by means of their oars (the brooms), hallooing and skirting worse than the Bogles, and each holding in her left hand a torch of fir. Whilst at other times they would swirl themselves into a row, and make profound obeisance to a large black ugly tyke, perched on a lofty rock, and who was no doubt the "muckle thief" himself, and who was pleased to acknowledge most graciously those expressions of their loyalty and devotion, by bowing, grinning, and clapping his paws.

Having administered to the bride some preliminary instructions, the impatient wives desired him to remain by the pool's side until they should commune with his Satanic Highness on the subject of her inauguration, directing her, as they proceeded on their voyage across the pool, to speed them in their master's name. To this order of the black pair the bride was resolved to pay particular attention. As soon as they were embarked in their riddles, and had wriggled themselves, by means of their brooms, into a proper depth of water, "Go," says he, "in the name of the Beast." A horrid yell from the Witches announced their instant fate—the magic spell was now dissolved—crash went the riddle, and down sank the two Witches, never more to rise, amidst the shrieks and lamentations of the Old Thief and all his infernal crew, whose combined power and policy could not save them from a watery end. All the torches were extinguished in an instant, and the affrighted company fled in different directions, in such forms and similitudes as they thought most convenient for them to adopt; and the wily bride returned home at his leisure, enjoying himself vastly at the clever manner in which he had executed the instructions of his deceased friends. On arriving at his house, he dressed himself in his own clothes, and, without immediately satisfying his wife's curiosity at the result of his excursion, he yoked his cattle, and commenced his morning labours with as little concern as usual.

His two neighbours, who were not even conscious of the absence of their wives (so ably substituted were they by the brooms), did the same. Towards breakfast-time, however, the two neighbours were not a little astonished that they observed no signs of their wives having risen from bed—notwithstanding their customary earliness—and this surprise they expressed to the late bride, their neighbour. The latter archly remarked that he had great suspicions, in his own mind, of their rising ever that day. "What mean you by that?" replied they. "We left our wives apparently in good health when we ourselves arose." "Find them now," was the reply—the bride setting up as merry a whistle as before. Running each to his bed, what was the astonishment of the husbands, when, instead of his wife, he only found an old broom? Their neighbour then told them that, if they chose to examine Polnain well, they would find both their dear doxies there. The grieving husbands accordingly proceeded thither, and with the necessary instruments dragged their late worthy partners to dry land, and afterwards privately interred them. The shattered vessels and oars of those unfortunate navigators, whirling about the pool, satisfied their lords of the manner by which they came to their ends; and their names were no longer mentioned by their kindred in the land. It need scarcely be added that the poor man gradually recovered his former opulence; and that, in the course of a short time, he was comparatively as rich as he was formerly poor.

The Old Lady of Littledean

The old tower of Littledean, on Tweedside, had long been haunted by the spirit of an old lady, once its mistress, who had been a covetous, grasping woman, and oppressive to the poor. Tradition averred that she had amassed a large sum of money by thrift or extortion, and now could not rest in her grave because of it. Spite of its ghost, however, Littledean Tower was inhabited by a Laird and his family, who found no fault with their place of abode, and were not much troubled by thoughts of the supernatural world.

One Saturday evening, however, a servant girl, who was cleaning shoes in the kitchen by herself, suddenly observed an Elf-light shining on the floor. While she gazed on it, it disappeared, and in its place stood an old woman wrapped in a brown cloak, who muttered something about being cold, and asked to warm herself at the fire. The girl readily consented, and seeing that her visitor's shoes were wet, and her toes peeping out blue and cold from their tips, she good-naturedly offered to dry and clean the shoes, and did so. The old lady, touched by this attention, confessed herself frankly to be the apparition that haunted the house. "My gold wudna let me rest," said she, "but I'll tell ye where it lies; 'tis 'neath the lowest step o' the Tower stairs. Take the Laird there, an' tell him what I now tell ye; then dig up the treasure, and put it in his hands. An' tell him to part it in two shares: one share let him keep, for he's master here now; the other share he maun part again, and gie half to you, for ye are a kind lassie and a true, and half he maun gie to the poor o' Maxton, the auld folk an' the fatherless bairns, and them that need it most. Do this an' I sall rest in my grave, where I've no rested yet; and never will I trouble the house mair till the day o' doom." The girl rubbed her eyes, looked again, and behold the old woman was gone!

Next morning the young servant took her master to the spot which had been indicated to her, and told him what had taken place. The stone was removed, and the treasure discovered, and divided according to the instructions given. The Laird, being blessed with a goodly family of sturdy lads and smiling maidens, found no difficulty in disposing of his share. The servant-girl, so richly dowered, found a good husband ere the year had passed. The poor of Maxton, for the first time in their lives, blessed the old lady of Littledean; and never was the ancient tower troubled again by ghost or apparition.

The Island Cave

More than a couple of hundred years ago, "Dhonnocha Reamhar", or "Stout Duncan", a near kinsman to M'Donald of Glengarry, immured and confined his wife, a daughter of M'Donald, Lord of the Isles, within a cave on an island in Loch Chon. The lady, who was both young and beautiful, had brought him, though their union, large tracts of land in the shires of Argyle and Ross. Dhonnocha Reamhar, who was then well advanced in years, and who had led a lawless life all his days, appropriated the prize greedily. Resembling in character Rob Roy, or Robin Hood, he considered nothing to become him ill, and various charges of hame-sucken and cattle-lifting were brought against him. Of a wild and roving disposition, he would never remain at rest, but was continually engaged in fighting, plundering and robbing the neighbouring clans.

Once, when hotly pursued by a party of M'Phersons in Rannoch, he came to the River Erichty, and finding it in full spate, swollen with recent rains, gave himself up for lost. Nevertheless, he started afresh, and, nothing daunted, ran down the river's edge until he reached a bend in the stream, where it takes a sharp and sudden turn. On either side were steep rocks, rising perpendicular from the water, and about sixteen feet apart. Between the rocks the water rushed with great velocity, throwing the foam and spray high into the air. Dhonnocha

Reamhar quailed before the means of escape, but was resolved at all hazards to make a desperate attempt for freedom. Rather than fall into the hands of the enemy, he determined there and then to leap into the roaring torrent, and so end for ever his warfare. Taking a run of a few yards, and leaping high into the air, he cleared the chasm, and landed safe on the opposite side. Having thus obtained a footing, he turned round upon his pursuers, defied them, and laughed them to scorn. Enraged beyond measure, the baffled enemy retired in disgust.

Shortly after this event his marriage took place. It proved a very unhappy one. Growing tired of the society of his wife, he resolved to get rid of her at once and for ever. Having chosen the island cave of Loch Chon as a fit place to perpetrate his awful and bloodthirsty deed, he succeeded, by wiles and other means known only to himself, in inducing his wife to accompany him in an expedition to the loch. On their arrival, he persuaded her to enter the cave, where, without a word of warning, he suddenly overpowered her and left her to perish. On his way out he blocked up the mouth of the cavern with stones, and, fearful lest the deed should be discovered, obliterated all trace of footprints in and around the cave's mouth. The island is only about fifteen yards from the shore of the loch, and is thickly studded with trees. All traces of the cave are now lost; but it is supposed to lie towards the west end, where the ground is very rocky. Times without number have I endeavoured to ascertain its whereabouts, but have always failed to discover it. Tradition declares that the lady was never seen again alive; but to this day her wraith is said to haunt the lonely shore of Loch Chon.

Dhonnocha Reamhar's Leap is about a mile and a half from Loch Chon, and about a quarter of a mile west from the junction of the Ault-na-Chon burn with the River Erichty. The rocks on either side of the stream, where he performed his remarkable feat, are now well worn with the inroads of the river; but they are still, as of old, lofty and dangerous.

The Spectre Piper

During the rebellion of 1745-46, in Prince Charles Edward Stuart's retreat, from Derby, the main body of his Highlanders were compelled, on their northward march through Badenoch, to make a short halt in the wild pass of Drumouchtdar, in order to enable the rear and other stragglers of the ill-fated army to overtake them. Being sorely harassed by a party of English cavalry, the men began to murmur and grumble at the Prince's stubbornness in not giving them permission to dislodge the horsemen, and at his seeming unwillingness to give the order to charge.

The unfortunate Prince, not wishing to risk a combat with the fresh and well-trained dragoons, owing to the deplorable condition of his own men, endeavoured to reason them out of such an insane idea, and explained to the best of his ability the utter foolishness of the strategic move in question. But the eager Highlanders paid no attention to his counsel, and determined on their own account to assail the enemy. Resolving at all hazards to dislodge them from the position they occupied on the hill, they straightway prepared for action, and about midday marched to the attack. The assaulting party consisted of two regiments of infantry—the clans M'Donald and M'Pherson—while the enemy mustered about six hundred men.

The battle commenced, and great was the carnage, as the

dismounted cavalry, in expectation of an attack, had during the night constructed earthworks and dug trenches. Every available stone and boulder had in this way been piled up to repel the onslaught of the fierce Gaels, who charged with terrible force, hewing and slashing everything that came in their way, and destroying all and sundry who impeded their progress. Savage and grim, they were determined either to conquer or die; and, charging again and again, they at last with difficulty gained a footing within the trenches. Once there, the dirk and claymore soon decided the fortune of the day, and eventually the enemy, completely routed, fled in all directions. Hamstringing the horses, the Celts immediately started in pursuit, and cut down the fugitives to a man. The last man of the English who met his death at the point of a Highland claymore fell on the banks of the Ault-na-Sassenach, or Englishman's burn. The burn is called by that name to this day; and the spot where the last survivor was killed is marked by an upright stone erected in the moss, about nine yards from the edge of the stream.

And it is said that persons who chance to pass over the moor at the hour of gloaming are suddenly startled by the wailing of a bagpipe, but find it impossible to tell from whence comes the melancholy strain. People also aver that, in the twilight, other sounds no less strange and weird are heard, and that spectres are seen engaged in mortal combat on the site of the old battleground. Various antique relics—claymores, dirks, musket-barrels, and the like—have been found in and about the trenches, a few of which I have myself seen.

Prince Charlie's Cave

On the summit of Meilchan, about three hundred yards off the main road between Rannoch and Dalnacardoch, is to be found a cave, where the bonnie but unfortunate Prince Charles Edward Stuart is said to have lurked previous to his embarkation for France. After the terrible massacre on Culloden (locally better known by the name of Drumossie) Moor, he wandered through the Highlands like a hare before the hounds. Pursued by the terrible sleuth-hounds of the Duke of Cumberland, he experienced many hair's-breadth escapes, and was several times on the point of being captured. But it is unnecessary for me here to dwell upon the unlucky Prince's many adventures. Enough to say that, hard pressed and hunted as he was, he succeeded in eluding his enemies, and the following year escaped to France. Over the length and breadth of Scotland the name of "Bonnie Prince Charlie" is a household word; and over all Albyn his fame is handed down in song and in story.

Prince Charlie's cave is situated on the summit of a small green hillock, and is composed of solid limestone rock. It is rather a difficult and hazardous matter to obtain access to it, the mouth of the cavern being flooded with water, and the arched entrance exceedingly low.

A young gentleman, a member of a shooting-party, then volunteered to enter it; and, with that object in view, started to creep on hands and knees into the cavern.

His exit was more rapid than his entrance, and he made his reappearance before his companions, pale and trembling. On being asked what he had heard or seen, he declared that he had beheld, crouching at the further end of the cave, the figure of a tall, lean man, dressed in the Highland garb; who had appeared to threaten him should he offer to penetrate further into the cavern.

Tradition says the cave possesses more than one entrance, the other being away in the direction of Loch Chon. Situated as it is, on mossy and treacherous ground, very few people trouble to visit the spot, notwithstanding the amount of interest which clings to it.

Adam Bell

This tale, which may be depended on as in every part true, is singular, from the circumstance of its being insolvable, either from the facts that have been discovered relating to it, or by reason; for though events sometimes occur among mankind, which at the time seem inexplicable, yet there being always some individuals acquainted with the primary causes of these events, they seldom fail of being brought to light before all the actors in them, or their confidants, are removed from this state of existence. But the causes which produced the events here related have never been accounted for in this world; even conjecture is left to wander in a labyrinth, unable to get hold of the thread that leads to the catastrophe.

Mr. Bell was a gentleman of Annandale, in Dumfriesshire, in the south of Scotland, and proprietor of the considerable estate in that district, part of which he occupied himself. He lost his father when he was an infant, and his mother, dying when he was about twenty years of age, left him the sole proprietor of the estate, besides a large sum of money at interest, for which he was indebted, in a great measure, to his mother's parsimony during his minority. His person was tall, comely, and athletic, and his whole delight was in war like and violent exercises. He was the best horseman and marksman in the county, and valued himself particularly upon his skill in the broadsword. Of this he often boasted aloud, and regretted that there was not one in the county whose skill was in some degree equal to his own.

In the autumn of 1745, after being for several days busily and silently employed in preparing for his journey, he left his own house, and went to Edinburgh, giving at the same time such directions to his servants as indicated his intention of being absent for some time.

A few days after he had left his home, one morning, while his housekeeper was putting the house in order for the day, her master, as she thought, entered by the kitchen door, the other being bolted, and passed her in the middle of the floor. He was buttoned in his greatcoat, which was the same he had on when he went from home; he likewise had the same hat on his head, and the same whip in his hand which he took with him. At sight of him she uttered a shriek, but recovering her surprise, instantly said to him, "You have not stayed so long from us, Sir." He made no reply, but went sullenly into his own room, without throwing off his greatcoat. After a pause of about five minutes, she followed him into the room. He was standing at his desk with his back towards her. She asked him if he wished to have a fire kindled, and afterwards if he was well enough; but he still made no reply to any of these questions. She was astonished, and returned into the kitchen. After tarrying about another five minutes, he went out of the front door, it being then open, and walked deliberately towards the bank of the River Kinnel, which was deep and wooded, and in that he vanished from her sight.

The woman ran out in the utmost consternation to acquaint the men who were servants belonging to the house; and coming to one of the ploughmen, she told him that their master was come home, and had certainly lost his reason, for that he was wandering about the house and would not speak. The man loosed his horses from the plough and came home, listened to the woman's relation, made her repeat it again and again, and then assured her that she was raving, for their master's horse was not in the stable, and of course he could not be come home. However, as she persisted in her asseveration with every appearance of sincerity, he went into the linn to see what was become of his mysterious master. He was neither to be seen nor heard of in the country. It was then concluded that the housekeeper had seen an apparition, and that something had befallen their master; but on consulting with some old people, skilled in these matters, they learned that when a "wraith", or apparition of a living person, appeared while the sun was up, instead of being a prelude of instant death, it prognosticated very long life; and, moreover, that it could not possibly be a ghost that she had seen, for they always chose the night season for making their visits. In short, though it was the general topic of conversation among the servants and the people in the vicinity, no reasonable conclusion could be formed on the subject.

The most probable conjecture was that as Mr. Bell was known to be so fond of arms, and had left his home on the very day that Prince Charles Stuart and his Highlanders defeated General Hawley on Falkirk Muir, he had gone either with him or the Duke of Cumberland to the north. It was, however, afterwards ascertained that he had never joined any of the armies. Week passed after week, and month after month, but no word of Mr. Bell. A female cousin was his nearest living relation; her husband took the management of his affairs; and concluding that he had either joined the army, or drowned himself in the Kinnel, when he was seen going into the linn, made no more inquiries after him.

About this very time, a respectable farmer, whose surname was M'Millan, and who resided in the neighbourhood of Musselburgh, happened to be in Edinburgh about some business. In the evening he called upon a friend who lived near Holyrood House; and being seized with an indisposition, they persuaded him to tarry with them all night. About the middle of the night he grew exceedingly ill, and not being able to find any rest or ease in his bed, imagined he would be the better of a walk. He put on his clothes, and, that he might not disturb the family, slipped quietly out at the back door, and walked in St. Anthony's Garden behind the house. The moon shone so bright, that it was almost as light as noonday, and he had scarcely taken a single turn, when he saw a tall man enter from the other side, buttoned in a drab-coloured greatcoat. It so happened that at that time M'Millan stood in the shadow of the wall, and perceiving that the stranger did not observe him, a thought struck him that it would not be amiss to keep himself concealed, that he might see what the man was going to be about. He walked backwards and forwards for some time in apparent impatience, looking at his watch every minute, until at length another man came in by the same way, buttoned likewise in a greatcoat, and having a bonnet on his head. He was remarkably stout made, but considerably lower in stature than the other. They exchanged only a single word; then turning both about, they threw off their coats, drew their swords, and began a most desperate and well-contested combat.

The tall gentleman appeared to have the advantage. He constantly gained ground on the other, and drove him half round the division of the garden in which they fought. Each of them strove to fight with his back towards the moon, so that it might shine full in the face of his opponent; and many rapid wheels were made for the purpose of gaining this position. The engagement was long and obstinate, and by the desperate thrusts that were frequently aimed on both sides, it was evident that they meant one another's destruction. They came at length within a few yards of the place where M'Millan still stood concealed. They were both out of breath, and at that instant a small cloud chancing to overshadow the moon, one of them called out, "Hold, we cannot see." They uncovered their heads, wiped their faces, and as soon as the moon emerged from the cloud, each resumed his guard. Surely that was an awful pause! And short, indeed, was the stage between it and eternity with the one! The tall gentleman made a lounge at the other, who parried and returned it; and as the former sprung back to avoid the thrust, his foot slipped, and he stumbled forward towards his antagonist, who dextrously met his breast in the fall with the point of his sword, and ran him through the body. He made only one feeble convulsive struggle, as if attempting to rise, and expired almost instantaneously.

M'Millan was petrified with horror; but conceiving himself to be in a perilous situation, having stolen out of the house at that dead hour of the night, he had so much presence of mind as to hold his peace, and to keep from interfering in the smallest degree.

The surviving combatant wiped his sword with great composure, put on his bonnet, covered the body with one of the greatcoats, took up the other, and departed. M'Millan returned quietly to his chamber without awakening any of the family. His pains were gone, but his mind was shocked and exceedingly perturbed; and after deliberating until morning, he determined to say nothing of the matter, and to make no living creature acquainted with what he had seen, thinking that suspicion would infallibly rest on him. Accordingly, he kept his bed next morning, until his friend brought him the tidings that a gentleman had been murdered at the back of the house during the night. He then arose and examined the body, which was that of a young man, seemingly from the country, having brown hair, and fine manly features. He had neither letter, book, nor signature of any kind about him that could in the least lead to a discovery of who he was; only a common silver watch was found in his pocket, and an elegant sword was clasped in his cold bloody hand, which had an A. and B. engraved on the hilt. The sword had entered at his breast, and gone out at his back a little below the left shoulder. He had likewise received a slight wound on the sword arm.

The body was carried to the dead-room, where it lay for eight days, and though great numbers inspected it, yet none knew who or whence the deceased was, and he was at length buried among the strangers in Greyfriars Churchyard.

Sixteen years elapsed before M'Millan mentioned to any person the circumstance of his having seen the duel, but at that period, being in Annandale receiving some sheep that he had bought, and chancing to hear of the astonishing circumstances of Bell's disappearance, he divulged the whole. The time, the description of his person, his clothes, and, above all, the sword with the initials of his name engraved upon it, confirmed the fact beyond the smallest shadow of doubt that it was Mr. Bell whom he had seen killed in the duel behind the Abbey. But who the person was that slew him, how the quarrel commenced, or who it was that appeared to his housekeeper, remains to this day a profound secret, and is likely to remain so, until that day when every deed of darkness shall be brought to light.

Some have even ventured to blame M'Millan for the whole, on account of his uncommon bodily strength and daring disposition, he being one of the boldest and most enterprising men of the age in which he lived; but all who knew him despised such insinuations, and declared them to be entirely inconsistent with his character, which was most honourable and disinterested; and besides, his tale has every appearance of truth.

The Winding Sheet

I was resolved to pay a visit to an English gentleman, Sir William Sacheverill, who had a commission from the English Court of Admiralty to give his best trial to find out gold or money, or any other thing of note, in one of the ships of the Spanish Armada, that was blown up in the bay of Tobbermory, in the Sound of Mull. And having condescended upon the number of men that were to go with me, one of the number was a handsome boy that waited upon my own person; and, about an hour before I made sail, a woman, that was also one of my own servants, spoke to one of the seamen, and bade him to dissuade me to take that boy along with me, or if I did I should not bring him back alive; the seaman answered, he had not confidence to tell me such unwarrantable trifles.

I took my voyage, and sailed the length of Tobbermory; and having stayed two or three nights with that liberal and ingenuous gentleman, who himself had collected many observations of the Second Sight in the Isle of Man, and compared his notes and mine together, I then took leave of him. In the meantime my boy grew sick of a vehement bloody flux, the winds turned cross, that I could neither sail nor row, and the boy died with me the eleventh night from his decumbiture. The next morning the wind made fair, and the seaman to whom the matter was foretold related the whole story when he saw it verified. I carried the boy's corpse aboard with me, and after my arrival, and his burial, I called suddenly for the woman, and asked her what warrant she had to foretell the boy's death. She said that she had no other warrant but that she saw, two days before I took my voyage, the boy walking with me in the fields, sewed up in his winding sheets from top to toe, and that she had never seen this in others but she found that they shortly thereafter died; and therefore concluded that he would die too, and that shortly.

The Tale of the Shifty Lad, the Widow's Son

There was at some time or other before now a widow, and she had one son. She gave him good schooling, and she was wishful that he should choose a trade for himself; but he said he would not go to learn any art, but that he would be a thief.

His mother said to him, "If that is the art that thou art going to choose for thine ownself, thine end is to be hanged at the Bridge of Baile Cliabh, in Eirinn."

But it was no matter, he would not go to any art, but to be a thief; and his mother was always making a prophecy to him that the end for him would be, hanging at the Bridge of Baile Cliabh, in Eirinn.

On a day of the days, the widow was going to the church to hear the sermon, and was asking the Shifty Lad, her son, to go with her, and that he should give over his bad courses; but he would not go with her, but said to her, "The first art of which thou hearest mention, after thou hast come out of the sermon, is the art to which I will go afterwards."

She went to the church full of good courage, hoping that she would hear some good thing.

He went away, and he went to a tuft of wood that was near to the church; and he went into hiding in a place where he could see his mother when she should come out of the church; and as soon as she came out he shouted, "Thievery! Thievery! Thievery!" She looked about, but she could not make out whence the voice was coming, and she went home. He ran by the way of a short cut, and he was at the house before her, and he was seated within beside the fire when she came home. He asked her what tale she had got; and she said that she had not got any tale at all, but that "Thievery, thievery, thievery!" was the first speech she heard when she came out of the church.

He said, "That was the art that he would have."

And she said, as she was accustomed to say, "Thine ending is to be hanged at the Bridge of Baile Cliabh, in Eirinn."

On the next day, his mother herself thought that, as nothing at all would do for her son but that he should be a thief, she would try to find him a good aid-to-learning; and she went to the Black Gallows Bird of Aachaloinne, a very cunning thief who was in that place; and though they had knowledge that he was given to stealing, they were not finding any way for catching him. The widow asked the Black Rogue if he would take her son to teach him roguery. The Black Rogue said that if he were a clever lad that he would take him, and if there were a way of making a thief of him that he could do it; and a covenant was made between the Black Rogue and the Shifty Lad.

When the Shifty Lad, the widow's son, was making ready for going to the Black Rogue, his mother was giving him counsel, and she said to him, "It is against my will that thou art going to thievery; and I was telling thee, that the end of thee is to be hanged at the Bridge of Baile Cliabh, Eirinn." But the Shifty Lad went home to the Black Rogue.

The Black Rogue was giving the Shifty Lad every knowledge he might for doing thievery; he used to tell him about the cunning things that he must do to get a chance to steal a thing; and when the Black Rogue thought that the Shifty Lad was good enough at learning to be taken out with him, he used to take him to do stealing; and on a day of these days the Black Rouge said to his lad:

"We are long enough thus, we must go and do something. There is a rich tenant near to us, and he has much money in his chest. It was he who bought all that there was of cattle to be sold in the country, and he took them to the fair, and he sold them; he has got the money in this chest, and this is the time to be at him, before the people are paid for their lot of cattle; and unless we go to seek the money at this very hour, when it is gathered together, we shall not get the same chance again."

The Shifty Lad was as willing as himself; they went away to the house; they got in at the coming on of the night, and they went up upon the loft, and went in hiding up there. It was the night of Savain (Hallowe'en); and there assembled many people within to keep the Savain hearty as they used to do. They sat together, and they were singing songs, and at fun burning the nuts, and at merrymaking.

The Shifty Lad was wearying that the company was not scattering; he got up and he went down to the byre, and he loosed the bands off the necks of the cattle, and he returned and he went up upon the loft again. The cattle began goring each other in the byre, and roaring. All that were in the room ran to keep the cattle from each other till they could be tied again; and in the time while they were doing this, the Shifty Lad went down to the room and he stole the nuts with him, and he went up upon the loft again, and he lay down at the back of the Black Rogue.

There was a great leathern hide at the back of the Black Rogue, and the Shifty Lad had a needle and thread, and he sewed the skirt of the Black Rogue's coat to the leathern hide that was at his back; and when the people of the house came back to the dwelling-room again, their nuts were away; and they were seeking their nuts; and they thought that it was some one who had come into play them a trick that had taken away their nuts, and they sat down at the side of the fire quietly and silently.

Said the Shifty Lad to the Black Rogue, "I will crack a nut."

"Thou shalt not crack one," said the Black Rogue, "they will hear thee, and we shall be caught."

Said the Shifty Lad, "I never yet was a Savain night without cracking a nut," and he cracked one.

Those who were seated in the dwelling-room heard him, and they said "There is some one up in the loft cracking our nuts; we will go and catch them."

When the Black Rogue heard that, he sprang off the loft and he ran out, and the hide dragging at the tail of his coat. Every one of them shouted that there was the Black Rogue stealing the hide with him. The Black Rogue fled, and the people of the house after him; and he was a great distance from the house before he got the hide torn from him, and was able to leave them. But in the time that the people of the house were running after the Black Rogue, the Shifty Lad came down off the loft; he went up about the house, he hit upon the chest where the gold and the silver was; he opened the chest, and he took out of it the bags in which the gold and silver was and he took with him a load of the bread, and of the butter, and of the cheese, and of everything that was better than another which he found within; and he was gone before the people of the house came back from chasing the Black Rogue.

When the Black Rogue reached his home, and he had nothing, his wife said to him, "How hast thou failed this journey?"

Then the Black Rogue told his own tale; and he was in great fury at the Shifty Lad, and swearing that he would serve him out when he got a chance at him.

Said the wife of the Black Rogue, "But I fancy that thou art the better thief!"

The Black Rogue said not a word till the Shifty Lad showed the bags that he had full of gold and silver; then said the Black Rogue, "But it is thou that wert the smart lad!"

They made two halves of the gold and silver, and the Black Rogue got the one half, and the Shifty Lad the other half. When the Black Rogue's wife saw the share that came to them, she said, "Thou thyself art the worthy thief!" and she had more respect for him after that than she had for the Black Rogue himself.

The Black Rogue and the Shifty Lad went on stealing till they had got much money, and they thought that they had better buy a drove of cattle, and go to the fair with it to sell, and that people would think that it was at drovering they had made the money that they had got. The two went, and they bought a great drove of cattle, and they went to a fair that was far on the way from them. They sold the drove, and they got the money for them, and they went away to go home. When they were on the way, they saw a gallows on the top of a hill, and the Shifty Lad said to the Black Rogue, "Come up till we see the gallows; some say that the gallows is the end for the thieves at all events."

They went up where the gallows was, and they were looking all about it. Said the Shifty Lad, "Might we not try what kind of death is in the gallows, that we may know what is before us, if we should be caught at roguery. I will try it myself first."

The Shifty Lad put the cord about his own neck, and he said to the Black Rogue, "Here, draw me up, and when I am tired above I will shake my legs, and then do thou let me down."

The Black Rogue drew the cord, and he raised the Shifty Lad aloft off the earth, and at the end of a little blink the Shifty Lad shook his legs, and the Black Rogue let him down.

The Shifty Lad took the cord off his neck, and he said to the Black Rogue, "Thou thyself hast not ever tried anything that is so funny as hanging. If thou wouldst try once, thou wouldst have no more fear for hanging. I was shaking my legs for delight, and thou wouldst shake thy leg for delight too if thou wert aloft."

Said the Black Rogue, "I will try it too, so that I may know what it is like."

"Do," said the Shifty Lad, "and when thou art tired above, whistle and I will let thee down."

The Black Rogue put the cord about his neck, and the Shifty Lad drew him up aloft; and when the Shifty Lad found that the Black Rogue was aloft against the gallows, he said to him, "Now, when thou wantest to come down, whistle, and if thou art well pleased where thou art, shake thy legs."

When the Black Rogue was a little blink above, he began to shake his legs and to kick; and the Shifty Lad would say, "Oh! Art thou not funny! Art thou not funny! Art thou not funny! When it seems to thee that thou art long enough above, whistle."

But the Black Rogue has not whistled yet. The Shifty Lad tied the cord to the lower end of the tree of the gallows till the Black Rogue was dead; then he went where he was, and he took the money out of his pouch, and he said to him, "Now, since thou hast no longer any use for this money, I will take care of it for thee." And he went away, and he left the Black Rogue hanging there. Then he went home where was the house of the Black Rogue, and his wife asked where was his master?

The Shifty Lad said, "I left him where he was, upraised above the earth."

The wife of the Black Rogue asked and asked him about her man, till at last he told her; but he said to her, that he would marry her himself. When she heard that, she cried that the Shifty Lad had killed his master, and he was nothing but a thief. When the Shifty Lad heard that he fled. The chase was set after him; but he found means to go in hiding in a cave, and the chase went past him. He was in the cave all night, and the next day he went another way, and he founds means to fly to Eirinn.

He reached the house of a wright, and he cried at the door, "Let me in."

"Who art thou?" said the wright.

"I am a good wright, if thou hast need of such," said the Shifty Lad.

The wright opened the door, and he let in the Shifty Lad, and the Shifty Lad began to work at carpentering along with the wright.

When the Shifty Lad was a day or two in their house, he gave a glance thither and a glance hither about the house, and he said, "O choin! What a poor house you have, and the King's storehouse so near you."

"What of that?" said the wright.

"It is," said the Shifty Lad, "that you might get plenty from the King's storehouse if you yourselves were smart enough."

The wright and his wife would say, "They would put us in prison if we should begin at the like of that."

The Shifty Lad was always saying that they ought to break into the King's storehouse, and they would find plenty in it; but the wright would not go with him; but the Shifty Lad took with him some of the tools of the wright, and he went himself and he broke into the King's storehouse, and he took with him a load of the butter and of the cheese of the King, and he took it to the house of the wright. The things pleased the wife of the wright well, and she was willing that her own husband should go there the next night. The wright himself went with his lad the next night, and they got into the storehouse of the King, and they took with them great loads of each thing that pleased them best of all that was within the King's storehouse.

But the king's people missed the butter and the cheese and the other things that had been taken out of the storehouse, and they told the King how it had happened.

The King took the counsel of the Seanagal about the best way of catching the thieves, and the counsel that the Seanagal gave them was that they should set a hogshead of soft pitch under the hole where they were coming in. That was done, and the next night the Shifty Lad and his master went to break into the King's storehouse.

The Shifty Lad put his master in before him, and the master went down into the soft pitch to his very middle, and he could not get out again. The Shifty Lad went down, and he put a foot on each of his master's shoulders, and he put out two loads of the King's butter and of the cheese at the hole; and at the last time when he was coming out, he swept the head off his master, and he took the head with him, and he left the trunk in the hogshead of pitch, and he went home with the butter and with the cheese, and he took home the head, and he buried it in the garden.

When the King's people went in to the storehouse, they found a body without a head into the hogshead of pitch; but they could not make out who it was. They tried if they could find any one at all that could know him by the clothes, but his clothes were covered with pitch so that they could not make him out. The King asked the counsel of the Seanagal about it; and the counsel that the Seanagal gave was, that they should set the trunk aloft on the points of the spears of the soldiers, to be carried from town to town, to see if they could find any one at all that would take sorrow for it; or to try if they could hear any one that would make a painful cry when they should see it; or if they should not see one that should seem about to make a painful cry when the soldiers should be going past with it. The body was taken out of the hogshead of pitch, and set on the points of the spears; and the soldiers were bearing it aloft on the points of their long wooden spears, and they were going from town to town with it; and when they were going past the house of the wright, the wright's wife made a tortured scream and swift the Shifty Lad cut himself with the adze; and he kept saying to the wright's wife, "The cut is not as bad as thou thinkest."

The commander-in-chief, and his lot of soldiers, came in and they asked,

"What ailed the housewife?"

Said the Shifty Lad, "It is that I have just cut my foot with the adze, and she is afraid of blood." And he would say to the wife of the wright, "Do not be so much afraid; it will heal sooner than thou thinkest."

The soldiers thought that the Shifty Lad was the wright, and that the wife whom they had seen was the wife of the Shifty Lad; and they went out, and they went from town to town; but they found no one besides, but the wife of the wright herself, that made cry or scream when they were coming past her.

They took the body home to the King's house; and the King took another counsel from his Seanagal, and that was to hang the body to a tree in an open place, and soldiers to watch it that none should take it away, and the soldiers to be looking if any should come the way that should take pity or grief for it.

The Shifty Lad came past them, and he saw them; he went and he got a horse, and he put a keg of whisky on each side of the horse in a sack, and he went past the soldiers with it, as though he were hiding from them. The soldiers thought that it was so, or that he had taken something which he ought not to have; and some of them ran after him, and they caught the old horse and the whisky; but the Shifty Lad fled, and he left the horse and the whisky with them. The soldiers took the horse and the kegs of whisky back to where the body was hanging against the mast. They looked what was in the kegs; and when they understood that it was whisky that was in them, they got a drinking cup, and they began drinking until at last every one of them was drunk, and they lay and they slept. When the Shifty Lad saw that, that the soldiers were laid down and asleep and drunk, he returned and took the body off the mast. He set it crosswise on the horse's back, and he took it home; then he went and he buried the body in the garden where the head was

When the soldiers awoke out of their sleep, the body was stolen away; they had nothing for it but to go and tell it to the King. Then the King took the counsel of the Seanagal; and the Seanagal said to them, all that were in his presence, that his counsel to them was, to take out a great black pig that was there, and that they should go with her from town to town; and when they should come to any place where the body was buried, that she would root it up.

They went and they got the black pig, and they were going from farm to farm with her, trying if they could find out where the body was buried. They went from house to house with her, till at last they came to the house where the Shifty Lad and the wright's widow were dwelling. When they arrived they let the pig loose about the grounds. The Shifty Lad said that he himself was sure that thirst and hunger was on them; that they had better go into the house, and that they should get meat and drink; and that they should let their weariness from off them, in the time when the pig should be seeking about his place.

They went in, and the Shifty Lad asked the wright's widow that she should set meat and drink before the men. The widow of the wright set meat and drink on the board, and she set it before them; and in the time while they were eating their meat, the Shifty Lad went out to see after the pig; and the pig had just hit upon the body in the garden; and the Shifty Lad went and he got a great knife and he cut the head off her, and he buried herself and her head beside the body of the wright in the garden.

When those who had the care of the pig came out, the pig was not to be seen. They asked the Shifty Lad if he had seen her; he said that he had seen her, that her head was up and she was looking upwards, and going two or three steps now and again; and they went with great haste to the side where the Shifty Lad said the pig had gone.

When the Shifty Lad found that they had gone out of sight, he set everything in such a way that they should not hit upon the pig. They on whom the care of the pig was laid went and they sought her every way that it was likely she might be. Then when they could not find her, they had nothing for it but to go to the King's house and tell how it had happened.

Then the counsel of the Seanagal was taken again; and the counsel that the Seanagal gave them was, that they should set their soldiers out about the country at free quarters; and at whatsoever place they should get pig's flesh, or in whatsoever place they should see pig's flesh, unless those people could show how they had got the pig's flesh that they might have, that those were the people who killed the pig, and that had done every evil that had been done.

The counsel of the Seanagal was taken, and the soldiers sent out to free quarters about the country; and there was a band of them in the house of the wright's widow where the Shifty Lad was. The wright's widow gave their supper to the soldiers, and some of the pig's flesh was made ready for them; and the soldiers were eating the pig's flesh, and praising it exceedingly. The Shifty Lad understood what was the matter, but he did not let on. The soldiers were set to lie out in the barn and when they were asleep the Shifty Lad went out and he killed them. Then he went as fast as he could from house to house, where the soldiers were at free quarters, and he set the rumour afloat amongst the people of the houses, that the soldiers had been sent out about the country to rise in the night and kill the people in their beds; and he found means to make the people of the country believe him, so that the people of each house killed all the soldiers that were asleep in their barns; and when the soldiers did not come home at the time they should, some went to see what had happened to them; and when they arrived, it was so that they found the soldiers dead in the barns where they had been asleep; and the people of each house denied that they knew how the soldiers had been put to death, or who had done it.

The people who were at the ransacking for the soldiers went to the King's house, and they told how it had happened; then the King sent word from the Seanagal to get counsel from him; the Seanagal came, and the King told how it had happened, and the King asked counsel from him. This is the counsel that the Seanagal gave the King, that he should make a feast and a ball, and invite the people of the country; and if the man who did the evil should be there, that he was the man who would be the boldest who would be there, and that he would ask the King's daughter herself to dance with him. The people were asked to the feast and the dance; and amongst the rest the Shifty Lad was asked. The people came to the feast, and amongst the rest came the Shifty Lad. When the feast was past, the dance began; and the Shifty Lad went and he asked the King's daughter to dance with him; and the Seanagal had a vial full of black stuff, and the Seanagal put a black dot of the stuff that was in the vial on the Shifty Lad. But it seemed to the King's daughter her hair was not well enough in order, and she went to a side chamber to put it right; and the Shifty Lad went in with her; and when she looked in the glass, he also looked in it, and he saw the black dot that the Seanagal had put upon him. When they had danced till the tune of music was finished, the Shifty Lad went and he got a chance to steal the vial of the Seanagal from him unknown to him, and he put two black dots on the Seanagal, and one black dot on twenty other men besides, and he put the vial back again where he found it.

Between that and the end of another while, the Shifty Lad came again and he asked the King's daughter to dance. The

King's daughter had a vial also, and she put a black dot on the face of the Shifty Lad; but the Shifty Lad got the vial whipped out of her pocket, unknown to her; and since there were two black dots on him, he put two dots on twenty other men in the company, and four black dots on the Seanagal. Then when the dancing was over, some were sent to see who was the man on whom were the two black dots. When they looked amongst the people, they found twenty men on whom there were two black dots, and there were four black dots on the Seanagal; and the Shifty Lad found means to go swiftly where the king's daughter was, and to slip the vial back again into her pocket. The Seanagal looked and he had his black vial; the King's daughter looked and she had her own vial; then the Seanagal and the King took counsel; and the last counsel that they made was that the King should come to the company, and say, that the man who had done every trick that had been done must be exceedingly clever; if he would come forward and give himself up, that he should get the King's daughter to marry, and the one half of the kingdom while the King was alive, and the whole of the kingdom after the King's death. And every one of those who had the two black dots on their faces came and they said that it was they who had done every cleverness that had been done. Then the King and his high counsel went to try how the matter should be settled; and the matter which they settled was, that all the men who had the two black dots on their faces should be put together in a chamber, and they were to get a child, and the King's daughter was to give an apple to the child, and the child was to be put in where the men with the two black dots on their faces were seated, and to whatsoever one the child should give the apple, that was the one who was to get the King's daughter.

That was done, and when the child went into the chamber in which the men were, the Shifty Lad had a shaving and a drone, and the child went to gave him the apple. Then the shaving and the drone were taken from the Shifty Lad, and he was seated in another place, and the apple was given to the child again; and he was taken out of the chamber, and sent in again to see to whom he would give the apple; and since the Shifty Lad had a shaving and the drone before, the child went where he was agin, and he gave him the apple. Then the Shifty Lad got the King's daughter to marry.

And shortly after that the King's daughter and the Shifty Lad were taking a walk to Baile Cliabh; and when they were going over the Bridge of Baile Cliabh, the Shifty Lad asked the King's daughter what was the name of that place; and the King's daughter told him that it was the bridge of Baile Cliabh, in Eirinn; and the Shifty Lad said, "Well, then, many is the time that my mother said to me, that my end would be to be hanged at the Bridge of Baile Cliabh, in Eirinn; and she made me that prophecy many a time when I might play her a trick."

And the King's daughter said, "Well, then, if thou thyself shouldst choose to hang over the little side wall of the bridge, I will hold thee aloft a little space with my pocket napkin."

And they were at talk and fun about it; but at last it seemed to the Shifty Lad that he would do it for sport, and the King's daughter took out her pocket napkin, and the Shifty Lad went over the bridge, and he hung by the pocket napkin of the King's daughter as she let it over the little side wall of the bridge, and they were laughing to each other.

But the King's daughter heard a cry, "The King's castle is going on fire!" and she started, and she lost her hold of the napkin; and the Shifty Lad fell down, and his head struck against a stone, and the brain went out of him; and there was in the cry but the sport of children; and the King's daughter was obliged to go home a widow.

Lothian Tom

Tom being grown up to years and age of man, thought himself wiser and slyer than his father; and there were several things about the house which he liked better than to work; so he turned to be a dealer amongst brutes, a cowper of horses and cows, etc., and even wet ware, amongst the brewers and brandy shops, until he cowped himself to the toom halter, and then his parents would supply him no more. He knew his grandmother had plenty of money, but she would give him none; but the old woman had a good black cow of her own, which Tom went to the fields one evening and catches, and takes her to an old waste house which stood at a distance from any other, and there he kept her two or three days, giving her meat and drink at night when it was dark, and made the old woman believe somebody had stolen the cow for their winter's mart, which was grief enough to the old woman, for the loss of her cow. However, she employs Tom to go to a fair that was nearby, and buy her another; she gives him three pounds, which Tom accepts very thankfully, and promises to buy her one as like the other as possibly he could get; then he takes a piece of chalk, and brays it as small as meal, and steeps it in a little water, and therewith rubs over the cow's face and back, which made her have black and white stripes.

So Tom in the morning takes the cow to a public house within a little of the fair, and left her till the fair was over, and then drives her home before him; and as soon as they came home, the cow began to low loudly as it used to do, which made the old woman to rejoice, thinking it was her own cow; but when she saw her white, sighed and said, "Alas! Thou'll never be like the kindly brute my Black Lady, and yet ye low as like her as ony ever I did hear." But says Tom to himself, "'Tis a mercy you know not what she says, or all would be wrong yet." So in two or three days the old woman put forth her bra' black and white cow in the morning with the rest of her neighbours' cattle, but it came on a sore day of heavy rain, which washed away all the white from her face and back; so the old woman's Black Lady came home at night, and her black and white cow went away with the shower, and was never heard of. But Tom's father having some suspicion, and looking narrowly into the cow's face, found some of the chalk not washed away, and then he gave poor Tom a hearty beating, and sent him away to seek his fortune with a skin full of sore bones.

Tom being now turned to his own shifts, considered with himself how to raise a little more money; and so gets a string as near as he could guess to be the length of his mother, and to Edinburgh he goes, to a wright who was acquainted with his father and mother. The wright asked him how he did; he answered him, very soberly, he had lost a good dutiful mother last night, and there's a measure for the coffin. Tom went out and stayed for some time, and then comes in again, and tells the wright he did not know what to do, for his father had ordered him to get money from such a man, whom he named, and he that day was gone out of town. The wright asked him how much he wanted. To which he answered, a guinea and a half. Then Tom gave him strict orders to be out next day against eleven o'clock with the coffin, and he should get his money altogether. So Tom set off to an ale house with the money, and lived well while it lasted. Next morning the wright and his two lads went out with the coffin; and as they were going into the house they met Tom's mother, who asked the master how he did, and where he was going with the fine coffin? Not knowing well what to say, being surprised to see her alive, at last he told her that her son brought in the measure the day before, and had got a guinea and a half from him, with which he said he was to buy some necessaries for the funeral. "Oh, the rogue!" said she. "Has he play'd me that?" So the wright got his lent money, and so much for his trouble, and had to take back his coffin with him again.

Tom being short of money, began to think how he could raise a fresh supply; so he went to the port among the shearers, and there he hired about thirty of them, and agreed to give them a whole week's shearing at tenpence a day, which was twopence higher than any had got that year; this made the poor shearers think he was a very honest, generous, and genteel master, as ever they met with; for he took them all into an ale house, and gave them a hearty breakfast. "Now," says Tom, "when there is so many of you together, and perhaps from very different parts, and being unacquainted with one another, I do not know but there may be some of you honest men and some of you rogues; and as you are all to lie in one barn together, any of you who has got money, you will be surest to give it to me, and I'll mark it down in my book with your names, and what I receive from each of you, and you shall have it all again on Saturday night, when you receive your wages."

"Oh, very well, goodman, there's mine; take mine," said every one faster than another. Some gave him five, six, seven, and eight shillings—even all that they had earn'd thro' the harvest which amounted to near seven pounds sterling. So Tom, having got all their money, he goes on with them till about three miles out of town, and coming to a field of standing corn, though somewhat green, yet convenient for his purpose, as it lay at some distance from any house so he made them begin work there, telling them he was going to order dinner for them, and send his own servants to join them. Then he sets off with all the speed he could, but takes another road into the town lest they should follow and catch him. Now then the people to whom the corn belonged saw such a band in their field, they could not understand the meaning of it. So the farmer whose corn it was went off, crying always as he ran to them to stop; but they would not, until he began to strike at them, and they at him, he being in a great passion, as the corn was not fully ripe. At last, by force of argument, and other people coming up to them, the poor shearers were convinced they had got the bite, which caused them to go away sore lamenting their misfortune.

Two or three days thereafter, as Tom was going down Canongate in Edinburgh, he meets one of the shearers, who knew and kept fast by him, demanding back his money, and also satisfaction for the rest. "Whisht, whisht," says Tom, "and you'll get yours and something else beside." So Tom takes him into the gaol, and calls for a bottle of ale and a dram, then takes the gaoler aside, as if he had been going to borrow some money from him, and says to the gaoler, "This man is a great thief. I and other two have been in search of him these three days, and the other two men have a warrant with them; so if you keep this rogue here till I run and bring them, you shall have a guinea in reward."

"Yes," says the gaoler, "go, and I'll secure the rogue for you." So Tom got off, leaving the poor innocent fellow and the gaoler struggling together, and then sets out for England directly.

Tom having now left his own native country, went into the country of Northumberland, where he hired himself to an old miser of a farmer, where he continued for several years, performing his duty in his service very well, though sometimes playing tricks on those about him. But his master had a naughty custom, he would allow them no candle at night, to see with when at supper. So Tom one night sets himself next his master, and as they were all about to fall on, Tom puts his spoon into the heart of the dish, where the crowdy was hottest, and claps a spoonful into his master's mouth. "A pox on you for a rogue," cried his master, "for my mouth is all burnt." "A pox on you for a master," says Tom, "for you keep a house as dark as Purgatory, for I was going to my mouth with the soup and missed the way, it being so dark. Don't think, master, that I am such a big fool as to feed you while I have a mouth of my own." So from that night that Tom burnt his master's mouth with the hot crowdy, they always got a candle to show them light at supper, for his master would feed no more in the dark while Tom was present.

There was a servant girl in the house, who always when she made the beds neglected to make Tom's, and would have him do it himself. "Well, then," says Tom, "I have harder work to do, and I shall do that too." So next day when Tom was at the plough, he saw his master coming from the house towards him. He left the horses and the plough standing in the field, and goes away towards his master, who cried, "What is wrong? Or is there anything broke with you?" "No, no," said Tom, "but I am going home to make my bed; it has not been made these two weeks, and now it is about the time the maid makes all the rest, so I'll go and make mine too." "No, no," says his master, "go to your plough and I'll cause it to be made every night." "Then," says Tom, "I'll plough two or three furrows more in the time." So Tom gained his end.

One day a butcher came and bought a fine fat calf from Tom's master, and Tom laid it on the horse's neck, before the butcher. When he was gone, "Now," says Tom, "what will you hold, master, but I'll steal the calf from the butcher before he goes two miles off?" Says his master, "I'll hold a guinea you don't." "Done," says Tom. Into the house he goes, and takes a good shoe of his master's, and runs another way across a field, till he got before the butcher, near the corner of a hedge, where there was an open and turning of the way; here Tom places himself behind the hedge, and throws the shoe into the middle of the highway.

So, when the butcher came up riding, with his calf before him, "Hey," said he to himself, "there's a good shoe! If I knew how to get on my calf again, I would light for it; but what signifies one shoe without its neighbour?" So on he rides and lets it lie. Tom then slips out and takes up the shoe, and runs across the fields until he got before the butcher, at another open of a hedge, about half a mile distant, and throws out the shoe again on the middle of the road; then up comes the butcher, and seeing it says to himself, "Now I shall have a pair of good shoes for the lifting." And down he comes, lays the calf on the ground, and tying his horse to the hedge, runs back thinking to get the other shoe, in which time Tom whips up the calf and shoe, and home he comes demanding his wager, which his master could not refuse, being so fairly won.

The poor butcher not finding the shoe, came back to his horse, and missing the calf, knew not what to do; but thinking it had broke the rope from about its feet, and had run into the fields, the butcher spent the day in search of it amongst the hedges and ditches, and returned to Tom's master's at night, intending to go in search again for it next day, and gave them a tedious relation how he came to lose it by a cursed pair of shoes, which he believed the devil had dropped in his way and taken the calf and shoes along with him, but he was thankful he had left his old horse to carry him home.

Next morning Tom set to work, and makes a fine white face on the calf with chalk and water; then brings it out and sells it to the butcher, which was good diversion to his master and other servants, to see the butcher buy his own calf again. No sooner was he gone with it, but Tom says, "Now, master, what will you hold but I'll steal it from him again ere he goes two miles off?" "No, no," says his master, "I'll hold no more bets with you; but I'll give you a shilling if you do it." "Done," says Tom, "it shall cost you no more." And away he runs through the fields, until he came before the butcher, hard by the place where he stole the calf from him the day before; and there he lies down behind the hedge, and as the butcher came past, he put his hand on his mouth and cries "baw, baw" like a calf.

The butcher hearing this, swears to himself that there was the calf he had lost the day before. Down he comes, and throws the calf on the ground, gets through the hedge in all haste, thinking he had no more to do but to take it up; but as he came in at one part of the hedge, Tom jumped out at another, and gets the calf on his back; then goes over the hedge on the other side, and through the fields he came safely home, with the calf on his back, while the poor butcher spent his time and labour in vain, running from hedge to hedge, and hole to hole, seeking the calf. So the butcher returning to his horse again, and finding his other calf gone, he concluded that it was done by some invisible spirit about that spot of ground, so went home lamenting the loss of his calf.

When Tom got home he washed the white face off the stolen calf, and his master sent the butcher word to come and buy another calf, which he accordingly did in a few days after, and Tom sold him the same calf a third time, and then told him the whole affair as it was acted, giving him back his money. So the butcher got fun for his trouble.

Cousin Mattie

At the lone farm of Finagle, there lived for many years an industrious farmer and his family. Several of his children died, and only one daughter and one son remained to him. He had besides these a little orphan niece, who was brought into the family, called Matilda; but all her days she went by the familiar name of Cousin Mattie. At the time this simple narrative commences, Alexander, the farmer's son, was six years of age, Mattie was seven, and Flora, the farmer's only daughter, about twelve.

How I do love a little girl about that age! There is nothing in nature so fascinating, so lovely, so innocent; and, at the the same time, so full of gaiety and playfulness. The tender and delicate affections, to which their natures are moulded, are then beginning unconsciously to form; and everything beautiful or affecting in nature claims from then a deep but momentary interest. They have a tear for the weaned lamb, for the drooping flower, and even for the travelling mendicant, though afraid to come near him. But the child of the poor female vagrant is to them, of all others, an object of the deepest interest. How I have seen them look at the little wretch, and then at their own parents alternately, the feelings of the soul abundantly conspicuous in every muscle of the face and turn of the eye! Their hearts are like softened wax, and the impressions then made on them remain for ever. Such beings approach nigh to the list where angels stand, and are, in fact, the connecting link that joins us with the inhabitants of a better world. How I do love a well-educated little girl of twelve or thirteen years of age!

As such an age was Flora of Finagle, with a heart moulded to every tender impression, and a memory so retentive that whatever affected or interested her was engraven there never to be cancelled.

One morning, after her mother had risen and gone to the byre to look after the cows, Flora, who was lying in a bed by herself, heard the following dialogue between the two children, who were lying prattling together in another bed close beside hers:

"Do you ever dream ony, little Sandy?"

"What is't like, cousin Mattie? Sandy no ken what it is til deam."

"It is to think ye do things when you are sleeping, when ye dinna do them at a'."

"Oh, Sandy deam a great deal yat way."

"If you will tell me ane o' your dreams, Sandy—I'll tell you ane o' mine that I dreamed last night; and it was about you, Sandy."

"Sae was mine, cousin. Sandy deamed that he fightit a gaet Englishman, an' it was Yobin Hood; an' Sandy ding'd him's swold out o' him's hand, an' noll'd him on ye face, an' ye back, till him geetit. An' yen thele comed anodel littel despelyate Englishman, an' it was littel John; an' Sandy fightit him till him was dead; an' yen Sandy got on ane gyand holse, an' gallompit away."

"But I wish that ye be nae making that dream just e'en now, Sandy?"

"Sandy thought it, atweel."

"But were you sleeping when you thought it?"

"Na, Sandy wasna' sleepin', but him was winking."

"Oh, but that's not a true dream; I'll tell you one that's a true dream. I thought there was a bonny lady came to me, and she held out two roses, a red one and a pale one, and bade me take my choice. I took the white one; and she bade me keep it, and never part with it, for if I gave it away, I would die. But when I came to you, you asked my rose, and I refused to give you it. You then cried for it, and said I did not love you; so I could not refuse you the flower, but wept too, and you took it.

"Then the bonny lady came back to me, and was very angry, and said, 'Did not I tell you to keep your rose? Now the boy that you have given it to will be your murderer. He will kill you; and on this day fortnight you will be lying in your coffin, and that pale rose upon your breast.'

"I said, 'I could not help it now.' But when I was told that you were to kill me, I liked you aye better and better, and better, and better."

And with these words Matilda clasped him to her bosom and wept. Sandy sobbed bitterly too, and said, "She be geat lial, yon lady. Sandy no kill cousin Mattie. When Sandy gows byaw man, an' gets a gyand house, him be vely good till cousin an' feed hel wi' gingerbead, an' yeam, an' tyankil, an' take hel in him's bosy yis way." With that the two children fell silent, and sobbed and wept till they fell sound asleep, clasped in each other's arms.

This artless dialogue made a deep impression on Flora's sensitive heart. It was part of her mother's creed to rely on dreams, so that it had naturally become Flora's too. She was shocked, and absolutely terrified, when she heard her little ingenious cousin say that Sandy was to murder her, and on that fortnight she should by lying in her coffin; and without informing her mother of what she had overheard, she resolved in her own mind to avert, if possible, the impending evil. It was on a Sabbath morning, and after little Sandy had got on his clothes, and while Matilda was out, he attempted to tell his mother Cousin Mattie's dream, to Flora's great vexation; but he made such a blundering story of it that it proved altogether incoherent, and his mother took no further notice of it than to bid him hold his tongue. "What was that he was speaking about murdering?"

The next week Flora entreated of her mother that she would suffer Cousin Mattie and herself to pay a visit to their aunt at Kirkmichael; and, though her mother was unwilling, she urged her suit so earnestly that the worthy dame was fain to consent.

"What's ta'en the gowk lassie the day?" said she. "I think she be gane fey. I never could get her to gang to see her aunt, and now she has ta'en a tirrovy in her head, that she'll no be keepit. I dinna like sic absolute freaks, an' sic langings, to come into the heads o' bairns; they're ower aften afore something uncannie. Gae your ways an' see your auntie, sin' ye will gang; but ye's no get little cousin w'ye, sae never speak o't. Think ye that I can do wantin' ye baith out o' the house till the Sabbath day be ower."

"Oh but, mother it's sae gousty, an' sae eiry, to lie up in yon loft ane's lane; unless Cousin Mattie gang wi' me, I canna' gang ava."

"Then just stay at hame, daughter, an' let us alane o' thae daft nories a' thegither."

Flora now had recourse to that expedient which never fails to conquer the opposition of a fond mother: she pretended to cry bitterly. The good dame was quite overcome, and at once yielded, though not with a very good grace. "Saw ever onybody sic a fie-gae-to as this? They that will to Cupar maun to Cupar! Gae your ways to Kirkmichael, an' take the hale town at your tail, gin ye like. What's this that I'm sped wi'."

"Na, na, mother; I's no gang my foot length. Ye sanna hae that to flyre about. Ye keep me working frae that taw year's end to the tither, an' winna gie me a day to mysel'. I's no seek to be away again, as lang as I'm aneath your roof."

"Whisht now, an' haud your tongue, my bonny Flora. Ye hae been ower good a bairn to me, no to get your ain way o' ten times mair nor that. Ye ken laith wad your mother be to contrair you i' ought, if she wist it war for your good. I'm right glad that it has come i' your ain side o' the house, to gang an' see your auntie. Gang your ways, an' stay a day or twa; an' if ye dinna like to sleep your lane, take billy Sandy w'ye, an' leave little cousin wi' me, to help me wi' bits o' turns till ye come back.'

This arrangement suiting Flora's intent equally well with the other, it was readily agreed to, and everything soon amicably settled between the mother and daughter. The former demurred a little on Sandy's inability to perform the journey; but Flora, being intent on her purpose, overruled this objection, though she knew it was but too well founded. Accordingly, the couple set out on their journey next morning, but before they were half way Sandy began to tire, and a short time after gave fairly in. Flora carried him on her back for a space, but finding that would never do, she tried to cajole him into further exertion. No, Sandy would not set a foot to the ground. He was grown drowsy, and would not move. Flora knew not what to do, but at length fell upon an expedient which an older person would scarcely have thought of. She went to a gate of an enclosure, and, pulling a spoke out of it, she brought that to Sandy, telling him she had now got him a fine horse, and he might ride all the way. Sandy, who was uncommonly fond of horses, swallowed the bait, and, mounting astride on his rung, he took the road at a round pace, and for the last two miles of their journey Flora could hardly keep in view of him.

She had little pleasure in her visit, further than the satisfaction that she was doing what she could to avert a dreadful casualty, which she dreaded to be hanging over the family; and on her return, from the time that she came in view of her father, she looked only for the appearance of Mattie running about the door; but no Mattie being seen, Flora's heart began to tremble, and as she advanced nearer, her knees grew so feeble that they would scarcely support her slender form; for she knew that it was one of the radical principles of a dream to be ambiguous.

"A's unco still about our hame the day, Sandy; I wish ilka ane there may be weel. It's like death."

"Sandy no ken what death is like. What is it like, Sistel Flola?"

"You will maybe see that ower soon. It is death that kills a' living things, Sandy.'

"Aye, Sandy saw a wee buldie, it could neilel pick, nol flee, nol dab. It was vely ill done o' death! Sistel Flola, didna' God make a' living things?"

"Yes; be assured he did."

"Then, what has death ado to kill them? If Sandy wele God, him wad fight him."

"Whisht, whist, my dear; ye dinna ken what you're sayin'. Ye maunna speak about these things."

"Weel, Sandy no speak ony maile about them. But if death should kill Cousin Mattie, Sandy wish him might kill him too!"

"Wha do ye like best i' this world, Sandy?"

"Sandy like sistel Flola best."

"You are learning the art of flattery already; for I heard ye telling Mattie the tither morning, that ye likit her better than a' the rest o' the world put thegither."

"But yan Sandy coudna help yat. Cousin Mattie like Sandy, and what could him say?"

Flora could not answer him for anxiety; for they were now drawing quite near to the house, and still all was quiet. At length Mattie opened the door, and, without returning to tell her aunt the joyful tidings, came running like a little fairy to meet them; gave Flora a hasty kiss; and then, clasping little Sandy about the neck, she exclaimed, in an ecstatic tone, "Ah,

Sandy man!" and pressed her cheek to his. Sandy produced a small book of pictures, and a pink rose knot that he had brought for his cousin, and was repaid with another embrace, and a sly compliment to his gallantry.

Matilda was far beyond her years in acuteness. Her mother was an accomplished English lady, though only the daughter of a poor curate, and she had bred her only child with every possible attention. She could read, she could sing, and play some airs on the spinnet; and was altogether a most interesting little nymph. Both her parents came to an untimely end, and to the lone cottage of Finagle was she then removed, where she was still very much caressed. She told Flora all the news of her absence in a breath. There was nothing disastrous had happened. But, so strong was Flora's presentiment of evil, that she could not get quit of it, until she had pressed the hands of both her parents. From that day forth, she suspected that little faith was to be put in dreams. The fourteen days was now fairly over, and no evil nor danger had happened to Matilda, either from the hand of Sandy or otherwise. However, she kept the secret of the dream locked up in her heart, and never either mentioned or forgot it.

Shortly after that she endeavoured to reason her mother out of her belief in dreams, for she would still gladly have been persuaded in her own mind that this vision was futile, and of no avail. But she found her mother staunch to her point. She reasoned on the principle that the Almighty had made nothing in vain, and if dreams had been of no import to man they would not have been given to him. And further, she said we read in the Scriptures that dreams were fulfilled in the days of old, but we didna read in the Scriptures that ever the nature of dreaming was changed. On the contrary, she believed that since the days of prophecy had departed, and no more warnings of futurity could be derived by man from that, dreaming was of doubly more avail, and ought to be proportionally more attended to, as the only mystical communication remaining between God and man. To this reasoning Flora was obliged to yield. It is no hard matter to conquer, where belief succeeds argument.

Time flew on, and the two children were never asunder. They read together, prayed together, and toyed and caressed without restraint, seeming but to live for one another. But a heavy misfortune at length befell the family. She who had been a kind mother and guardian angel to all the three was removed by death to a better home. Flora was at that time in her eighteenth year, and the charge of the family then devolved on her. Great was their grief, but their happiness was nothing abated; they lived together in the same kind love and amity as they had done before. The two youngest in particular fondled each other more and more, and this growing fondness, instead of being checked, was constantly encouraged, Flora still having a lurking dread that some deadly animosity might breed between them.

Matilda and she always slept in the same bed, and very regularly told each other their dreams in the morning— dreams pure and innocent as their own stainless bosoms. But one morning Flora was surprised by Matilda addressing her as follows, in a tone of great perplexity and distress:

"Ah, my dear cousin, what a dream I have had last night ! I thought I saw my aunt, your late worthy mother, who was kind and affectionate to me, as she always wont to be, and more beautiful than I ever saw her. She took me in her arms, and wept over me; and charged me to go and leave this place instantly, and by all means to avoid her son, otherwise he was destined to be my murderer, and on that day seven night I should be lying in my coffin. She showed me a sight too that I did not know, and cannot give a name to. But the surgeons came between us, and separated us, so that I saw her no more."

Flora trembled and groaned in spirit; nor could she make

any answer to Matilda for a long space, save by repeated moans. "Merciful Heaven!" said she at length. "What can such a dream portend? Do not you remember, dear Mattie, of dreaming a dream of the same nature once long ago?"

Mattie had quite forgot of ever having dreamed such a dream; but Flora remembered it well; and thinking that she might formerly have been the mean, under Heaven, of counterworking destiny, she determined to make a further effort; and, ere ever she arose, advised Matilda to leave the house, and avoid her brother until the seven days had elapsed. "It can do nae ill, Mattie," said she, "an' mankind hae whiles muckle i' their ain hands to do or no to do; to bring about, or to keep back." Mattie consented, solely to please the amiable Flora; for she was no more afraid of Sandy than she was of one of the flowers of the field. She went to Kirkmichael, stayed till the week was expired, came home in safety, and they both laughed at their superstitious fears. Matilda thought of the dream no more, but Flora treasured it up in her memory, though all the coincidence that she could discover between the two dreams was that they had both happened on a Saturday, and both precisely at the same season of the year, which she well remembered.

At the age of two and twenty, Flora was married to a young farmer, who lived in a distant corner of the same extensive parish, and of course left the charge of her father's household to Cousin Mattie, who, with the old farmer, his son, and one maidservant, managed and did all the work of the farm. Still, as their number was diminished, their affections seemed to be drawn the closer; but Flora scarcely saw them any more, having the concerns of a family to mind at home.

One day, when her husband went to church, he perceived the old beadle standing bent over his staff at the churchyard gate, distributing letters to a few as they entered. He held out one to the husband of Flora, and, at the same time, touched the front of his bonnet with the other hand; and without regarding how the letter affected him who received it, began instantly to look about for others to whom he had letters directed.

The farmer opened the letter, and had almost sunk down on the earth, when he read as follows:

Sir

The favour of your company, at twelve o'clock, on Tuesday next, to attend the funeral of Matilda A——, my niece, from this, to the place of interment, in the churchyard of C——, will much oblige, Sir, your humble servant,

James A——.

Finagle, April 12th.

Think of Flora's amazement and distress, when her husband told her what had happened, and showed her this letter. She took to her bed on the instant, and wept herself into a fever for the friend and companion of her youth. Her husband became considerably alarmed on her account, she being in that state in which violent excitement often proves dangerous. Her sickness was, however, only temporary; but she burned with impatience to learn some particular of her cousin's death. Her husband could tell her nothing; only, that he heard one say she died on Saturday.

This set Flora a-calculating, and going over in her mind reminiscences of their youth; and she soon discovered, to her utter astonishment and even horror, that her Cousin Matilda had died precisely on that day fourteen years that she first dreamed the ominous dream, and that day seven years that she dreamed it again!

Here was indeed matter of wonder! But her blood ran cold to her heart when she thought what might have been the manner of her death. She dreaded, nay, she almost calculated upon it as certain, that her brother had poisoned, or otherwise made away privately with the deceased, as she was sure such an extraordinary coincidence behoved to be fulfilled in all its parts. She durst no more make any inquiries concerning the circumstances of her cousin's death; but she became moping and unsettled, and her husband feared for her reason.

He went to the funeral; but dreading to leave Flora long by herself, he only met the procession a small space from the churchyard; for his father-in-law's house was distant fourteen miles from his own. On his return, he could still give Flora very little additional information. He said he had asked his father-in-law what had been the nature of the complaint of which she died; but he had given him an equivocal answer, and seemed to avoid entering into any explanation; and that he had then made inquiry at others, who all testified their ignorance of the matter. Flora at length, after long hesitation, ventured to ask if her brother was at the funeral and was told that he was not. This was a death-blow to her lingering hopes, and all but confirmed the hideous catastrophe that she dreaded; and for the remainder of that week she continued in a state of mental agony.

On the Sunday following, she manifested a strong desire to go to church to visit her cousin's grave. Her husband opposed it at first, but at last consenting, in hopes she might be benefited by an overflow of tenderness, he mounted her on a pad, and accompanied her to the churchyard gate, leaving her there to give vent to her feelings.

As she approached the new grave, which was by the side of her mother's, she perceived two aged people whom she knew, sitting beside it busily engaged in conversation about the inhabitant below. Flora drew her hood over her face, and came with a sauntering step towards them, to lull all suspicion that she had any interest or concern in what they were saying; and finally she leaned herself down on a flat gravestone close beside them, and made as if she were busied in deciphering the inscription. There she heard the following dialogue, one may conceive with what sort of feelings.

"An' then she was aye say kind, an' sae lively, an' sae affable to poor an' rich, an' then sae bonny an' sae young. Oh, but my heart's sair for her! When I saw the mortclaith drawn off the coffin, an' saw the silver letters kythe, Aged 21, the tears ran down ower thae auld wizzened cheeks, Janet; an' I said to mysel', 'Wow but that is a bonny flower cut off i' the bloom!' But, Janet, my joe, warna ye at the corpse-kisting?"

"An' what suppose I was, Matthew? What's your concern wi' that?"

"Because I heard say that there was nane there but you an' another that ye ken weel. But canna you tell me, kimmer, what was the corpse like? Was't a' fair an' bonny, an' nae blueness nor demmish to be seen?"

"An' what wad an auld fool body like you be the better, gin ye kend what the corpse was like? Thae sights are nae for een like your to see; an' thae subjects are nae fit for tongues like yours to tattle about. What's done canna be undone. The dead will lie still. But oh, what's to come o' the living?"

"Ay, but I'm sure she had been a lusty weel plenished corpse, Janet; for she was heavy ane; an' a deeper coffin I never saw."

"Haud your auld souple untackit tongue. Gin I hear sic another hint come ower the foul tap o't, it sal be the waur for ye. But lown be it spoken, an' little be it said. Weel might the corpse be heavy, an' the coffin deep! Ay, weel might the coffin be made deep, Matthew, for there was a stout lad bairn, a poor little pale flower, that hardly even saw the light o' heaven, was streekit on her breast at the same time wi' hersel'."

Elphin Irving

The romantic vale of Corriewater, in Annandale, is regarded by the inhabitants, a pastoral and unmingled people, as the last Border refuge of those beautiful and capricious beings, the Fairies. Many old people yet living imagine they have had intercourse of good words and good deeds with the "good folk"; and continue to tell that in the ancient of days the Fairies danced on the hill, and revelled in the glen, and showed themselves, like the mysterious children of the deity of old, among the sons and daughters of men. Their visits to the earth were periods of joy and mirth to mankind, rather than of sorrow and apprehension. They played on musical instruments of wonderful sweetness and variety of note, spread unexpected feasts, the supernatural flavour of which overpowered on many occasions the religious scruples of the Presbyterian shepherds, performed wonderful deeds of horsemanship, and marched in midnight processions, when the sound of their Elfin minstrelsy charmed youths and maidens into love for their persons and pursuits; and more than one family of Corriewater have the fame of augmenting the number of the Elfin chivalry. Faces of friends and relatives, long since doomed to the battle-trench or the deep sea, have been recognised by those who dared to gaze on the Fairy march. The maid has seen her lost lover and the mother her stolen child; and the courage to plan and achieve their deliverance has been possessed by at least one

Border maiden. In the legends of the people of Corrievale there is a singular mixture of Elfin and human adventure, and the traditional story of the Cupbearer to the Queen of the Fairies appeals alike to our domestic feelings and imagination.

In one of the little green loops, or bends, on the banks of the Corriewater, mouldered walls, and a few stunted wild plum trees and vagrant roses, still point out the site of a cottage and garden. A well of pure spring-water leaps out from an old tree root before the door; and here the shepherds, shading themselves in summer from the influence of the sun, tell to their children the wild tale of Elphin Irving and his sister Phemie; and, singular as the story seems, it has gained full credence among the people where the scene is laid.

When Elphin Irving and his sister Phemie were in their sixteenth year, for tradition says they were twins, their father was drowned in Corriewater, attempting to save his sheep from a sudden swell, to which all mountain streams are liable; and their mother, on the day of her husband's burial, laid down her head on the pillow, from which, on the seventh day, it was lifted to be dressed for the same grave. The inheritance left to the orphans may be briefly described: seventeen acres of plough and pasture land, seven milk cows, and seven pet sheep (many old people take delight in odd numbers); and to this may be added seven Bonnet-pieces of Scottish gold, and a broadsword and spear, which their ancestor had wielded with such strength and courage in the Battle of Dryfe Sands, that the minstrel who sang of the deed of arms ranked him only second to the Scotts and Johnstones.

The youth and his sister grew in stature and in beauty. The brent bright brow, the clear blue eye, and frank and blithe deportment of the former gave him some influence among the young women of the valley; while the latter was no less the admiration of the young men, and at fair and dance and at bridal, happy was he who touched but her hand or received the benediction of her eye. Like all other Scottish beauties, she was the theme of many a song; and while tradition is yet busy with the singular history of her brother, song has taken all the care that rustic minstrelsy can of the gentleness of her spirit and the charms of her person.

But minstrel skill and true love tale seemed to want their usual influence when they sought to win her attention; she was only observed to pay most respect to those youths who were most beloved by her brother; and the same hour that brought these twins to the world seemed to have breathed through them a sweetness and affection of heart and mind, which nothing could divide. If, like the virgin queen of the immortal poet, she walked "in maiden meditation fancy free", her brother Elphin seemed alike untouched with the charms of the fairest virgins in Corrie. He ploughed his field, he reaped his grain, he leaped, he ran, and wrestled, and danced, and sang, with more skill and life and grace than all other youths of the district; but he had no twilight and stolen interviews; when all other young men had their loves by their side, he was single, though not unsought, and his joy seemed never perfect save when his sister was near him. If he loved to share his time with her, she loved to share her time with him alone, or with the beasts of the field, or the birds of the air. She watched her little flock late, and she tended it early; not for the sordid love of the fleece, unless it was to make mantles for her brother, but with the look of one who had joy in its company. The very wild creatures, the deer and the hares, seldom sought to shun her approach, and the bird forsook not its nest, nor stinted its song, when she drew nigh; such is the confidence which maiden innocence and beauty inspire.

It happened one summer, about three years after they became orphans, the rain had been for awhile withheld from the earth, the hillsides began to parch, the grass in the vale to wither, and the stream of Corrie was diminished between its banks to the size of an ordinary rill. The shepherds drove their flocks to moorlands, and marsh and tarn had their reeds invaded by the scythe to supply the cattle with food. The sheep of his sister were Elphin's constant care; he drove them to the moistest pastures during the day, and he often watched them at midnight, when flocks, tempted by the sweet dewy grass, are known to browse eagerly, that he might guard them from the fox, and lead them to the choicest herbage. In these nocturnal watchings he sometimes drove his little flock over the water of Corrie, for the fords were hardly ankle-deep; or permitted his sheep to cool themselves in the stream, and taste the grass which grew along the brink. All this time not a drop of rain fell, nor did a cloud appear in the sky.

One evening, during her brother's absence with the flock, Phemie sat at her cottage door, listening to the bleatings of the distant folds and the lessened murmur of the water of Corrie, now scarcely audible beyond its banks. Her eyes, weary with watching along the accustomed line of road for the return of Elphin, were turned on the pool beside her, in which the stars were glimmering fitful and faint. As she looked she imagined the water grew brighter and brighter; a wild illumination presently shone upon the pool, and leaped from bank to bank, and suddenly changing into a human form, ascended the margin, and, passing her, glided swiftly into the cottage. The visionary form was so like her brother in shape and air, that, starting up, she flew into the house, with the hope of finding him in his customary seat. She found him not, and, impressed with the terror which a wraith or apparition seldom fails to inspire, she uttered a shriek so loud and so piercing as to be heard at Johnstone Bank, on the other side of the vale of Corrie.

It is hardly known how long Phemie Irving continued in a state of insensibility. The morning was far advanced, when a neighbouring maiden found her seated in an old chair, as white as monumental marble; her hair, about which she had always been solicitous, loosened from its curls, and hanging disordered over her neck and bosom, her hands and forehead. The maiden touched the one, and kissed the other; they were as cold as snow; and her eyes, wide open, were fixed on her brother's empty chair, with the intensity of gaze of one who had witnessed the appearance of a spirit. She seemed insensible of anyone's presence, and sat fixed and still and motionless. The maiden, alarmed at her looks, thus addressed her:

"Phemie, lass, Phemie Irving! Dear me, but this be awful! I have come to tell ye that seven of your pet sheep have escaped drowning in the water; for Corrie, sae quiet and sae gentle yestreen, is rolling and dashing frae bank to bank this morning. Dear me, woman, dinna let the loss of the world's gear bereave ye of your senses. I would rather make ye a present of a dozen mug-ewes of the Tinwald brood myself; and now I think on't, if ye'll send over Elphin, I will help him hame with them in the gloaming myself. So, Phemie, woman, be comforted."

At the mention of her brother's name she cried out, "Where is he? Oh, where is he?' gazed wildly round, and, shuddering from head to foot, fell senseless on the floor. Other inhabitants of the valley, alarmed by the sudden swell of the river, which had augmented to a torrent, deep and impassable, now came in to inquire if any loss had been sustained, for numbers of sheep and teds of hay had been observed floating down about the dawn of the morning. They assisted in reclaiming the unhappy maiden from her swoon; but insensibility was joy compared to the sorrow to which she awakened. "They have ta'en him away, they have ta'en him away," she chanted, in a tone of delirious pathos, "him that was whiter and fairer than the lily on Lyddal Lee. They have long sought, and they have long sued, and they have the power to prevail against my prayers at last. They have ta'en him away; the flower is plucked from among the weeds, and the dove is slain amid a flock of ravens. They came with shout, and they came with song, and they spread the charm, and they placed the spell, and the baptised brow has been bowed down to the unbaptised hand. They have ta'en him away, they have ta'en him away; he was too lovely, and too good, and too noble, to bless us with his continuance on earth; for what are the sons of men compared to him—the light of the moonbeam to the morning sun, the glow-worm to the eastern star. They have ta'en him away, the invisible dwellers of the earth. I saw them come on him with shouting and with singing, and they charmed him where he sat, and away they bore him; and the horse he rode was never shod with iron, nor owned before the mastery of human hand. They have ta'en him away over the water, and over the wood, and over the hill. I got but ae look of his bonnie blue ee, but ae, ae look. But as I have endured what never maiden endured, so will I undertake what never maiden undertook; I will win him from them all. I know the invisible ones of the earth; I have heard their wild and wondrous music in the wild woods, and there shall a christened maiden see him, and achieve his deliverance."

She paused, and glancing around a circle of condoling faces, down which the tears were dropping like rain, said, in a calm and altered but still delirious tone: "Why do you weep, Mary Halliday? And why do you weep, John Graeme? Ye think that Elphin Irving—oh, it's a bonnie, bonnie name, and dear to many a maiden's heart as well as mine—ye think he is drowned in Corrie, and ye will seek in the deep, deep pools for the bonnie, bonnie corse, that ye may weep over it, as it lies in its last linen, and lay it, amid weeping and wailing, in the dowie kirkyard. Ye may seek but ye shall never find; so leave me to trim up my hair, and prepare my dwelling and make myself ready to watch for the hour of his return to upper earth." And she resumed her household labours with an alacrity which lessened not the sorrow of her friends.

Meanwhile the rumour flew over the vale that Elphin Irving was drowned in Corriewater. Matron and maid, old man and young, collected suddenly along the banks of the river, which now began to subside to its natural summer limits, and commenced their search; interrupted every now and then by calling from side to side, and from pool to pool, and by exclamations of sorrow for this misfortune. The search was fruitless: five sheep, pertaining to the flock which he conducted to pasture, were found drowned in one of the deep eddies; but the river was still too brown, from the soil of its moorland sources, to enable them to see what its deep shelves, its pools, and its overhanging and hazely banks concealed. They remitted further search till the stream should become pure; and old man taking old man aside, began to whisper about the mystery of the youth's disappearance; old women laid their lips to the ears of their coevals, and talked of Elphin Irving's Fairy parentage, and his having been dropped by an unearthly hand into a Christian cradle. The young men and maids conversed on other themes; they grieved for the loss of the friend and the lover, and while the former thought that a heart so kind and true was not left in the vale, the latter thought, as maidens will, on his handsome person, gentle manners, and merry blue eye, and speculated with a sigh on the time when they might have hoped a return for their love. They were soon joined by others who had heard the wild and delirious language of his sister. The old belief was added to the new assurance, and both again commented upon by minds full of superstitious feelings, and hearts full of supernatural fears, till the youths and maidens of Corrievale held no more love trysts for seven days and nights, lest, like Elphin Irving, they should be carried away to augment the ranks of the unchristened chivalry.

It was curious to listen to the speculations of the peasantry. "For my part," said a youth, "if I were sure that poor Elphin escaped from that perilous water, I would not give the Fairies a pound of hiplock wool for their chance of him. There has not been a Fairy seen in the land since Donald Cargil, the

Cameronian, conjured them into the Solway for playing on their pipes during one of his nocturnal preachings on the tip of the Burnswark Hill."

"Preserve me, bairn," said an old woman, justly exasperated at the incredulity of her nephew. "If ye winna believe what I both heard and saw at the moonlight end of Craigyburnwood on a summer night, rank after rank of the Fairy folk, ye'll at least believe a douce man and a ghostly professor, even the late minister of Tinwaldkirk. His only son—I mind the lad weel, with his long yellow locks and his bonnie blue eyes— when I was but a gilpie of a lassie, he was stolen away from off the horse at his father's elbow, as they crossed that false and fearsome water, even Locherbriggflow, on the night of the Midsummer Fair of Dunfries. Ay, ay—who can doubt the truth of that? Have not the godly inhabitants of Almsfieldtown and Tinwaldkirk seen the sweet youth riding at midnight, in the midst of the unhallowed troop, to the sound of flute and of dulcimer, and though meikle they prayed, naebody tried to achieve his deliverance?"

"I have heard it said by douce folk and sponsible," interrupted another, "that every seven years the Elves and Fairies pay kane, or make an offering of one of their children, to the grand enemy of salvation, and that they are permitted to purloin one of the children of men to present to the fiend a more acceptable offering, I'll warrant, than one of their own infernal brood that are Satan's sib allies, and drink a drop of the Deil's blood every May morning. And touching this lost lad, ye all ken his mother was a hawk of an uncannie nest, a second cousin of Kate Kimmer, of Barfloshan, as rank a Witch as ever rode on ragwort. Ay, sirs, what's bred in the bone is ill to come out of flesh."

On these and similar topics, which a peasantry full of ancient tradition and enthusiasm and superstition readily associate with the commonest occurrences of life, the people of Corrievale continued to converse till the fall of evening, when each, seeking their home, renewed again the wondrous subject, and illustrated it with all that popular belief and poetic imagination could so abundantly supply.

The night which followed this melancholy day was wild with wind and rain; the river came down broader and deeper than before, and the lightning, flashing by fits over the green woods of Corrie, showed the ungovernable and perilous flood sweeping above its banks. It happened that a farmer, returning from one of the Border fairs, encountered the full swing of the storm; but mounted on an excellent horse, and mantled from chin to heel in a good grey plaid, beneath which he had the further security of a thick great-coat, he sat dry in his saddle, and proceeded in the anticipated joy of a subsided tempest and a glowing morning sun. As he entered the long grove, or rather remains of the old Galwegian forest, which lines for some space the banks of the Corriewater, the storm began to abate, the wind sighed milder and milder among the trees; and here and there a star, twinkling momentarily through the sudden rack of the clouds, showed the river raging from bank to braw. As he shook the moisture from his clothes, he was not without a wish that the day would dawn, and that he might be preserved on a road which his imagination beset with greater perils than the raging river; for his superstitious feeling let loose upon his path Elf and Goblin, and the current traditions of the district supplied very largely to his apprehension the ready materials of fear.

Just as he emerged from the wood, where a fine sloping bank, covered with short greensward, skirts the limit of the forest, his horse made a full pause, snorted, trembled, and started from side to side, stooped his head, erected his ears, and seemed to scrutinise every tree and bush. The rider, too, it may be imagined, gazed round and round, and peered warily into every suspicious-looking place. His dread of a supernatural visitation was not much allayed when he observed a female shape seated on the ground at the root of a huge old oak-tree, which stood in the centre of one of those patches of verdant sward, known by the name of "Fairy-rings", and avoided by all peasants who wish to prosper. A long thin gleam of eastern daylight enabled him to examine accurately the being who, in this wild place and unusual hour, gave additional terror to his haunted spot. She was dressed in white from the neck to the knees; her arms, long and round and white, were perfectly bare; her head, uncovered, allowed her long hair to descend in ringlet succeeding ringlet, till the half of her person was nearly concealed in the fleece. Amidst the whole, her hands were constantly busy in shedding aside the tresses which interposed between her steady and uninterrupted gaze down a line of old road which winded among the hill to an ancient burial-ground.

As the traveller continued to gaze, the figure suddenly rose, and, wringing the rain from her long locks, paced round and round the tree, chanting in a wild and melancholy manner an equally wild and delirious song:

The Fairy Oak of Corriewater

The small bird's head is under its wing,
The deep sleeps on the grass;
The moon comes out, and the stars shine down,
The dew gleams like the glass:
There is no sound in the world so wide,
Save the sound of the smitten brass,
With the merry cittern and the pipe
Of the Fairies as they pass.
But oh, the fir maun burn and burn,
And the hour is gone, and will never return.

The green hill cleaves, and forth, with a bound,
Comes Elf and elfin steed;
The moon dives down in a golden cloud,
The stars grow dim with dread;
But a light is running along the earth,
So of heaven's they have no need:
O'er moor and moss with a shout they pass,
And the word is spur and speed—
But the fire maun burn, and I maun quake,
And the hour is gone that will never come back.

And when they came to Craigyburnwood,
The Queen of the Fairies spoke:
"Come, bind your steeds to the rushes so green,
And dance by the haunted oak:
I found the acorn on Heshbon Hill,
In the nook of a palmer's poke,
A thousand years since; here it grows!"
And they danced till the greenwood shook:
But oh, the fire, the burning fire,
The longer it burns, it but blazes the higher.

"I have won me a youth," the Elf Queen said,
"The fairest that earth may see;
This night I have won young Elph Irving
My cupbearer to be.
His service lasts but for seven sweet years,
And his wage is a kiss of me."
And merrily, merrily, laughed the wild elves
Round Corrie's greenwood tree.
But oh, the fire it glows in my brain,
And the hour is gone, and comes not again.

The Queen she has whispered a secret word,
    "Come hither, my Elphin sweet,
And bring that cup of the charmed wine,
    Thy lips and mine to weet."
But a Brown Elf shouted a loud, loud shout,
    "Come, leap on your courses fleet,
For here comes the smell of some baptised flesh,
    And the sounding of baptised feet."
But oh, the fire that burns, and maun burn;
For the time that is gone will never return.

On a steed as white as the new-milked milk,
    The Elf Queen leaped with a bound,
And young Elphin a steed like December snow
    'Neath him at the word he found.
But a maiden came, and her christened arms
    She linked her brother around,
And called on God, and the steed with a snort
    Sank into the gaping ground.
But the fire maun burn, and I maun quake,
And the time that is gone will no more come back.

And she held her brother, and lo, he grow
    A wild bull waked in ire;
And she held her brother, and lo, he changed
    To a river roaring higher;
And she held her brother, and he became
    A flood of the raging fire;
She shrieked and sank, and the wild Elves laughed
    Till the mountain rang and mire.
But oh, the fire yet burns in my brain,
And the hour is gone, and comes not again.

"O maiden, why waxed thy faith so faint,
Thy spirit so slack and slaw?
Thy courage kept good till the flame waxed
Then thy might began to thaw;
Had ye kissed him frae 'mang us a'.
New bless the fire, the elfin fire,
That made thee faint and fa';
Now bless the fire, the elfin fire,
The longer it burns it blazes the higher."

At the close of this unusual strain the figure sat down on the grass, and proceeded to bind up her long and disordered tresses, gazing along the old and unfrequented road. "Now God be my helper," said the traveller, who happened to be the Laird of Johnstone Bank, "can this be a trick of the fiend, or can it be bonnie Phemie Irving who chants this dolorous sang? Something sad has befallen, that makes her seek her seat in this eerie nook amid the darkness and tempest: through might from aboon I will go on and see." And the horse, feeling something of the owner's reviving spirit in the application of spur-steel, bore him at once to the foot of the tree. The poor delirious maiden uttered a yell of piercing joy as she beheld him, and, with the swiftness of a creature winged, linked her arms round the rider's waist and shrieked till the woods rang. "Oh, I have ye now, Elphin, I have ye now," and she strained him to her bosom with a convulsive grasp. "What ails ye, my bonnie lass?" said the Laird of Johnstone Bank, his fears of the supernatural vanishing when he beheld her sad and bewildered look. She raised her eyes at the sound, and, seeing a strange face, her arms slipped their hold, and she dropped with a groan on the ground.

The morning had now fairly broke: the flock shook the rain from their sides, the shepherds hastened to inspect their charges, and a thin blue smoke began to stream from the cottages of the valley into the brightening air. The laird carried Phemie Irving in his arms, till he observed two shepherds ascending from one of the loops of Corriewater, bearing the lifeless body of her brother. They had found him whirling round and round in one of the numerous eddies, and his hands, clutched and filled with wool, showed that he had lost his life in attempting to save the flock of his sister. A plaid was laid over the body, which, along with the unhappy maiden in a half-lifeless state, was carried into a cottage, and laid in that apartment distinguished among the peasantry by the name of the chamber. While the peasant's wife was left to take care of Phemie, old man and matron and maid had collected around the drowned youth, and each began to relate the circumstances of his death, when the door suddenly opened, and his sister advancing to the corpse with a look of delirious serenity, broke out into a wild laugh and said, "Oh, it is wonderful, it's truly wonderful! That bare and death-cold body, dragged from the darkest pool of Corrie, with its hands filled with fine wool, wears the perfect similitude of my own Elphin! I'll tell ye the spiritual dweller of the earth, the fairyfolk of our evening tale, have stolen the living body, and fashioned this cold and inanimate cold to mislead your pursuit. In common eyes this seems all that Elphin Irving would be, had he sunk in Corriewater; but so it seems not to me. Ye have sought the living soul, and ye have found only its garment. But oh, if ye had beheld him, as I beheld him tonight, riding among the elfin troop, the fairest of them all; had you clasped him in your arms, and wrestled for him with spirits and terrible shapes from the other world, till your heart quailed and your flesh was subdued, then would ye yield no credit to the semblance which this cold and apparent flesh bears to my brother. But hearken! On Hallowmass Eve, when the spiritual people are let loose on earth for a season, I will take my stand in the burial-ground of Corrie; and when my Elphin and his unchristened troop come past, with the sound of all their minstrelsy, I will leap on him and win him, or perish of ever."

All gazed aghast on the delirious maiden, and many of the auditors gave more credence to her distempered speech than to the visible evidence before them. As she turned to depart, she looked round, and suddenly sunk upon the body, with tears steaming from her eyes, and sobbed out, "My brother! Oh, my brother!" She was carried out insensible, and again recovered; but relapsed into her ordinary delirium, in which she continued till the Hallow Eve after her brother's burial. She was found seated in the ancient burial-ground, her back against a broken gravestone, her locks white with frost-rime, watching with intensity of look the road to the kirkyard; but the spirit which gave life to the fairest form of all the maids of Annandale was fled for ever.

Such is the singular story which the peasants know by the name of "Elphin Irving, the Fairies' Cupbearer"; and the title, in its fullest and most supernatural sense, still obtains credence among the industrious and virtuous dames of the romantic vale of Come.

The Haunted Ships

"Alexander (Sandie) Macharg, besides being the laird of three acres of peatmoss, two kale gardens, and the owner of seven good milch cows, a pair of horses, and six pet sheep, was the husband of one of the handsomest women in seven parishes. Many a lad sighed the day he was brided; and a Nithsdale laird and two Annandale moorland farmers drank themselves to their last linen, as well as their last shilling, through sorrow for her loss. But married was the dame; and home she was carried, to bear rule over her home and her husband, as an honest woman should. Now ye maun ken that, though the flesh-and-blood lovers of Alexander's bonnie wife all ceased to love and to sue her after she became another's, there were certain admirers who did not consider their claim at all abated, or their hopes lessened by the kirk's famous obstacle of matrimony. Ye have heard how the devout minister of Tinwald had a fair son carried away, and bedded against his liking to an unchristened bride, whom the elves and fairies provided; ye have heard how the bonnie bride of the drunken laird of Soukitup was stolen by the fairies out at the back window of the bridal chamber, the time the bridegroom was groping his way to the chamber door; and ye have heard—but why need I multiply? Such things in ancient days were as common as candlelight. So ye'll no hinder certain Water Elves and Sea Fairies, who sometimes keep festival and summer mirth in these old haunted hulks, from falling in love with the weel-faured wife of Laird Macharg; and to their plots and contrivances they went, how they might accomplish to sunder man and wife; and sundering such a man and such a wife was like sundering the green leaf from the summer, or the fragrance from the flower.

So it fell on a time that Laird Macharg took his half-net on his back, and his steel spear in his hand, and down to Blawhooly Bay gade he, and into the water he went right between the two haunted hulks, and, placing his net, awaited the coming of the tide. The night, ye maun ken, was mirk, and the wind lowne, and the singing of the increasing waters among the shells and the peebles was heard for sundry miles. All at once lights began to glance and twinkle on board the two Haunted Ships from every hole and seam, and presently the sound as of a hatchet employed in squaring timber echoed far and wide. But if the toil of these unearthly workmen amazed the laird, how much more was his amazement increased when a sharp shrill voice called out, "Ho! brother, what are you doing now?" A voice still shriller responded from the other haunted ship, "I'm making a wife to Sandie Macharg!" and a loud quavering laugh, running from ship to ship, and from bank to bank, told the joy they expected from their labour.

Now the laird, besides being a devout and a Godfearing man, was shrewd and bold; and in plot, and contrivance, and skill in conducting his designs, was fairly an overmatch for any dozen Land Elves. But the Water Elves are far more subtle; besides, their haunts and their dwellings being in the great deep, pursuit and detection is hopeless if they succeed in carrying their prey to the waves. But ye shall hear. Home flew the laird, collected his family around the hearth, spoke of the signs and the sins of the times, and talked of mortification and prayer for averting calamity; and finally, taking his father's Bible, brass clasps, black print, and covered with calf-skin, from the shelf, he proceeded without let or stint to perform domestic worship. I should have told ye that he bolted and locked the door, shut up all inlet to the house, threw salt into the fire, and proceeded in every way like a man skilful in guarding against the plots of Fairies and Fiends. His wife looked on all this with wonder; but she saw something in her husband's looks that hindered her from intruding either question or advice, and a wise woman was she.

Near the mid-hour of the night the rush of a horse's feet was heard, and the sound of a rider leaping from its back, and a heavy knock came to the door, accompanied by a voice, saying, "The cummer drink's hot, and the knave bairn is expected at Laird Laurie's tonight; sae mount, Gudewife, and come."

"Preserve me!" said the wife of Sandie Macharg, "that's news indeed! Who could have thought it? The laird has been heirless for seventeen years! Now Sandie, my man, fetch me my skirt and hood."

But he laid his arm round his wife's neck, and said, "If all the lairds in Galloway go heirless, over this door threshold shall you not stir tonight; and I have said, and I have sworn it. Seek not to know why or wherefore—but, Lord, send us thy blessed mornlight." The wife looked for a moment in her husband's eyes, and desisted from further entreaty.

"But let us send a civil message to the gossips, Sandie; and had nae ye better say I am sair laid with a sudden sickness? Though it's sinful-like to send the poor messenger a mile agate with a lie in his mouth without a glass of brandy."

"'To such a messenger, and to those who sent him, no apology is needed," said the austere Laird Macharg, "so let him depart." And the clatter of a horse's hoofs was heard, and the muttered imprecations of its rider on the churlish treatment he had experienced.

"Now Sandie, my lad," said his wife, laying an arm particularly white and round about his neck as she spoke, "are you not a queer man and a stern? I have been your wedded wife now these three years; and, beside my dower, have brought you three as bonnie bairns as ever smiled aneath a summer sun. O man, you a douce man, and fitter to be an elder than even Willie Greer himself—I have the minister's ain word for't,—to put on these hardhearted looks, and gang waving your arms that way, as if ye said, 'I winna take the counsel of sic a hempie as you.' I'm your ain leal wife, and will and maun have an explanation."

To all this Sandie Macharg replied, "It is written. 'Wives, obey your husbands.' but we have been stayed in our devotion, so let us pray." And down he knelt. His wife knelt also, for she was as devout as bonnie; and beside them knelt their household, and all lights were extinguished.

"Now this beats a', muttered his wife to herself. "However, I shall be obedient for a time; but if I dinna ken what all this is for before the morn by sunket-time, my tongue is nae langer a tongue, nor my hands worth wearing."

The voice of her husband in prayer interrupted this mental soliloquy; and ardently did he beseech to be preserved from the wiles of the Fiends, and the snares of Satan, "from Witches, Ghosts, Goblins, Elves, Fairies, Spunkies, and Water-Kelpies; from the Spectre Shallop of Solway; from spirits visible and invisible; from the Haunted Ships and their unearthly tenants; from maritime spirits that plotted against godly men, and fell in love with their wives."

"Nay, but His presence be near us!" said his wife in a low tone of dismay. "God guide my gudeman's wits; I never heard such a prayer from human lips before. But Sandie, my man, Lord's sake, rise. What fearful light is this? Barn, and byre, and stable, maun be in a blaze; and Hawkie and Hurley, Doddie, and Cherrie, and Damson Plum will be smoored with reek, and scorched with flame."

And a flood of light, but not so gross as a common fire, which ascended to heaven and filled all the court before the house, amply justified the good wife's suspicions. But, to the terrors of fire, Sandie was as immovable as he was to the imaginary groans of the barren wife of Laird Laurie; and he held his wife, and threatened the weight of his right hand, and it was a heavy one, to all who ventured abroad, or even unbolted the door. The neighing and prancing of horses, and the bellowing of cows, augmented the horrors of the night; and to any one who only heard the din, it seemed that the whole farmstead was in a blaze, and horses and cattle perishing in the flame. All wiles, common or extraordinary, were put in practice to entice or force the honest farmer and his wife to open the door; and when the like success attended every new stratagem, silence for a little while ensured, and a long, loud, and shrilling laugh wound up the dramatic efforts of the night.

In the morning, when Laird Macharg went to the door, he found standing against one of the pilasters a piece of black ship oak, rudely fashioned into something like human form and which skilful people declared would have been clothed with seeming flesh and blood, and palmed upon him by elfin adroitness for his wife, had he admitted his visitants. A synod of wise men and women sat upon the woman of timber, and she was finally ordered to be devoured by fire, and that in the open air. A fire was soon made, and into it the Elfin sculpture was tossed from the prongs of two pairs of pitchforks. The blaze that arose was awful to behold; and hissings, and burstings, and loud crackling, and strange noises, were heard in the midst of the flame; and when the whole sank into ashes, a drinking cup of some precious metal was found; and this cup, fashioned no doubt by elfin skill, but rendered harmless by the purification with fire, the sons and daughters of Sandie Macharg and his wife drink out of to this very day. Bless all bold men, say I, and obedient wives!